P1

PATHWAYS

PATHWAYS

NICHOLAS RUDD-JONES & DAVID STEWART

JOURNEYS ALONG BRITAIN'S
HISTORIC BYWAYS, FROM
PILGRIMAGE ROUTES
TO SMUGGLERS' TRAILS

guardianbooks

Published by Guardian Books 2011

2 4 6 8 10 9 7 5 3 1

Text and pictures (except pictures on pages 98 and 166) copyright ©
Nicholas Rudd-Jones and David Stewart 2011.

Maps and format copyright © Guardian News and Media Ltd 2011.

Contains Ordnance Survey data © Crown copyright and database right 2010

First published in Great Britain in 2011 by

Guardian Books

Kings Place, 90 York Way

London N1 9GU

www.guardianbooks.co.uk

A CIP catalogue record for this book is available from the British Library

ISBN 978 0 85265 226 8

Edited by Phil Daoust

Designed by Two Associates

Maps by Darren Bennett

Production management by Artypeeps

Printed and bound in China by C&C Offset Printing Co., Ltd

The Random House Group Limited supports The Forest Stewardship Council (FSC), the leading
international forest certification organisation. All our titles that are printed on Greenpeace approved
FSC certified paper carry the FSC logo. Our paper procurement policy can be
found at www.rbooks.co.uk/environment.

CONTENTS

	Introduction	7
	Who were the walkers?	9
Chapter 1	Ridgeways	11
Chapter 2	Processions	27
Chapter 3	Roman roads	41
Chapter 4	Dykes and ditches	55
Chapter 5	Wetland tracks	71
Chapter 6	Monks' trods	81
Chapter 7	Pilgrimage routes	95
Chapter 8	Forest tracks	109
Chapter 9	The corpse road	123
Chapter 10	Packhorse routes	137
Chapter 11	Drovers' roads	151
Chapter 12	Village walks	163
Chapter 13	Smugglers' trails	179
Chapter 14	Stalkers' tracks	197
Chapter 15	Miners' tracks	213
Chapter 16	Canal towpaths	231
Chapter 17	Promenades	249
Chapter 18	Municipal parks	265
Chapter 19	Leisure trails	281
Chapter 20	Pedestrian zones	297
	Index	312
	A note about terminology	316

INTRODUCTION

We are both footpath fanatics. When we arrive in a new place we can spend hours poring over an Ordnance Survey map, scouring it for signs of a Roman road, an old tramway or a packhorse route over the hills. Then we drag our families out to tramp along it and discover what it is like on the ground. Yet despite a passion for paths that has lasted several decades, we have often found we know remarkably little about them or the people who have walked them before us.

History has tended to focus on sites and on the powerful individuals who controlled them. So much more has been written on Iron Age hill forts, Norman castles, medieval churches, stately homes and even modern towns than on the tracks, ways and roads walked by millions of ordinary people through the ages. Deep down, however, most of us know that pathways are important. It feels wrong to visit an ancient site by car; it always seems better to approach on foot, as our ancestors would have done. There is something uplifting about coming upon Uffington Castle hill fort and its accompanying White Horse after a few hours' walk along the Ridgeway. By contrast, arriving by the A303 at Stonehenge, however magnificent and extraordinary a monument it is, is always just a mite dissatisfying.

Maybe we unconsciously recognise that these places never stood in splendid isolation: they were always linked into a network of paths, tracks and ways. What's more, these pathways were not just for the traffic of people, animals and goods. Before the telephone, radio, television and the internet they were the sole channel for communication. Paths were what joined people together socially, politically and economically.

It is no exaggeration to say that pathways made our nation. On a personal level they were incredibly important to those who walked them, as they formed a map of every relationship – social, familial and commercial – in their lives. In a wider sense they were integral to every shift in power, every "revolution", every change in consciousness that took place in the British Isles for hundreds, even thousands, of years. A world without paths would be a world without any history.

This book is our effort to redress the balance, to uncover the story of the paths themselves and the people who used them. It has been a fascinating journey.

We expected to find routes used for the transport of goods. Packhorse trails, drovers' roads and miners' tracks helped to fuel the industrial revolution, although they were eventually superseded by canals, railways and well-surfaced roads. We also discovered pathways that were created specifically for the easier exercise of power: roads built to move armies; dykes thrown up for protection and to establish tribal boundaries; monks' "trods" cut across the land to control monastic orders as they spread across Europe. But, outside of these very practical purposes, we were surprised to uncover so many paths with a strong spiritual dimension, from prehistoric processional avenues to the tracks travelled by medieval pilgrims, to the grim roads used to carry corpses to their final resting place. Closer to our own time we found more and more places where people strolled purely for pleasure: on the seaside promenades, in gardens and in the public parks. These quite formal walking environments sit at the beginning of a

)

movement that culminates in the waymarked paths and open-access areas that so many of us enjoy for leisure walking today.

It is one thing to appreciate the significance of these pathways in the development of our nation. But to really understand their history you have to try to get into the heads of the people who walked them, to know what is was like to use these thoroughfares for daily work or for that special individual journey. This is not always easy, as the stories of ordinary walkers are so often unwritten. But the paths remain, and they can still be walked. With some research and a little imagination we can go a long way towards reliving the experiences of earlier travellers.

It helps that we have a clear affinity with our walking ancestors. We seem to have a strong emotional attachment to the land that can only be satisfied by travelling through it on foot. Our reasons for wanting to own dogs – animals that have to be walked – is difficult to fathom in purely objective terms. There is something passed down to us through our ancestry that tells us – some of us, at least – that a dog is the right thing to have on a walk. When we put on our walking boots, gather our weatherproof gear around us, fill our sacks with emergency rations, call our dogs to our side and wait for our leader's instructions, it mirrors in so many ways the setting-out of a hunting party, many centuries ago. We may not come back with felled prey strapped across our backs but the perfect day out still ends around an open fire, with food in our bellies and a drink in our hands.

A great deal of the history of our pathways, as indeed of the land as a whole, lives on in our own minds. The "enclosure movement", peaking in the late 18th and early 19th centuries, defined the attitudes of the British people to ownership of the land. The indignation the Victorian poacher felt at not being able to snare a hare to go in his hungry family's pot resurfaces in the struggles by ramblers to gain access to the countryside – battles that are running to this day. Likewise, the heady blend of exhaustion and elation experienced by medieval pilgrims chimes with our own feelings after a charity walk.

So it is our fervent belief that the essence of a path can still be captured by walking it, even though much has changed. For each chapter of this book, then, as well as giving some wider historical background, we focus on an individual path. We delve a little more into its history and, most importantly, we experience it first hand, travelling the same way as our forebears. We invite you to do the same, whether by following the same path as us or by finding your own example nearer to home.

With this book, all we have given is a template for a much longer adventure, in which everyone can participate. We hope you enjoy the process of discovery as much as we have done.

David Stewart and Nicholas Rudd-Jones

Go to walkingworld.com to download detailed route guides for the paths featured in the book, find others nearer to you, keep up-to-date with new information and ideas and join in the discussion.

WHO WERE THE WALKERS?

For thousands of years the vast majority of people in the British Isles travelled everywhere on foot. We can tell how ubiquitous the act of walking was, and the significance attached to it, by the number of words that have entered the English language to describe it. Every nuance of gait, purpose and effort can be captured: hobble, amble, saunter, stride, clomp, stagger, bound, limp, march, lope, strut, march, stroll, hike and that most glorious of Scottish words, stravaig, meaning to wander aimlessly. The list goes on and on.

What is noticeable is how often these words contain an implicit judgement. In almost every case we can learn something about the speaker's attitude to the person being observed. Perhaps most telling of all is the word "pedestrian". It has an underlying sense of being rather slow and dull: we talk disparagingly of someone's mental approach, or the plot of a film, as being "a bit pedestrian". Yet for most of our history the pedestrian rate of around three miles an hour was what everyone, apart from a very small minority, was familiar with.

The pedestrian is inevitably set in contrast to those travelling in a "superior" way. In the last car-dominated century we saw the relentless rise of the "driver", itself a much more dynamic, positive-sounding word. In earlier times it would have been those travelling on horse, or in a carriage pulled by horses, who immediately gained higher status. It is no accident that the word "chivalry" comes from the French word "cheval" for horse, or that one of two aristocratic orders in ancient Rome was the "equestrian". These riders literally looked down on those who walked, while their horses added their manure to the mire through which they had to wade.

But walking has not been entirely consigned to the lower classes. A growing distinction has been made between whether you were on foot for work or for leisure – or indeed because you were on pilgrimage, in which case walking when you could afford to do otherwise was a deliberate sign of humility. Being on foot for work – whether it was trudging to the fields, carrying goods to market or being a footsoldier in an army – meant stepping through the mud and the dirt. It also meant being at risk, as being on the road rather than riding above it conferred a lack of worth. At one time being run down by a stage coach was one of the commonest ways of being killed on a British road.

Walking for leisure came to acquire an altogether different status, but it depended utterly on being in the right place. The trend began many centuries ago. Wealthy Romans avoided walking around their dangerous, dirty towns, preferring to send slaves and messengers to carry out their business for them. But when they left for their country villas they took to strolling around their gardens, chatting or simply thinking, as the philosopher Pliny was known to do. The private garden remained a place for "promenading" through the centuries, but only for those who could afford it. It was only with the arrival of public gardens and seaside resorts that the activity worked its way down through the classes.

Even the Romantics like Wordsworth and Coleridge were highly selective about where they walked, in spite of the importance they attached to it as a way of understanding the location you were in. Thanks to an improving network of roads leading into their favoured spots, they were able to get to places where it was good to walk.

Only recently has walking begun to lose its stigma. It is changing in our towns and cities, where finally the supremacy of the car is being questioned. More than anything it is changing in an economic sense. Walkers are now deemed to be valuable, particularly for rural tourism. A recent study estimated the value of "nature-based" tourism in Scotland alone at £1.4 billion a year.

Until the past couple of centuries and the rise in leisure walking over that period, first-hand accounts by walkers can prove rather elusive. Foot travellers, especially those of the lower classes, did not generally leave diaries or chronicles. This was a largely undocumented world, precisely because it was so normal and everyday, and because those who walked were often illiterate. Some information can be gleaned from official documents: court papers, registrations of ownership, records of transactions, employment or trading contracts. However, we have to be somewhat wary of the tale these documents tell. Whether it's the indictments of smugglers or poachers, the record of a benevolent gift of land for a municipal park, or an Anglo-Saxon chronicle lauding the achievements of a great king, there is always another story left untold: the account that might have been given by the pedestrians themselves.

In the few cases where snippets of first-hand experience can be found, the very fact that they were written down marks the authors down as out of the ordinary. So there does remain a conundrum: that the people you would most like to hear from are those who have left no record, either because they couldn't write or wouldn't have seen the point if they could. It makes the tracing of their history all the more challenging – and important.

Background reading

The chapters of this book are arranged in broadly chronological order from early prehistoric times to the present day. To gain a wider historical view of the same period, the following books are recommended.

The History of the Countryside (Oliver Rackham, Phoenix) is a classic survey of Britain's landscape, explaining in great detail how it has come to look the way it does, with a particular emphasis on flora and fauna. Francis Pryor, as an archaeologist, offers a slightly different perspective of the same subject in *The Making of the British Landscape* (Allen Lane).

The Tribes of Britain (David Miles, Phoenix) is a readable study of the origins of the British people, charting the various influxes and movements of population through the centuries.

On Foot: a History of Walking (Joseph Amato, New York University Press) is one of the few books focusing directly on the history of walking. Although written by an American academic, it concentrates on walking in Europe as well as North America.

1 Ridgeways

The great sheets of ice and snow from the last glacial phase began to recede around 14,000 years ago, slowly opening up the British landmass to new vegetation, an influx of wildlife and, ultimately, human habitation. The change in climate was remarkably quick – temperatures rose to near current levels within around 50 years – but the thaw took several centuries longer. With so much water locked up in ice, sea levels remained low. The first hunter-gatherers to colonise the land from the continent found the easiest living on the low-lying terrain that is now under the North Sea. Dubbed "Doggerland" (after Dogger Bank) by archaeologists, the gently undulating landscape, with winding rivers, areas of marshland and stumpy hills, would have formed a rich hunting ground.

The Ridgeway starts from Overton Hill near Avebury

During this Mesolithic, or Middle Stone Age period, lasting from roughly 9000 BC to 4000 BC, the majority of paths would have formed through the simple pounding of feet. Animals make tracks to get from their lairs or burrows to forage for food and water. These regularly followed pathways have the insistence of a river. When a tree has fallen down or the route becomes too muddy to pass easily, creatures start to make tracks on either side of the obstruction. The phrase "desire line" has been coined to encapsulate this tendency to get from A to B by the most straightforward route possible. Over time the route becomes a habit – feet like to follow footsteps – and a semi-permanent track is created. The earliest human pathways would have been just the same.

But a more planned approach to path-making may have started to emerge, even at this early date. As hunter-gatherers, Mesolithic people left few lasting marks on the landscape, but excavations at a handful of settlements, including Starr Carr in East Yorkshire, suggest that family groups were beginning to lay claim to tracts of land. From Starr Carr they travelled to collect flint from the coast near Flamborough Head, from which they could make axes to clear woodland and cut pathways. It is possible that some Mesolithic folk practised an early form of transhumance – a short seasonal migration between summer and winter pastures. If so, they may have done more than simply follow where their herded animals went: they may have started to lay down timber to make bridges over streams and trackways over marshy ground. They may have created the first "manmade" paths.

As sea levels rose, eventually to cut Britain off from the continent, the pressure on the remaining land increased. This may have generated a greater need to mark territory out as one's own. The arrival of a farming economy around 4000 BC, in the time we call the Neolithic or New Stone Age, witnessed a sudden increase in settlements and of more permanent, deliberately routed, tracks. The people cleared large areas of trees for fields and began to trade, often over great distances.

They also started to create monuments. Communal burial mounds, such as the long barrows with their stone-built compartments, indicate that they pursued some sort of "cult of the ancestors". Whatever the spiritual dimension, these mounds almost certainly served a more practical purpose: sited at the boundaries of their cultivated land, they helped the living to lay claim to their ancestral rights.

The large circular henges, consisting of raised banks and ditches and sometimes ringed with wooden posts or upright stones, must have served a wider community, bringing people together for special occasions. People may have travelled many miles from their places of everyday living to attend an important event at a stone circle. The practice was astonishly widespread: there are around a thousand documented stone circles and henges in Great Britain, of which Avebury and Stonehenge are merely the best known.

All these activities required the movement of materials and of people. A network of local tracks must have evolved to serve the developments in agriculture, husbandry and social structure. However, the "communication highways" would have been the ridgeways. In southern Britain these typically ran along a ridge of chalk, with steep slopes on each side and a dry stony surface above the "spring line", the level at which the first tiny streams emerge from the ground. The ridgeway path must have initially come into being through the continuing passage of people, animals and goods, taking the easiest, driest route. The underlying structure was of course nature's own work, but it is striking how similar in concept it is to the Roman road 3,000 or so years later, with its raised bed, cambered surface and parallel ditches – or, 2,000 or so years after that, to the modern motorway, with its embankment, tarmac surface and elaborate drainage systems.

As well as being dry, ridgeways must have offered significant navigational advantages. There would not have been dense woodland or foliage to block the way, or streams and rivers to cross. And in an

Looking north towards The Manger, which was formed by melting glacial ice. The white horse is said to come down from its hill to feed here on moonlit nights.

era before maps and compasses, a series of ridges would have been easy enough to follow, in much the same way as coastlines guided seafarers. From the Neolithic period onwards the Atlantic seaways carried people and cargo huge distances, from the coasts of modern Spain, Portugal and France all the way north to the Orkneys and beyond. Safe passage would have been accomplished by hopping between recognisable points on the coast, never straying too far out into the open ocean. Knowledge of how to pilot one's way along these seaways must have been passed down from one generation to the next and was no doubt extremely valuable to the enterprising trader – more valuable in many ways than the boat itself.

Likewise a ridgeway path, followed simply by keeping to the high ground and basic orientation by the sun and stars, must have been a godsend. Just as the intrepid Victorian explorers of Africa were mostly drawn from the Royal Navy, so perhaps the first long-

distance users of ridgeways were seafarers extending their trading routes using methods of navigation with which they were already familiar.

Ridgeways continued in regular use for centuries. Until at least the Middle Ages they would have been much broader swaths of passage than they are today. In places they could have been as much as a mile wide, along which each traveller chose the best route available, avoiding the worst of the ruts. Regular side tracks would have allowed those with animals to dip down into the valley from time to time to reach a water course. But since the "enclosure" movement of 200 or so years ago, which saw much common land transferred into private hands, most of the ridgeway routes have themselves become enclosed tracks. This is generally how we experience them today – as relatively narrow trackways, separated by hedges or fences from the fields on either side.

OUR WALK | The Ridgeway

Standing in a clump of tall beech trees on the north side of the Ridgeway, Wayland's Smithy is a truly evocative ancient site.

For at least 6,000 years drovers, traders and invaders have walked or ridden along what we now call *the* Ridgeway, which runs from Overton Hill, near Avebury in Wiltshire, to Ivinghoe Beacon, near Aylesbury in Buckinghamshire. As the key central section of a linked series of prehistoric tracks, once stretching some 250 miles from the Dorset coast to the Wash on the Norfolk coast, it provided a route over the high ground that was less wooded and considerably drier than the alternatives through the spring line settlements below.

As elsewhere it was the Neolithic farmers who left the first lasting remains on this great trackway. Their long barrows can be found both west and east of the Thames, itself an important artery in the nascent transport and communication network, cutting through the line of the Ridgeway just north-west of Reading. People from the later Neolithic period dragged the huge sandstone blocks known as sarsen stones from the surrounding hills and formed the gigantic Avebury Circle, found at the western end of the classic Ridgeway route. Ease of access to Avebury via the Ridgeway must been a significant factor in its choice as a ritual centre.

During the Bronze and Iron ages the Ridgeway continued to be a significant trading route. A series of Iron Age hill forts were built along it, including Liddington Castle and Barbury Castle, both just south of Swindon. The forts no doubt played a vital role in protecting and controlling trade along the route.

The Ridgeway continued to be an important thoroughfare well into medieval times. In the Dark Ages it was a main route for the Saxons and Vikings during their advances into Wessex, where bitter battles were fought. During the medieval period it was used by drovers taking livestock from Wales and the West Country to the markets in the Home Counties and London (see Chapter 11).

Until the local Enclosure Acts of 1750, the Ridgeway consisted of a broad band of tracks along the crest of the downs. During the enclosures its exact course and width were finally defined by the building of earth banks and the planting of thorn hedges to prevent livestock straying into the newly cultivated fields. Since 1973 the Ridgeway has enjoyed the status of a National Trail; having once suffered badly from off-roading, it is now well signposted and maintained.

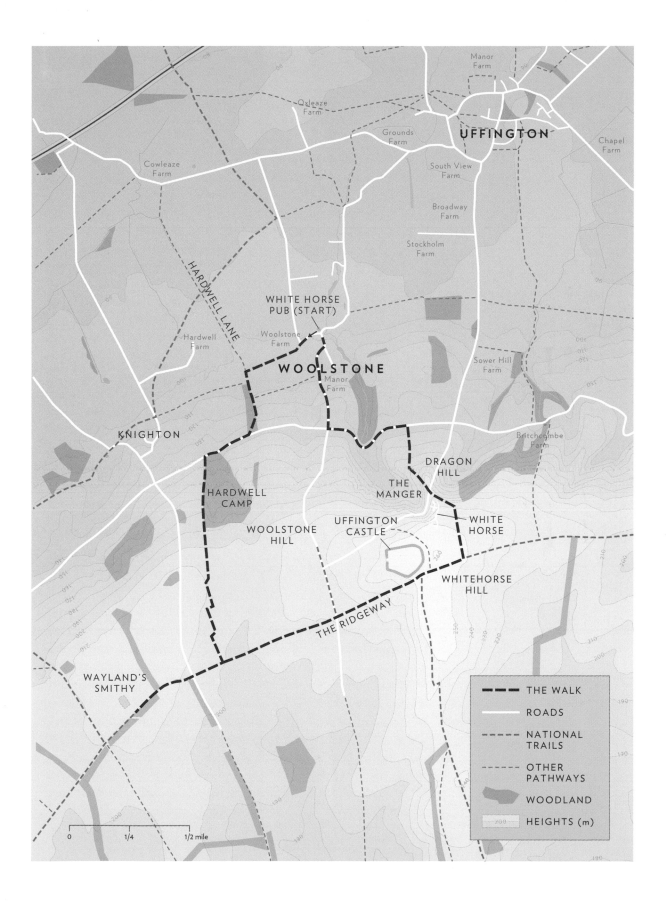

MANOR
FARM

OXLEAZE
FARM

UFFINGTON

GROUNDS
FARM

SOUTH VIEW
FARM

CHAPEL
FARM

COWLEAZE
FARM

BROADWAY
FARM

HARDWELL
LANE

STOCKHOLM
FARM

HARDWELL
FARM

WHITE HORSE
PUB (START)

Woolstone
Farm

SOWER HILL
FARM

WOOLSTONE

Manor
Farm

KNIGHTON

BRITCHCOMBE
FARM

DRAGON
HILL

THE
MANGER

HARDWELL
CAMP

UFFINGTON
CASTLE

WHITE
HORSE

WOOLSTONE
HILL

WHITEHORSE
HILL

THE RIDGEWAY

WAYLAND'S
SMITHY

	THE WALK
	ROADS
	NATIONAL TRAILS
	OTHER PATHWAYS
	WOODLAND
200	HEIGHTS (m)

0   1/4   1/2 mile

THE ROUTE | Wayland's Smithy and Uffington Castle

Nicholas Rudd-Jones sets out with his friend Kate Mere on a wet and windy day, to visit the Ridgeway near Uffington Castle.

Our six-mile walk begins at the quaint White Horse pub, a 16th-century coaching inn in the village of Woolstone. Neither of us quite expected the wetness and windiness of the day, and we are short of proper waterproof clothing. The pub looks much more inviting than the soggy path that will take us out of the village, and we are sorely tempted by the sign "Coffee served all day". But our hopes are dashed as we turn the door handle to discover that it is locked. So we set out through a horse's muddy field, beginning our journey much as any wild day out on the road would have begun through the ages – both dreading what is to come and a little proud of ourselves for showing the resolve to get under way.

We skirt the edge of Woolstone, a hamlet that dates back at least to 950, when the boundary was recorded in an old Saxon record. The fields that we are now crossing could well be the ones that were the subject of a famous dispute in 1327. The owner of Woolstone, the Bishop of Winchester, came into conflict with the Abbot of Abingdon (who owned the adjoining village of Uffington) over the rights to graze some pasture land called Summerlease. It was decided that it should be resolved by combat; the bishop's man lost.

At the end of two fields we step over a stile into Hardwell Lane, the subject of a more recent land dispute – though this was settled in the courts. Hardwell Lane is an ancient route mentioned in three Anglo-Saxon charters as having equal status with the Ridgeway and the Icknield Way. In 1987 the Countryside Commission charged all local highway authorities with ensuring that every footpath was unblocked by the millennium. When 2000 came an audit report estimated that a quarter of all paths were still blocked or unusable, and Hardwell Lane was one of them. It was cited by the Ramblers as "blocked and impenetrable"; the landowner, on the other hand, claimed that "Hardwell Lane does not exist as a path". Access to the lane was successfully defended and today we find Hardwell Lane quite open to walk along, if rather poorly looked after.

We turn right at the road and then in a hundred yards or so turn left onto a footpath going uphill along the edge of a coppice. Tucked away in the trees are the remains of Hardwell Camp, an Iron Age

This stretch of the Ridgeway represents the highest point in Oxfordshire, with superb views in all directions.

valley fort. It was built using a combination of rampart banks, ditches and enhanced natural features to enclose an area roughly 220 yards square, with two enclosed spurs extending to the north. We rootle around, getting very wet as we brush against the rain-sodden branches and make our way along some clearly visible earthworks. The site has never been excavated, so we can only surmise its original purpose: its location, tucked into the side of the hill and not easily visible, suggests a convenient place to gather and protect surplus crops, or perhaps a discreet vantage point from which to keep an eye on the traffic coming along Hardwell Lane from the north.

Ten minutes later, pushing our way irritably through a sodden rape field, we emerge at the top of the slope. We finally set foot on the Ridgeway. Whereas in ancient times it would have stretched across the breadth of the hill, what we see today is the path created by enclosure in the 18th century. The route is hemmed in between hedges, and the surface was probably also added at that time. But whichever era you walked it in, you would have felt ... well, above it all. This is the highest point in Oxfordshire, with superb views in all directions. We set off along it, the shiny chalk surface beneath our feet.

Standing in a clump of tall beech trees on the north side of the Ridgeway, Wayland's Smithy is only a short diversion from our route and is a truly evocative ancient site. It is a fine example of a Neolithic long barrow, built over 5,000 years ago as a communal burial chamber. It may be as much as 1,000 years older than the oldest parts of Stonehenge and shares a similar structure to that found at West Kennet Long Barrow near Avebury. During excavations a smaller long barrow of an earlier date was discovered beneath the mound, with burials in wooden chambers. The main entrance is flanked by four high sarsen stones, probably dragged here from the Marlborough Downs to the south-west.

It was the Saxons who gave this ancient barrow its name. Wayland was a Saxon smith god and local legend has it that his magic forge is contained in the barrow. It is said that if you leave your horse overnight with suitable payment by the tomb, the animal will have been reshod on your return the next day.

As we are exploring the site we come across a group of Scouts – the only other folk braving the weather. They are learning how to use a compass, and have a massive version that everyone can gather around and peer at. There's no doubt up here on the Ridgeway which way is east and west, so their job is made a little easier.

Coming back along the Ridgeway, Uffington Castle stands on the

The main entrance of Wayland's Smithy is flanked by four high sarsen stones, probably dragged here from the Marlborough Downs.

horizon – its robustness and scale impressive even from a mile away. The chalky track leads past its southernmost edge, so we turn off the Ridgeway to climb up and around its grassy ramparts. The fort, standing at the very peak of Whitehorse Hill, offers a chance to absorb the view in all directions. A single-track road cuts across the face of Uffington Hill, leading to a car park, so Uffington Castle always has plenty of visitors. It's a great place to fly a kite.

Uffington Castle is an Iron Age hill fort built around 700 BC, on top of an earlier Bronze Age earthwork. Originally the steep ramparts would have been bare white chalk, topped by a timber palisade and sarsen stones, with the ridgeway track running directly through gateways at either end. It must have looked spectacular. No evidence of buildings within Uffington Castle has been found, but pottery, animal bone and loom weights from the period do suggest some form of occupation. After the Iron Age the Romans used the castle as a fortress or trading place, and Saxons farmed within its ramparts.

Turning left just past the castle, we come down to the head of the Uffington White Horse. This is the oldest and most famous of the hill figures carved into the chalk hills over which the Ridgeway runs. It is a magnificent creature, 360 feet long by 160 feet high, slender and beautifully proportioned, seeming to gallop uphill. As if on cue, the sun bursts through the clouds and the head and oval eye of the horse burn brilliant white at our feet.

Most chalk figures are at most a few centuries old, created by landowners to lend an aura of antiquity to their country estates or, more recently, to commemorate a regiment or a war. The Uffington Horse, however, has always been accepted as ancient. In the past historians speculated that it was cut in the Iron Age as a tribal emblem by those who constructed the hill fort above, or that it commemorated one of King Alfred's victories over the Danes. Excavations during the 1990s finally established that the figure is older, almost certainly dating from the Bronze Age. Core samples taken by archaeologists, tested for the length of time they had been hidden from sunlight, gave dates between 1400 BC and 600 BC.

Its age may now be known – if only roughly – but mystery still surrounds its purpose. The shape is not easily made out from the top of the hill; it is better seen from the bottom of Woolstone Hill or further north still. However, by far the best place to view it is from the air, prompting the thought that those who made it wanted it to be seen by the gods as well as by mortals. It is such a recognisable landmark that it was covered up during the second world war, to prevent it being used

The Ridgeway leads from Wayland's Smithy to Uffington Castle, which stands on the horizon.

HILL FORTS are iconic features of the British landscape, moulded into the crest of a hill or on a commanding promontory. They were mostly built during the Iron Age from around 700 BC, although some, like Uffington, have foundations that date back to the Bronze Age. Construction peaked within a couple of centuries and most had fallen out of use by around 100 BC. Some were reoccupied briefly at the time of the Roman invasion and again, during times of strife, after the Romans left.

Despite the name, hill forts were not universally dedicated to military purposes, though their construction coincided with a dramatic increase in population and therefore pressure on the land. Some contained substantial settlements, no doubt providing a safe haven for farming surpluses and a good meeting point for trading. The elaborate entrances to some forts, like Maiden Castle in Dorset, indicate that a good part of the purpose was to impress rather than simply to defend. Danebury in Hampshire, which was studied by the archaeologist Barrie Cunliffe over two decades from the late 1960s, is one fort that does appear to have been attacked, as there is evidence of at least two serious fires.

as a navigation point by enemy aircraft.

Other animals have been suggested, but it is generally assumed to be the representation of a horse. Horses feature frequently in ancient mythology. Epona was a horse-goddess widely worshipped in Roman times; the derivation of the name suggests that the cult developed first in Gaul. There was a more or less contemporary Welsh counterpart to Epona called Rhiannon, though rather than being a goddess she is usually referred to as a queen. Both post-date the creation of the White Horse, but it remains possible that Bronze Age people held horses in similar regard.

Whatever the original conception, what strikes us today is its uncanny resemblance to modern logos – the one for insurance giant Prudential springs to mind. More than anything, the White Horse stands out as a bold and powerful tribal symbol, proclaiming to anyone approaching Uffington Hill: "This is our place and this is where we stand."

The shape was originally made by cutting a trench into the hillside and filling it with chalk blocks. For centuries local people have cared for the figure by "scouring" the surface and renewing the chalk infill to keep the horse white. In the 18th and 19th centuries, the Lord of the Manor provided food and entertainment for the scourers, which became a great annual celebration called the Pastime. Thousands came to see the stalls and sideshows, taking part in games such as wrestling, cheese rolling and pig chasing.

Standing at the head of the horse, we get a stunning view of the Manger, curving below us. This deep bowl was formed by melting glacial ice; the white horse is said to come down from its hill to feed here on moonlit nights. In the Manger is a curious flat-topped pedestal called Dragon Hill. Tradition has it that St George fought and slew the dragon here. Given its plinth-like shape, one feels it must have been created for some important purpose and a dragon-slaying is as good as any.

We drop down the steep slope and walk back quickly to the pub to dry out, soaked in rain and ancient history. Our boots and clothes soon recover but the camera takes a little longer – 24 hours in the airing cupboard to nurse it back to life.

The White Horse stands out
as a bold and powerful tribal
symbol, proclaiming to anyone
approaching Uffington Hill:
"This is our place and this is
where we stand." Dragon Hill
sits below.

Other ancient tracks to follow

Shorter trackways taking advantage of a ridge of higher ground can be found the length and breadth of the British Isles; one has only to look at a map with contour lines to pick them out. As well as the Ridgeway, there are other longer routes.

The *Icknield Way*, starting in the north Chilterns, is as ancient as the Ridgeway, of which it is a continuation, passing through Royston, Newmarket and Thetford and making its way eventually to the Wash. The route is marked by numerous ancient sites. The way seldom follows the highest ground to avoid the clay that often caps the chalk ridges in this part of the country. The route was originally complex and up to a mile wide; it is now best followed as a 110-mile long-distance footpath. Find out more at icknieldwaypath.co.uk

The *Harrow Way* is in the West Country, leading eastwards from Stonehenge to the North Downs to join the Pilgrims' Way. The *Exmoor Ridgeway* runs across the moor north of the B3223 and B3358. The *Kerry Hills Ridgeway* leads into Bishop's Castle in mid-Wales. The *Portway* makes its way along the top of the Long Mynd in Shropshire, while the *Old Portway*, running south from Mam Tor in Derbyshire, is close to our walk in Chapter 10.

Further reading

Roads & Tracks for Historians (Paul Hindle, Phillimore) contains a whole chapter on ancient tracks that lays out the evidence with the minimum of speculation.

The Oldest Road: An Exploration of the Ridgeway (JRL Anderson & Fay Godwin, Wildwood House) is a classic, with lots of good detail on the route itself.

The Icknield Way Path: A Walker's Guide can be bought from the Icknield Way Association at icknieldwaypath.co.uk.

The Icknield Way (Edward Thomas, Wildwood) was originally published in 1916, and paints a vivid picture of the route and the people that lived along it a century ago. It begins: "Much has been written of travel, far less of the road..."

More walks, ideas and discussion can be found on the *Walkingworld* website at walkingworld.com

2 Processions

Some time around 6,000 years ago the inhabitants of Britain embarked on a wholesale transformation of their environment. Using a combination of slash and burn and the swinging of heavy stone axes, Neolithic folk felled vast areas of wild wood and converted it to grassland and farmland. Along with this exercise of control over the land must have come a significant change in consciousness. Now humans were not just part of the environment but increasingly the masters of it.

The circle of standing stones in the Avebury henge are part of an outstanding prehistoric site.

The new methods of living must have been very successful, as they created surpluses of food, of labour and of time. Communities started to come together with the resources and social structure to create large-scale edifices dedicated to something beyond mere survival. Prehistoric monuments of varying kinds, constructed from stone, wood or simple earth, are found the length and breadth of the British Isles. The culture that gave rise to these structures was passed from people to people over long distances, suggesting that ideas about veneration of the dead and communal gatherings travelled along with traded goods. There's a remarkable conformity in these hundreds of stone circles, chambered tombs, barrow mounds and stone rows, although communities almost always gave their structures a local twist.

Dating evidence is difficult to come by. Stones, of themselves, give no clue as to when they were erected, and the mounds and ditches of prehistoric enclosures have tended to yield little in the way of dateable artefacts. It does not help that many sites have been plundered. Driven by a desire to discover the truth behind these mysterious constructions, generations have dug, scraped and blasted their way through them. Even quite recent archaeological excavations have been badly recorded, if at all. This is unfortunate, as once the earth is disturbed, the really important evidence is destroyed for ever. Outside what archaeologists call their "context", artefacts alone tell us very little. Without careful planning and meticulous recording, most excavation is worse than useless.

It is only within the past few decades that an appropriate degree of attention has been applied to the excavation and surveying of these important ancient monuments. At the same time a focus on the entire landscape rather than on individual structures has helped to generate some fascinating new theories.

The earliest chambered tombs, long barrows and single-chamber tombs known as dolmens date from around 3500 BC and were clearly dedicated to the veneration of the dead. Human bones have been found in many, sometimes in quite large numbers. We cannot know for sure if the dead were placed in them whole and allowed to decompose, or the bones were reburied there after a while elsewhere, or if collections of bones were moved in and out at intervals. In some cases the bones have been carefully organised, with different parts of the body piled together in separate portions of the tomb. What we can say is that the number of bodies that could be buried in these tombs does not match the headcount of the communities who made them. A tomb burial, in whatever form it took, was a sign of distinction.

The position of these tombs, in prominent locations overlooking the surrounding landscape, suggests not just an interest in the afterlife but also a desire, conscious or not, to lay claim to the land. A tomb or barrow is a clear indicator to anyone who passes that the land has been handed down to the living generation by their ancestors.

The later henges, avenues and cursuses, constructed in the latter stages of the Neolithic and early Bronze Age, are even more enigmatic. Some are built on a staggeringly large scale. A number of cursuses, consisting of long parallel banks with enclosed ends, are several miles long. The largest, the Dorset Cursus on Cranbourne Chase, is over six miles long and over 330 feet wide. Excavations on cursus monuments have revealed tantalisingly few clues as to their date or purpose: dating evidence is mainly gained from their relationship to other monuments. Some archaeologists feel they have come closest to discerning their meaning by walking them and observing the ways in which vistas open up and close down along the enclosed pathway.

Altogether the linear monuments of the Neolithic speak to us of organised processions, whether from one monument to another – as may well have taken place at Stonehenge – or along the length of an individual processional route. What these ceremonies consisted of we can only speculate. They may have involved rites of passage or veneration of the dead or, as some have suggested, a tribute to the alternately life-giving and destructive power of the river. The presence of water is a recurring theme in prehistoric ritual landscapes.

From around 2200 BC onwards, we see the emergence of a new burial tradition among the elite of the communities living in Britain. Bronze Age mounds, of which there are more than 6,000 in

Clumps of trees known as 'hedgehogs' sit over Bronze Age burial mounds, a mile from Avebury.

the West Country alone, appear to be once-only burials of important personages, not the site of continual revisiting witnessed with the chamber tombs many centuries earlier. Mound burials continued into the Iron Age and even into the post-Roman period. The large-scale linear monuments of earlier centuries were no longer constructed. However, this does not mean that gathering together and processing ceased to take place. Processions may have been shorter and not required a line of stones, banks or ditches to define their route.

The act of procession has continued to this day. It is an integral part of many religious ceremonies, both inside buildings such as churches and through towns and across the landscape. It also survives as a secular expression of togetherness and resolution. Few political rallies take place without a preceding march through the streets. The notion of walking together with a common aim is clearly deeply rooted in our psyche.

OUR WALK | The ritual landscape around Avebury

The surviving stones of the West Kennet avenue, leading south from Avebury, have been re-erected.

Avebury sits in a wide valley that is the catchment area for the River Kennet. The village and its famous henge sit on a slight rise at the northern end of a lozenge-shaped lump called Waden Hill, with a stream running close by that flows into the nascent river. Archaeological evidence from soil samples – essentially involving counting the number and type of snails through the ages – suggests that the woodland of the valley and the surrounding hills was cut down around 4000 BC, creating an open grassland landscape suitable for herding animals and farming. Significantly too perhaps, Avebury sits at one end of the ancient Ridgeway track, discussed in the preceding chapter.

Packed into a relatively confined area around Avebury, in its valleys and on its hills and ridges, we find prehistoric structures spanning more than two millennia. A mile or so to the north-west stands the early causewayed camp at Windmill Hill, and to the south is the magnificent chambered tomb at West Kennet, both constructed around 3500 BC. In the succeeding years the entire landscape must have attained a lasting ritual significance.

It is almost impossible to tell which monument preceded which, when and why they were altered and adapted, and whether they were in use at the same time. But during this period some of the most impressive and mysterious monuments in Britain were constructed: the Avebury henge and its standing stones; the wooden and subsequent stone henge at the Sanctuary; two long avenues leading from the Avebury henge; and Silbury Hill, the largest manmade mound in Europe.

Over such a long timescale it is quite possible that the meaning of the monuments mutated. In an oral tradition it would be hard to maintain a rigid ritual doctrine. Purposes may have evolved and sites may have fallen in and out of use. There is plentiful evidence that the people felt the need to regenerate sites, building new structures alongside old ones or replacing them, and no doubt investing them with their own interpretations and ideas. Indeed, the act of rebuilding may have been as important as the finished artefact – a way of thinking that is somewhat alien to our modern culture.

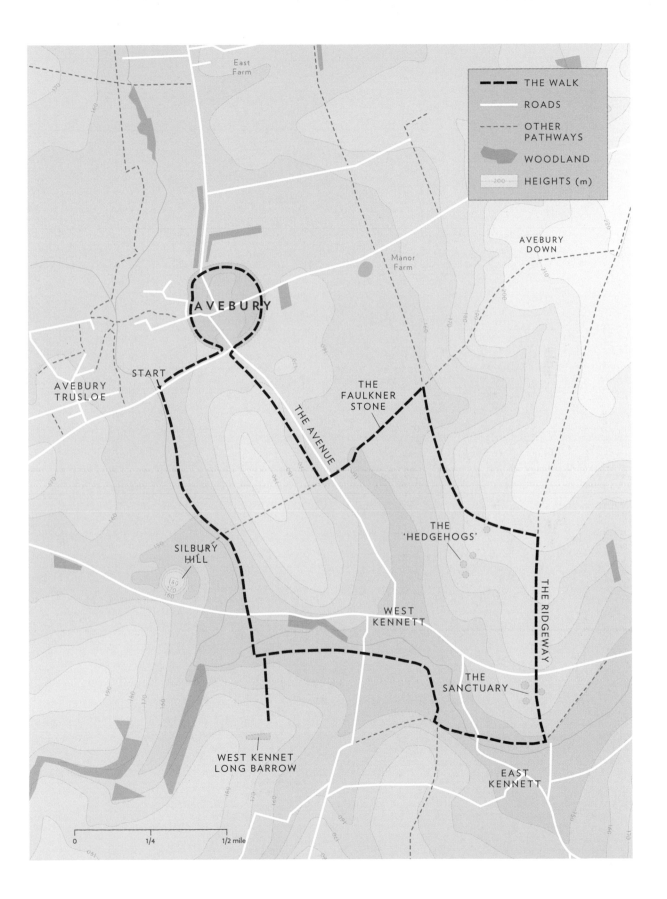

THE WALK

ROADS

OTHER
PATHWAYS

WOODLAND

200 HEIGHTS (m)

East
Farm

AVEBURY
DOWN

Manor
Farm

AVEBURY

START

THE FAULKNER
STONE

AVEBURY
TRUSLOE

THE AVENUE

THE
'HEDGEHOGS'

SILBURY
HILL

180
170
160

WEST
KENNETT

THE RIDGEWAY

THE
SANCTUARY

WEST KENNET
LONG BARROW

EAST
KENNETT

0   1/4   1/2 mile

THE ROUTE | Around Avebury's monuments

David Stewart, accompanied by his wife Chris and their Jack Russell Brough, undertake their own procession through the ritual landscape of Avebury.

Coming from the National Trust car park at Avebury, we set off south towards Silbury Hill. As we follow a small stream through the meadows, the hill looms like a strange bulb before us. Archaeologists have speculated that in its original prehistoric form it was a bright white upside-down bowl of chalk; it must have looked astonishing. Having been taken to see Silbury Hill as a young boy by my father, who was keen on all things archaeological, I have been lucky enough to stand on its oddly flattened summit and look across to the henge at Avebury. My small feet will have added to the erosion that has dogged it. It is not accessible now.

Passing around Silbury Hill, with the stream as a constant barrier, we cross the main road and climb up to **West Kennet Long Barrow**, a journey back from Silbury Hill of maybe 1,000 years. We navigate around a herd of frisky young cows, dog barking madly, and head up a gentle slope to the barrow, just visible on the horizon.

Chambered tombs are found across Britain, though most are clustered in the upland areas of Wales and Scotland. They date from around 3500 BC. Such tombs were clearly not designed for regular visiting; entering them may have only been for the privileged few. West Kennet Long Barrow is one of the most impressive, with great standing stones guarding the entrance and a tapering barrow extending way beyond the chamber within.

One thing that strikes us is that the view from a chambered tomb is always notable. In Orkney one tomb, that of Isbister, sits on the spectacular cliffs looking out to sea. Another is on a small promontory jutting into the lake on whose shores are found the huge standing stones of the Ring of Brodgar. Others again are on hillsides with long views over the surrounding countryside or across to other Orkney islands. Likewise, the barrow at West Kennet dominates its surroundings. Later, visiting the Wansdyke earthwork several miles to the south, we could still pick it out in the distance, sitting proudly on the apex of its ridge.

West Kennet Long Barrow is near enough to the busy A4 to attract a steady stream of visitors. For its builders it must have been a place of deep significance and power. Now children clamber over it, hide in the chambers and jump out from the dark at their parents; the once

The entrance to West Kennet Long Barrow is guarded by huge sarsen stones.

THE AVEBURY HENGE

Avebury's great stone and earth-bank henge was constructed, possibly in a series of stages, some time around 2500 BC. It is clear that these are not defensive earthworks, as the ditch is on the inside, a characteristic feature of the circular henge (though not, interestingly, at Stonehenge, where the ditch is on the outside). Inside the ditch only around a third of the original stones remain. More than 70 have been lost through centuries of neglect and wilful destruction.

The damage started in medieval times when the Church encouraged the breaking up of the stones, perhaps because the place remained a focus for pagan rites. Others were removed to build houses and walls. When the antiquarian John Aubrey visited the site in the 1640s almost all the stones were still standing. By the 1720s, William Stukeley was horrified to discover the site rapidly disappearing. In one of his illustrations he shows the process of breaking up one of the great stones using fire and runnels of water. Most of the remaining fallen stones were re-erected by Alexander Keiller in the 1930s, after he bought the whole village and its surrounding land.

sacred site has become a playground. We dig out a torch and try to take photographs, whlle the dog looks on with a bemused expression. Surely this hole is too big for rabbits?

Retracing our steps towards the A4, we turn right onto a path running along the Kennet valley, now part of the White Horse Way. We work our way through the meadows and the outskirts of a small village, over the Kennet, and finally up a track towards the A4 again and the site of **the Sanctuary**.

The Sanctuary will be missed by the drivers as they shoot by, though they'll find it harder to ignore the great lump of Silbury Hill just a mile further on. There's nothing left of the wooden posts that formed a series of circles within the henge, either as a succession of separate structures or as part of a single, possibly roofed, building. The later stone circle is known to have been dug up in the 1800s. The positions of the post-holes found by the excavators are marked on the ground. Apart from that there's nothing to see.

The intriguing possibility exists that the Sanctuary and the Avebury henge were linked elements in a ritual complex. Not far away, in the lush river valley through which we have just passed, evidence has been found of an unusual grouping of wooden palisades. Pits within them had been filled with bones and pots, the detritus of human feasting. In that other famous ritual complex around Stonehenge a similar link between the wooden henges at Durrington Walls and the stone edifice at Stonehenge has been suggested. If the monuments are indeed contemporary, the passage between them may have been of considerable significance.

One of the lead archaeologists on a recent major excavation within the Stonehenge complex, Michael Parker Pearson, has theorised that the wooden structures represented the place of the living, while stone ones were the place of the dead. Ceremonies in or near the wooden henge may have been joyous occasions of feasting, laughter and song, followed at the appropriate moment by a procession along the riverside and then up a stone avenue to venerate the dead in the place of hard stone. If the theory has any merit at all, then surely we can see the same configuration here at Avebury – and we are about to follow the very same route ourselves.

Vehicles thunder down the A4, making it difficult to cross, especially when accompanied by a tyre-biting Jack Russell. We join the **Ridgeway** path as it sweeps away from its end point at the Sanctuary. On the right a group of bare Bronze Age barrows stand just off the path, complete with explanatory panel. We are only on the Ridgeway

The West Kennet stone avenue meanders back to Avebury, which remains hidden until the last minute by a shallow ridge.

for a short while and then we turn left to join another track contouring round the side of the hill. On the way we pass a cluster of "hedgehogs". These Bronze Age barrows, of around the same age as those we have just passed, have resisted being ploughed out, perhaps because of the stands of trees that have sprouted from them. Looking out across the valley we can easily pick out Silbury Hill just behind the falling ridgeline of Waden Hill.

Turning off the track, we take the path leading directly downhill to the **Falkener Stone**, the sole survivor of yet another small stone circle. Rather stunted and standing all alone beside a ploughed field, it looks quite forlorn, despite sitting in a patch of beautifully mown grass carefully tended by its National Trust guardians. We continue on downwards towards the remaining stones of the West Kennet avenue.

We cross a minor road and start to make our way along the **West Kennet stone avenue** leading towards Avebury. This is one of two avenues linked to the henge, the other running in a more westerly direction towards Beckhampton. The Beckhampton avenue has almost completely disappeared, while the West Kennet one we are on is sadly depleted, the missing stones marked by concrete blocks. It is commonly assumed that the avenue stretched all the way back to the Sanctuary.

But the stones behind us have been removed, so our own route to the end of the existing avenue has been something of a detour from the original line.

The avenue is by no means straight. In fact it follows a sinuous serpentine track, at one point veering out over the modern road and then back again. Avebury generally defies attempts to reveal the kind of astronomical alignments found at Stonehenge, and this is certainly no alignment. The avenue winds like a lazy river on its path along one flank of Waden Hill. One can't help feeling that the avenue deliberately mirrors the sinuous flow of the small stream we followed earlier on the other side of the hill. The notion is strangely satisfying, although the idea is somewhat undermined by recent archaeological evidence suggesting that the Winterbourne was not so much a stream in Neolithic times as damp boggy ground. Even so, it's difficult to avoid the supposition that this is a route for walking along, either as a way of approaching the Avebury monument or of leaving it, and that its shape is somehow related to movement through nature.

We arrive back at **Avebury**, and spend some time walking the circumference of the henge. The stones come in all shapes and sizes, some of them estimated to weigh over 40 tons. Some people have posited that there is a distinction between the tall thinner ones and the rounder or more diamond-shaped ones, as they are often found in pairs. They could be representations of male and female – or they could just be positioned thus by chance. Walking along the top of the earthwork, one becomes very aware of its size and the depth of the ditches, even more so when you consider that they have, over time, become partly filled with silt.

Our five-mile walk has set us up nicely for expensive tea and cakes in the National Trust cafe, and a visit to the small museum.

Avebury's henge has its deep ditch on the inside of the earthworks, indicating a ritual rather than defensive purpose.

Other prehistoric sites to visit

Orkney has one of the highest concentrations of significant prehistoric monuments in the world, enough to secure its status as a world heritage site. Skara Brae is a well-preserved Neolithic village, a cluster of tiny circular houses cut out of earth and spoil, cleverly protecting its inhabitants from the harsh sea winds. Inland, on the banks of a loch, is a ritual landscape containing the extraordinary stone chambered tomb of Maeshowe, a settlement similar in style to Skara Brae, the magnificent Stones of Stenness and the stone circle called the Ring of Brodgar. A number of chambered tombs can be found nearby.

On the neighbouring island of Rousay, just a short ferry ride away from the Orkney mainland, a string of chambered tombs can be found in the space of a few miles, each slightly different in construction. The Broch of Midhowe is found perched on the rocks by the sea, one of a number of robustly built circular Iron Age towers found in the region, surrounded by its own small settlement. The broch looks across to its counterpart on the other side of the Eynhallow Sound, the equally impressive Broch of Gurness.

Dartmoor National Park has 18 recorded stone circles and over 70 stone rows. The stone rows seem much more open to the landscape than the cursuses, which were deliberately enclosed. However, it's quite possible that in their day they accentuated a processional path cut through woodland, exuding an even more claustrophobic sense of enclosure and of journey to some climactic end point. One of these rows, at Cut Hill on the northern side of the park, has been dated to around 3500 BC, although it's possible that it was standing even earlier.

Further reading

Hengeworld (Michael Pitts, Arrow Books) is a readable survey of the latest archaeology and theories surrounding Britain's henge monuments.

Britain BC (Francis Pryor, Harper Perennial) gives a good background to the relative sophistication of the societies in Britain before the arrival of the Romans.

The Council of British Archaeology publishes an excellent magazine, *British Archaeology*, sent to you six times a year when you become a member. There are also extensive online resources on the council's website: britarch.ac.uk

More walks, ideas and discussion can be found on the *Walkingworld* website at walkingworld.com

3 Roman roads

The Romans were the first to build a planned network of roads across Britain, a feat of engineering and construction that proved to be way ahead of its time. Nearly 2,000 years elapsed before there was once again a systematic effort to develop and improve the road system in Britain, with the construction of the toll-charging turnpike roads in the 18th century. Looking at a map of Roman roads at the height of the occupation, it is striking how similar it is to our road network today, with the majority of trunk roads radiating from London. This was the product of a national, rather than local, road-building strategy.

The Roman roads were designed primarily to facilitate military control. They dramatically increased speed of passage and were seldom impassable in bad weather. A journey that might previously have taken several days could, with regular changes of horses, be done in a matter of hours. It is no surprise, then, that the earliest Roman roads were built to consolidate the new frontiers. The very first major road, the Fosse Way, linked Exeter and Lincoln, passing through Bath, Gloucester and Leicester. Within a few decades of the invasion in 43 AD the frontier had been pushed out to include Lincoln, York, Wroxeter, Chester and Caerleon and new military roads were built to link them. Later the military network extended into what is now Scotland, past Hadrian's Wall to the Antonine Wall even further north.

But this was not just about the imposition of military might. As time went by and the conquered regions became settled, the roads increasingly became trading routes. Side roads were built to connect important commercial and industrial centres, for instance to the iron-mining area of the Weald. The Romans were masters of the art of assimilation, so the roads brought luxury goods and fine foods to the elite class of the indigenous population. The network was also a method of raising revenues, with a tax (*portorium*) imposed of some 2–2.5 per cent of the value of the goods passing along it.

In their heyday Roman roads stretched throughout the land, an estimated 10,000 miles in total. They were the motorways of their time but, just like modern motorways, they were by no means the only pathways across the country. They were additional to an already extensive track and path network. Often, however, the Roman road was quite isolated from the indigenous web of paths and population. The Romans favoured high ground and their routes were driven, at least initially, by military rather than local communication needs.

Stane Street heads south towards Chichester (Regnum), with the Halnaker windmill to the south west.

Following the collapse of Roman rule around 410 AD, the roads ceased to be properly maintained. Many of those with minimal engineering simply disappeared back into the landscape. Bridges, largely of wooden construction, were often the first things to give way. Inevitably some stretches of road were washed away by floods.

However, large chunks of the major routes survived and were in use up to medieval times, albeit often on a much more localised basis. Some of the well-known Roman road names, such as Watling Street and Ermine Street, are probably Anglo-Saxon, suggesting that they continued in regular use well into the post-Roman period. Some were eventually improved as turnpikes in the 18th century, having been pretty much neglected for over a millennium and a half.

Numerous Roman roads are still in evidence today, whether as main roads such as the A5, country lanes, parish boundaries (so used because of their longevity and prominence) or simply tracks and footpaths. Some, such as the Peddars Way, have become long-distance footpaths. In one way or another they have remained a key element of the British landscape and its pathways.

Change of use: sheep graze happily on the agger where once Roman soldiers and traders trod.

OUR WALK | Stane Street in West Sussex

Sit back, relax and take in the view from a Roman sofa at Bignor Roman Villa.

Stane Street connects Chichester – then called Regnum, the tribal capital of Roman Sussex – with London. It is likely to have carried inter-town traffic and facilitated the distribution of corn from the rich agricultural area of southern Sussex to London and the rest of Britain. There were, no doubt, lots of tracks criss-crossing Stane Street, especially on the crest of the Downs, which would have formed an east-west thoroughfare long before the Romans arrived.

The street took the most direct route that the lie of the land allows; it is a good example of the skill and thoroughness with which these roads were planned by the Roman engineers. They saw, for example, that by building the road a little east of the direct alignment from London to Chichester at Pulborough they could take advantage of a convenient descent from the South Downs between Gumber Corner and Bignor. The best place to see this descent is looking south from the Roman villa. There is a point in the field where in dry weather you can see the merest shadow of its form.

Every 13 miles or so there would be a "posting station", equivalent to the motorway stop of today. These were rectangular enclosures through which the road ran. Inside were whatever buildings were needed to service the traffic passing through, in particular stabling for a change of horses for high-speed message carriers. The nearest posting station to Bignor Hill is a few miles north, on the road to Pulborough, at Harding.

It is reckoned that Stane Street was maintained for well over three centuries, until the Romans left, at which point it started to fall into disrepair. It was, however, still in use in the 13th century, when it was mentioned in a "feet of fines", an agreement to end a legal dispute or establish a property ownership.

The road is still being used today, but for leisure only – walkers, cyclists and horse riders make good use of the firm ground and level surface. The South Downs is now a national park, which should ensure that the road is preserved for centuries to come.

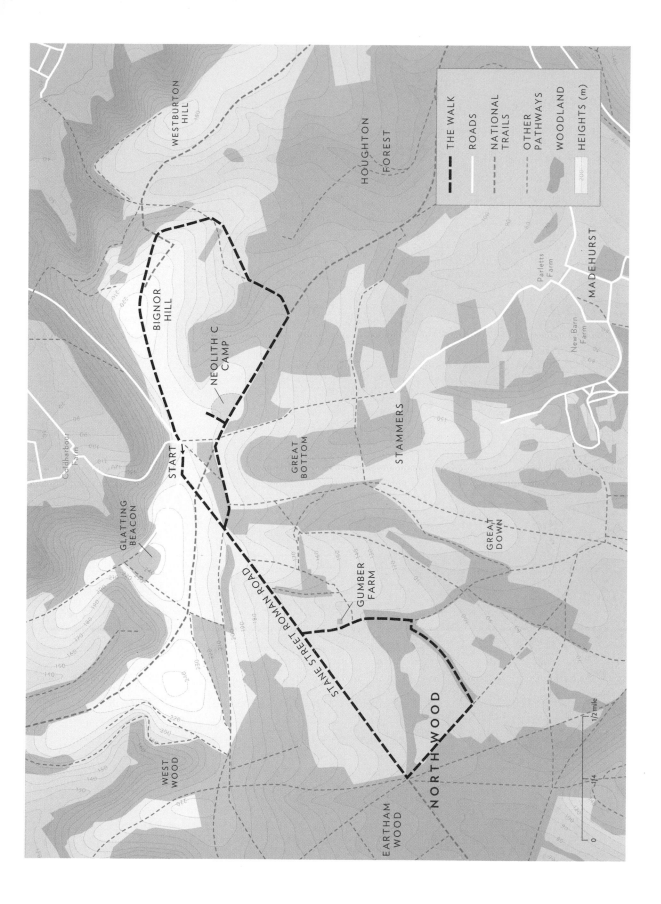

WESTBURTON HILL

HOUGHTON FOREST

MADEHURST

Parletts Farm

New Barn Farm

BIGNOR HILL

NEOLITH C CAMP

STAMMERS

GREAT BOTTOM

Coldharbour Farm

START

GLATTING BEACON

GREAT DOWN

GUMBER FARM

STANE STREET ROMAN ROAD

WEST WOOD

NORTHWOOD

EARTHAM WOOD

THE WALK
ROADS
NATIONAL TRAILS
OTHER PATHWAYS
WOODLAND
HEIGHTS (m)

0   1/4   1/2 mile

THE ROUTE | Stane Street at Bignor Hill

Nicholas Rudd-Jones travels back to the stamping ground of his youth.

This walk is about more than the Romans: it is as much about a sense of place, the beauty of Bignor Hill and its environs. This is a place that has been special to people throughout the ages. It was auspicious to the Neolithic people, who created a camp on the crest of the hill. It was highly appealing to some travelling Romans, who spied the fertile fields of Bignor and decided to turn off the road and start farming. Eventually they created one of Roman Britain's grandest private villas.

It was the hunting ground of one Toby after he had retired from the sea, immortalised in Toby's Stone, passed in the latter part of the walk. It is special to me, as the place where I grew up and explored every nook and cranny, latterly dragging my children along with me. It was special to my mother, who rode up here and used to bring a good friend for a walk along the top (a good friend who incidentally lived in the house of John Hawkins, the man who led the excavation of Bignor Roman Villa). It was a memorable place in the summer of 1977, when as teenagers we climbed up the adjacent Duncton Down to celebrate the Queen's Silver Jubilee, lighting a beacon as one of a network of flaming lights across the country, an ancient tradition most famously put to use to warn of the approaching Spanish Armada.

On the day I walk it again, it is certainly special to the many hikers, bikers and horse riders who are enjoying themselves, especially the father and son perched on a bench looking down towards the sea, deep in conversation and crisps.

My seven-mile walk begins at the top of **Bignor Hill**. Instantly there are glorious views to the south: you can see the sea glistening and on a clear day the Isle of Wight. To the north you can pick out the Hog's Back and the North Downs, the route that Stane Street takes towards London. Bignor Hill is now part of the Slindon Estate, run by the National Trust. It is an exquisite piece of country, running south to the village of Slindon, and criss-crossed by myriad well-kept paths.

Walking west along the main chalk ridge path, the path soon reaches **Stane Street**. Clamber up on to its embankment, or "agger", and it is easy to imagine yourself as a Roman soldier or aristocrat heading home to Regnum. If you had rested at Harding the night before, as most travellers did, it would probably be about lunchtime now. What better place to stop than the point you reach in a few minutes, where you get the first proper view of your destination and the end of your journey?

Walking along the agger, it is easy to imagine yourself as a Roman soldier or aristocrat heading home to Regnum.

Nowadays you can just spy the spire of Chichester Cathedral, marking the very centre of the old Roman settlement.

The track here opens out onto a great expanse of downland. On a fine day in almost any season the Sussex Downs are utterly beautiful, and this is one of the best spots. This being early October, I am lucky enough to see a Clouded Yellow butterfly, an immigrant from southern Europe, blown in on a southerly wind. Just like the Romans themselves, really.

As the track enters the wood there is a vast array of footpath choices. If you continue straight on you eventually get to Chichester, but here we leave our imaginary Roman companions and cut back via **Gumber Farm**, which is run by the National Trust and has a bothy and camping field where you can stay overnight. It's in an exquisite remote setting and would make the perfect base for exploring the area. Iron Age lynchets can be found in front of the farm cottages – banks of earth formed on the slope of a field through endless ploughing, making a series of wide steps. Hilaire Belloc (1870–1953), the writer, poet and walker, was a frequent visitor to Gumber Farm and the South Downs. There is a blue plaque in his memory on the bothy wall, with the inscription, "Lift up your hearts in Gumber."

Heading back up to Stane Street on the left are the remains of a second world war decoy airfield disguised as an RAF base. I wonder how the farmer felt about being a target? I retrace my steps back onto Stane Street, and at the pedestrian gate peel right towards the **Neolithic camp**. I clamber over a metal gate and stroll around the area of the camp. One's imagination needs to work overtime here, as there are just a few undulations, like waves in the sea, to indicate the signs of past human activity. But if you look up and around, it's easy to appreciate what a splendid spot its inhabitants chose, right on the top of the hill with views in all directions. The site may have been first occupied about 6,000 years ago, when settled farming replaced hunting and gathering as the main source of food. Dips left by old flint mines can be seen in several places.

I walk on and swing left down through a wood, back up the other side of a dip and join the South Downs Way. To the right of the track there's a dew pond, a typical feature of the South Downs. They were built with clay-lined bottoms, often at the top of hills above the water line. Despite the name, the primary source of water is believed to be rainfall rather than dew or mist.

From here it's a delightful stroll back to the car park, with wide views in every direction. On the way, there's **Toby's Stone** – a mounting block commemorating a local huntsman who, just like Hilaire Belloc,

HOW THE ROMANS BUILT THEIR ROADS

A cut-away view of a Roman road must be one of the most popular wall posters to be found in classrooms, illustrating the construction in graphic detail, usually with a proud Roman centurion posing alongside.

A Roman road typically comprised an embankment ("agger"), up to about 35ft wide, with a ditch on either side. The ditch was for drainage and also the consequence of quarrying for materials for the agger. The road metal was then laid on top, sometimes as a single layer of flint, gravel or other stony material, sometimes with layers of foundation material too, depending on the terrain. The surface was generally cambered to let the rainwater drain off easily.

We think of the completed roads as being absolutely straight and, all things being equal, they were. This tells us something about the Roman demand for efficiency, but it can also be seen as an expression of power. As conquerors, there were no considerations of land ownership or local objections to deter them from taking the most direct line. However, straightness was not an absolute rule: larger natural obstacles or steep gradients were sometimes avoided, with the road diverting around them before reverting back to its original line.

Gumber Farm was a favourite place for writer and walker Hilaire Belloc.

fell in love with the spirit of the place. Toby's inscription reads:

Here he lies
Where he longed to be
Home is the sailor
Home from the sea
And the hunter home from the hill.

Toby, incidentally, was Toby Fitzwilliam, master of the Leconfield Hunt, and his son Richard (also on the inscription) used to live in the house that my family later inhabited.

I round off my walk with a visit to Bignor Roman Villa. The site was discovered in 1811 by a farmer, Mr Tupper, who was ploughing his field and hit a large stone. It was fully excavated almost immediately and turned into a major tourist attraction during the Victorian era. The villa was one of the most opulent in Roman Britain, though considerably smaller than nearby Fishbourne Roman Palace. It was inhabited by a Romano-British farming family, who took advantage of the ridge of fertile greensand soil on which it sat to make themselves wealthy. It was linked to Stane Street by a metalled track.

The villa complex grew in a series of stages, from an original timber building dating from around 200 AD. Over the following two centuries it expanded to more than 60 rooms, several of which house fine mosaics, now protected under a thatched roof. There is an example of Roman underfloor heating and a sumptuous bath complex, complete with warm rooms, hot room, cold plunging pool and changing area.

There is little or no evidence of when or why the property was abandoned. It was not damaged by fire, like Fishbourne Palace, so it may simply have fallen into disuse after the end of the Roman occupation, in around 410 AD.

Here the agger is at its best preserved. Layers of flint and gravel were quarried from either side of the track to create a raised embankment up to 35ft wide, providing a robust and dry surface.

Other Roman roads

Roman roads can be found in just about every part of the country; just get out your OS map and start planning. But here are some favourites.

The *Peddars Way* in north Norfolk is now a long-distance footpath that joins up with the Norfolk Coast Path. Combining these two is a delight, taking you through rich farming land, old villages and a stunning stretch of coastline.

To get an idea of lofty Roman ambition, where better to go than *High Street* in the Lake District? The route follows the line of the Roman road that connected the fort of Brocavum at Penrith and Galava at Ambleside. This was the highest road that the Romans built in Britain. As Ivan Margary, the historian, somewhat wistfully commented: "It is in some respects an unusual Roman road, for it involves itself in prodigies of mountain climbing, passing for six miles over a succession of hills well above the 2,000ft [600 metre] level... and all to no real purpose as far as we can see."

If you want to see a Roman road just as it might have been during the Roman occupation, there's no better place to go than Blackstone Edge between Manchester and Ilkley. The surface of the road is intact, including a central line of stones with a deep groove in them, generally believed to have been created by the use of poles as brakes.

Further reading
Roads & Tracks for Historians (Paul Hindle, Phillimore). This is a superb book, with an excellent chapter on just about every era of road building. The section on Roman roads looks carefully at the evidence and is suitably questioning about some of the myths.

Roman Ways in the Weald and Roman Roads in Britain, volumes I and II (all Ivan D. Margary, Phoenix House). These seminal texts have formed the basis of our understanding of Roman roads in Britain, although not all the theories have stood the test of time. Out of print and hard to come by, but worth the effort if you really want to get into the subject.

To find out about Bignor Roman Villa, go to bignorromanvilla. co.uk or call 01798 869259.

More walks, ideas and discussion can be found on the Walkingworld website at walkingworld.com

4 Dykes and ditches

In the centuries after the Romans left Britain and before the arrival of the Normans in 1066, a considerable number of long linear earthworks were constructed across the country, of which Offa's Dyke is the best known. They were clearly designed as defensive barriers, but who built them and against what threat is largely lost in the mists of time. This was, after all, the period that we call the Dark Ages.

In the past many of these formidable structures were attributed to the Anglo-Saxons and presumed to be fortifications against the invading Danes and Norsemen. Certainly many of the names by which they are now known would appear to have Anglo-Saxon derivations. But, Offa apart, these names usually refer to legendary rather than historical figures or places, suggesting that the original purpose of the structure was very quickly superseded and forgotten, even by Anglo-Saxon times.

In Cambridgeshire a well-preserved linear earthwork now called the Devil's Dyke does appear to be Anglo-Saxon, dating from the sixth or seventh centuries. The dyke stretches seven miles to the west of Newmarket, from the fen edge at Reach to the claylands at Woodditton, and is the last in a series of defensive linear earthworks that stretch south-west, including Fleam Dyke, Brent Ditch and Bran Ditch. However, this dyke may have been one of the later constructions, along with Offa's to the west. Archaeological excavations suggest that many of the other dykes were built during the last years of Roman occupation in Britain, or soon after the Romans left the country to its own devices some time around 410 AD.

Wat's Dyke, for instance, which sometimes runs parallel to Offa's Dyke, was once considered to be the work of Offa's predecessor Aethelbald, predating it by just a few decades. Now there is some evidence that it was built several centuries earlier. Likewise, archaeological evidence from the eastern section of Wansdyke in Wiltshire suggests it was made in the fifth or sixth centuries, after the withdrawal of the Romans but before the arrival of the Anglo-Saxons. When the Saxons came upon the dyke, they named it after their god Woden; hence it became Woden's Dyke and, eventually, Wansdyke.

It is possible, then, that the earlier dykes tell a quite different story, one of inter-tribal warfare in the decades following the withdrawal of central Roman power. They would coincide with the refortification of some of the Iron Age forts. What we have is a picture of the disintegration of a country into a host of factions, with the rapid resurfacing of tribal loyalties held at bay during the Roman occupation. It must have been very similar to Yugoslavia falling apart in the late 20th century.

The sheer number of dykes indicates widespread disruption to the British economy, with loss of trade and communication between the opposing groups. Some of the dykes appear to protect major trade routes, but others cut through them, as Fleam Dyke in East Anglia does the Icknield Way. The aim may have been to control trade, but equally it may have been to prevent it altogether. In the latter case it would not have taken long for the whole damaged and dissected country to descend into isolated subsistence farming and a bitter fight for survival between scores of small tribes.

Such a situation may have made it easier for the Anglo-Saxon incomers to move in and take control of an attractively fertile land. Although the Dark Ages were dark in the sense that there were several centuries without written records or even a minted currency, it was not long before parts of the country regained their prosperity and long-distance trading resumed. There were, of course, new threats from around 800 onwards from Norse and Danish invaders (the "Vikings") keen to snatch riches but also to settle. There is little evidence, however, that dykes played a major role in the sometimes bitter warfare that ensued: in fact it was King Alfred's "burhs", a series of well-fortified towns, that saw off the Viking armies towards the end of the ninth century.

The massive earthworks of Wansdyke in Wiltshire were probably constructed soon after the Roman withdrawal.

OUR WALK | Offa's Dyke

Offa's Dyke is now a popular National Trail.

If many of the dykes were thrown up by British tribes before or soon after the Roman withdrawal, Offa's Dyke must have been one of the last of these grand linear structures to be built. It is recorded as the masterwork of Offa, King of Mercia from 757 to 796. There is no contemporary record of the construction but Bishop Asser writes a hundred years later that "a vigorous king called Offa... had a great dyke to be constructed between Wales and Mercia, stretching from sea to sea". There is some argument over whether Offa's creation actually did join the Bristol Channel to the Irish Sea, or whether this was simply in conjunction with Wat's Dyke and other earlier ditches.

The role of the dyke is still something of a mystery but there are clues in its construction. There are no forts or garrisons on its entire length, which would indicate that it was not intended to be defended. There would, however, have been clear sightlines for signalling, so warning of a Welsh force gathering at the border could have been communicated very quickly. Equally importantly, it would have provided a swift route for bringing an opposing force directly to the point of danger.

These would have been entirely practical functions, but no doubt the dyke also served a purpose as a statement of power and ownership. There was no capital to the Mercian kingdom: Offa was an itinerant leader and had to be. Only by making your presence felt on a regular basis could your supremacy be maintained. This was kingship by travelling about, complete with your entire retinue, tents for stays where there was no suitable lodging, treasure and money for gifts and of course men at arms for security. He would have travelled by poorly maintained Roman road and by any manner of rough track and way. It must have been incredibly tiring. Offa's reign is extraordinary therefore for its length – many kings only lasted a few years before dying of natural causes or worse.

Establishing your land rights by walking was pretty standard practice at the time, at every level. On a local scale pacing the land was integral to the doling out of property rights. In a world without maps, parcels of land granted to followers and religious houses were defined in charters. Hundreds of these Anglo-Saxon documents have been incorporated into succeeding deeds, so although the original may no longer exist the gist has been maintained. A charter involving a piece of land had a section describing its boundaries, tracing natural features and linking

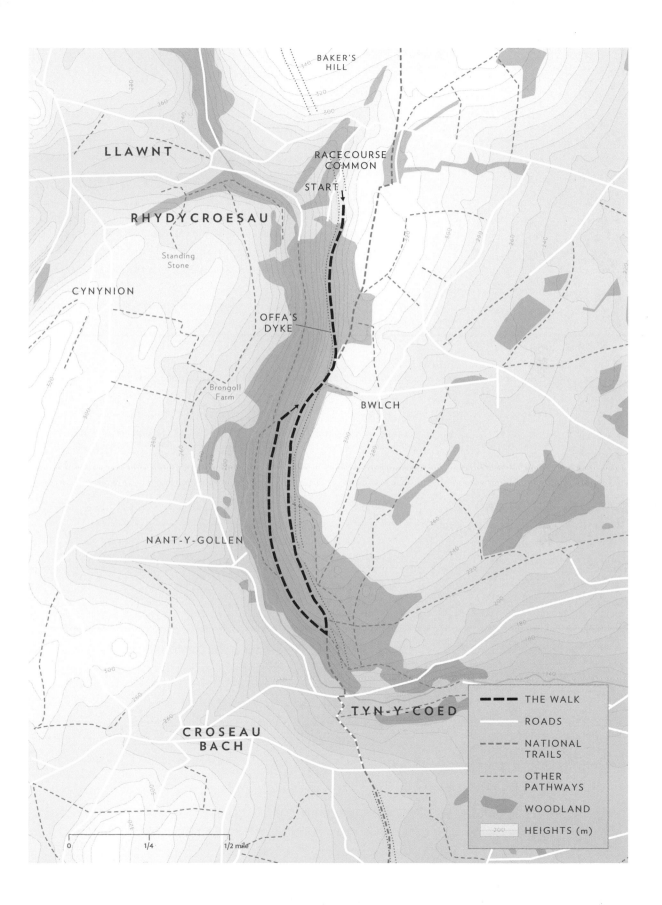

BAKER'S
HILL

LLAWNT

RACECOURSE
COMMON

START

RHYDYCROESAU

Standing
Stone

CYNYNION

OFFA'S
DYKE

Brongoll
Farm

BWLCH

NANT-Y-GOLLEN

TYN-Y-COED

CROSEAU
BACH

0   1/4   1/2 mile

THE WALK

ROADS

NATIONAL
TRAILS

OTHER
PATHWAYS

WOODLAND

200   HEIGHTS (m)

prominent landmarks. In a few parishes the tradition is maintained with the "beating of the bounds", with the youngsters of the village alternately beaten (very gently nowadays) and given rewards as they circuit the parish boundary. The idea was that younger villagers would be forced to remember the defining waypoints of the parish boundary, should there ever be a dispute in later years.

It is quite possible, then, that the dyke served an important purpose as the delineator of a national boundary – a property charter but on a very large scale. Natural borders to Offa's realm, like the Channel and to a lesser extent the Humber estuary to the north, were relatively simple to identify and defend. Elsewhere, Offa would have had to deal with endlessly troublesome neighbours. Having decided, after a number of fruitless campaigns, that he couldn't conquer the Welsh he opted instead to draw a line in the sand and define his kingdom rather than extend it.

So Offa would have known his land intimately and in a very practical way, because he paced much of it with his own feet. Walking along the parapet of the dyke today, it's intriguing to think that the man who ordered its construction might have done the very same. All along it makes use of the natural boundaries that do exist, linking and reinforcing them rather than inventing an entirely manmade line. Perhaps this is an integral part of its function: to make the image of a significant natural boundary where one didn't really exist before.

The dyke would certainly have reinforced a sense of belonging on "this side of the fence". It is likely that the construction was done by gangs from tribes offering annual service to the dominant king. By bringing in tribes from across Mercian-controlled England, it is conceivable that Offa completed the job in a single year, with every group returning with tales of how they built something incredible to keep the rebels out.

It's a nationalist sentiment that has endured, giving rise to the notion that "it was customary for the English to cut off the ears of every Welshman who was found east of the dyke, and for the Welshman to hang every Englishman whom they found west of it" (George Borrow, *Wild Wales*, 1862). This assertion almost certainly has no basis in reality, but the idea of setting up those "beyond the pale" as dangerous outsiders would certainly have been in the mental armoury of a ruthless leader like Offa. Significantly, the word "Welsh" derives from the Germanic word for "foreigner". "Cymry", on the other hand, is probably derived from the Celtic word "combrogi", meaning "fellow countrymen". The dyke was not just a physical partition; it was a cultural one.

In places Offa's Dyke is overgrown with trees, but in Offa's time the ground would have been clear to give a good sight of the enemy.

The dyke has been used as the line for a much more recent boundary wall.

THE ROUTE | Along Offa's Dyke near Oswestry

David Stewart takes a short three-mile walk along the ramparts of Offa's great dyke with his wife Chris and dog Brough.

We are still deliberating on which section of Offa's Dyke to walk when I find myself summonsed to Shrewsbury Crown Court as a prosecution witness. It seems a good opportunity to visit a section of the dyke we have not walked before. As the Crown Prosecution Service will be contributing to our overnight expenses, we splash out on a posh country house hotel right on the Welsh border. The Pen-y-Dyffryn promises fine food and drink, is happy to house the dog, and sits just a stone's throw from the dyke.

We know that Anglo-Saxon kings set great store by being able to provide their followers with great feasts and quantities of ale: it was part of the deal that helped to see them through the hardships of battle, travelling and hunger. The packed mead halls described in the epic poem *Beowulf*, which some commentators think may have been written for King Offa himself, spring vividly to mind. It seems appropriate somehow to be tucking into a lavish dinner at the Queen's expense, in return for services rendered at court the next day.

The court appearance turns out to be a slightly disconcerting affair. My memory of the incident, involving two young men racing on the motorway, has faded after more than a year. I strain to recall the details. The defending barrister asks if I recall seeing a silver Ford Fiesta. I don't but, trying to be helpful, I venture that it could have been one of the cars in front, hidden behind a cloud of burning rubber. The judge chides me gently: "Please don't speculate, Mr Stewart. Just stick to what you saw." After 10 minutes of doing my best I am dismissed. It's a salutary reminder of how unreliable memory can be. The fact that no one recalls the purpose of a clutch of imposing post-Roman earthworks begins to seem less surprising.

We make our way from our hotel in Rhydycroesau up onto **Racecourse Common**. Here Offa's Dyke runs along the edge of a ridge beside the grass strips of Oswestry's old race course. From the car park we soon join a wide band of well-cut grass as it arches round to a tight right-hand bend before a long open run along the top of the common. A bulky stone statue with horses' heads facing both ways, placed here in the 1990s, commemorates its history as a sporting venue and as the boundary between England and Wales.

For a good century from the early 1700s this was a popular horse

At times Brough is able to scamper along the top of the raised rampart of the dyke.

A modern statue, with one head facing towards England and one towards Wales, stands on Oswestry's old race course.

racing circuit for the local gentry. The annual meetings were a big event, with horses charging around a two-mile loop on this plateau 300 metres above sea level. In the early 19th century things were still going well – so much so that a stone grandstand was built at the southern end by the dramatic final bend before the finishing line.

But this was the beginning of the end. By the 1840s the gentlemen race-goers were getting increasingly disenchanted. Gambling, drinking and pick-pocketing were rife, the whole affair was becoming rowdy and, worst of all, the lower classes were winning the races. The arrival of the railway in Oswestry was the final blow, allowing spectators, horses and competitors to travel elsewhere for their fun. In 1848 the course was abandoned. Stone from the grandstand was plundered for housebuilding, though the foundations remain as a good spot for a picnic.

From the racecourse we take a path through the woods, which drops down to meet **Offa's Dyke**. The wide, deep ditch of the dyke still stands out, even though erosion and the pounding of many feet have done their best to level it. In places great trees have grown up in its banks, their root tentacles helping to hold it together. The path runs along its line, sometimes on the apex of the banks, sometimes within the ditch and sometimes on the outer edge. It must have been a popular walk in past decades as strange grottos and seating areas have been built from stone blocks, providing resting places and viewpoints along the way.

Walking along the dyke, as we do now for a mile or more, it's clear that this was no agreed boundary. The earthworks are substantial – 65 feet across and 10 feet deep in place – and they all favour the Mercians rather than the Welsh. Rubble dug up to make the ditch was all piled on the Mercian side. Rather than running along the ridge of the hill, the dyke is frequently built into the Welsh-facing slope, so the advantage lies with a Mercian force above the dyke as well as on it. Here the dyke sits 100 yards or more to the west of the ridge, on the side of a reasonably steep hill. Nowadays the hillside is wooded but no doubt a corridor of bare ground was maintained either side of the dyke during its working life, allowing the Mercians a clear view of the enemy. The top of the bank may well have had a wooden palisade, making it an even more formidable barrier.

Reaching the southern end of our section of the dyke, we cut back on a lower path, dropping through woods towards the stream below. The dyke swiftly disappears into the trees above. However, as we climb up again along a gentle incline we meet it again, its great banks

OFFA THE BRETWALDA

Far from being a petty tribal chief, Offa could lay claim to being an overlord – a "bretwalda" or "wide ruler" in Anglo-Saxon terminology. This was not the king of a single country in the sense that we would recognise it now, but rather the dominant overlord of all the minor kings and leaders of the realm under his command. And dominant he certainly was, bringing much of current-day England from the south coast to the Humber under his control.

The job called for constant vigilance, as other kings would flex their muscles from time to time. The people of Kent, occupying a valuable link to the continent, had a habit of falling out of line. In 775 Offa raised a force and attempted to put them right. On this occasion, in a battle at Otford near Sevenoaks, he seems to have been defeated. In 785 he tried again with more success. The process of subjugation would have involved a good measure of brutality, followed often by much conciliation and displays of renewed friendship and generosity.

Offa had a keen sense of the importance of PR and was determined to reinforce the legitimacy of his reign. This was particularly necessary as he had come to power in a coup d'état, seizing the throne from Aethelbald's successor Beornred, about whom little is known. He made a great show of his friendship with the powerful Charlemagne. He also understood the importance of being anointed by the Church, although like many Anglo-Saxons leaders his Christianity was half-baked. When the Kentish Archbishop Jaenberht failed to supply sufficient assurances of support, Offa went over his head to Rome and got his own archbishopric established in Lichfield.

As far as his currency was concerned, Offa went to exceptional lengths to have coins of ostensible quality. Some of the beautifully struck portraits show him almost in the guise of Roman emperor. He also had coins made with the image of his wife Cynethryth, just as Roman emperors used to do. Offa's Dyke fits in with all these endeavours to be recognised beyond the boundaries of his kingdom as well as within it.

now experienced from below – the Welsh perspective. The earthwork has been used as the line for a dry-stone wall, no doubt for the simple purpose of keeping stock on one side, though this too has tumbled down and now any animals are free to roam at will. A wooden gate lies uselessly, propped up against a pile of mossy stones. From here we rejoin our outward path and head back to our hotel.

The dyke's purpose was undoubtedly short-lived, partly because Offa's family swiftly lost its grip on power. Offa went to great lengths to have his son anointed as his successor with the blessing of the Church, but after his death his carefully laid plans crumbled away. Offa died in June 796 and his son outlived him by just a few months. Without a surviving dynasty to maintain them, the wooden palisades on Offa's Dyke probably rotted away, or were filched for timber or firewood, within a few short winters. It may not have been long before Offa's Dyke, like all those other great ditches, was simply a weird earthwork, built by strangers.

Odd stone seats and grottos suggest that a walk along the dyke was a popular diversion for race course visitors.

The Devil's Dyke stands out from the flat surrounding terrain.

THE DEVIL'S DYKE

Cambridgeshire's Devil's Dyke may have been constructed by Penda, the Saxon king of the East Angles, to protect the East Anglian Saxons from the Britons to the west. Stretching across the open chalk lands between the impassable fens to the north and the thickly wooded land to the south, it would have formed an effective barrier. The Britons often fought on horseback while the Saxons were usually on foot, so the dyke and ditch, possibly filled with thorny bushes, would have prevented the use of cavalry in a confrontation.

The monument has had several recorded names. During the Middle Ages it was regularly known as St Edmund's Dyke, because it marked the limit of the jurisdiction of the abbots of Bury St Edmunds. There are also references around the same time to the Great Ditch. During the 11th-century siege of Ely by William the Conqueror, it is referred to as Reach Dyke.

Devil's Dyke or Ditch is a post-medieval name: as so often, a supernatural provenance is ascribed to a monument, landform or structure whose original purpose is lost in the past. One local legend is that the Devil came uninvited to a wedding, perhaps at Reach church, and was chased away by the guests. In anger he formed the groove of the dyke with his fiery tail. In another a king called Hrothgar made the dyke with some local giants to ward off a fire god, or fire demon, who had taken a fancy to his daughter Hayenna. In the early stages of the conflict the fire demon looked to have got his way, at which point the giants fled. But Hrothgar had the presence of mind to scratch a breach from the river, allowing a thundering cascade of water to flow into the ditch, extinguishing the fire demon and freeing the daughter.

Other earthworks to explore

Offa's Dyke can be walked in its entirety, so there are plenty of other parts of it to see. The section above Tintern Abbey is particularly beautiful and dramatic.

Its Roman predecessor, *Hadrian's Wall*, can be walked end to end on a very popular National Trail. A shorter excursion along the wall can be combined with a visit to one of the fascinating Roman forts, like Housesteads or Vindolanda.

Sections of the more northerly Roman earthwork, the *Antonine Wall*, which achieved Unesco world heritage status in 2008, can also be accessed on foot.

The *Devil's Dyke*, or Ditch, runs just west of Newmarket in Suffolk between the villages of Woodditton and Reach. It is in places an impressive structure over 10 metres high, with a footpath running its full 7.5-mile length.

Around half as long, nearby *Fleam Dyke*, near Fulbourn just east of Cambridge, also has a footpath along its entire length. Sherds of Bronze Age pottery found in Fleam Dyke suggest that it, and Devil's Dyke, may have an earlier history before being rebuilt in Anglo-Saxon times.

A superb section of the *Wansdyke* can be walked just south of Avebury in Wiltshire. The section is on the White Horse Trail and can be reached either from the Avebury complex or from a car park near Walkers Hill. The area is littered with prehistoric tumuli, barrows, enclosures and forts.

Further reading

In Search of the Dark Ages (Michael Woods, BBC) gives a good account of a period that is often overlooked for lack of written evidence.

More walks, ideas and discussion can be found on the Walkingworld website at walkingworld.com

5 Wetland tracks

Odd though it may seem to us today, wetlands and marshy coastland areas were highly attractive places to live for the earliest inhabitants of our isles. Proximity to water provided a wider diversity of foodstuffs, whether through fishing, hunting for fowl or scavenging for cockles on the sea shore. We have already seen how Mesolithic folk populated the low-lying region known as Doggerland, now sunk under the North Sea.

Starr Carr, the Mesolithic "camp" discovered in East Yorkshire, sat on the shore of an inland lake (now completely drained so the ancient level has to be worked out from soil samples). The water would have been a magnet for herds of animals as well as a fine place to fish; a fragment of a wooden oar suggests the occupants used some type of boat. Numerous other settlements dating from around 9000 BC have been found around the edge of the lake, as well as on islands within it. The site may have been a seasonal hunting camp for a number of family groups.

Similar evidence for habitation during this period is found in the Severn estuary. Here footprints of animals, men, women and children living some 6,500 years ago have been found impressed into clay, very fortunately preserved under another layer of clay, in the Gwent levels. These prints are an extraordinary physical record of ancient people stepping across the tidal mudflats. The presence of the children's prints is particularly poignant, as it suggests that with their lighter weight they were valuable in gathering shellfish and seaweed among the dangerous quicksands.

In Scotland from around 5,000 years ago people constructed artificial islands a few yards from the loch shore, usually connected by a narrow causeway. The platforms were created with timber on log piles driven into the loch bed, or sometimes by depositing tons of rocks to create a solid foundation. These "crannogs" would have been used as homesteads, fishing stations and quite possibly as refuges in times of trouble. They may even have been a status symbol. Some were in use right up to the 17th century.

There is evidence that wooden trackways were being laid across boggy ground from the very earliest times. At Starr Carr a deliberately constructed platform of split and worked timbers has been found preserved in the peat by the original lake edge. In the later Neolithic era the inhabitants of the Somerset Levels constructed a network of timber tracks across the marshland, one of which, the "Sweet Track", has been excavated. The track appears to have been in use for only

The fens have always been a rich agricultural resource – and full of sky!

10 years or so, an indication of how volatile the water levels must have been at that time. Most famous of all is the slightly later wooden causeway and platform found at Flag Fen, near Peterborough.

It's a reminder of how smart early folk could be that this idea of laying wood across marshes was exactly the same as that adopted by George Stephenson over 3,000 years later when he constructed the Liverpool-to-Manchester Railway over Chat Moss Bog in 1830. To this day the track still floats on the hurdles that Stephenson's men laid, and trains 25 times the weight of the original Rocket are able to speed across it.

OUR WALK | The Fens

Holding back the water: the sluice at Willingham Drain.

Until east England's Fens were drained, first in medieval times and then more extensively in the 17th century, they were Great Britain's largest wetland, covering about a million acres, or 1,500 square miles. This was essentially a vast marshy swamp with just a few islands of higher ground, of which the Isle of Ely would have been one of the most prominent.

In 1630 the Earl of Bedford employed the Dutch engineer Vermuyden to drain the southern fenland to create land for agriculture. The drained soil exposed to the air was mostly composed of peat, which began to shrink and waste, and the ground level fell further. Over the years it became necessary to pump rainwater from the fields up into the rivers, which remained at the pre-drainage levels.

Thanks to this engineering the Fens became a rich agricultural region. But even before being drained they were blessed with abundant natural resources, with vast expanses of summer grazing, reeds for thatch and great stands of timber. The inhabitants were able to take advantage of plentiful stocks of fish and eels, and a wealth of wildfowl.

Folk tended to settle on the drier islands and around the edges of the wetlands. Here their houses were free from flooding but they were still able to benefit easily from the area's resources. This is one reason why so many prosperous medieval towns appeared along the Fens' margins: King's Lynn, Cambridge, Huntingdon, Peterborough, Lincoln, Spalding and Boston.

From the earliest times the Fens were also favoured by religious communities, perhaps because of the relative freedom they could enjoy from outside meddling. There are many monastic sites, of which Peterborough and Ely are the most famous. The disproportionately large cathedral at Ely, given the size of the community, is known locally as the Ship of the Fens as it towers over the flat landscape.

In a region of fens and rivers (in the words of Daniel Defoe, "the soak of no less than 13 counties"), rights of way took on special importance, providing vital pathways through the landscape. They were also the key to defence and economic control. Trackways were built across the Fens as far back as the Bronze Age, both from timber and from the piling up of earthwork banks. The more solid earthwork causeways have been continuously repaired and improved over the centuries, so in many cases it is difficult to establish a date of origin. Many have become the trunk roads of today, having been the first pathways to utilise the contours and the lie of the land to best advantage.

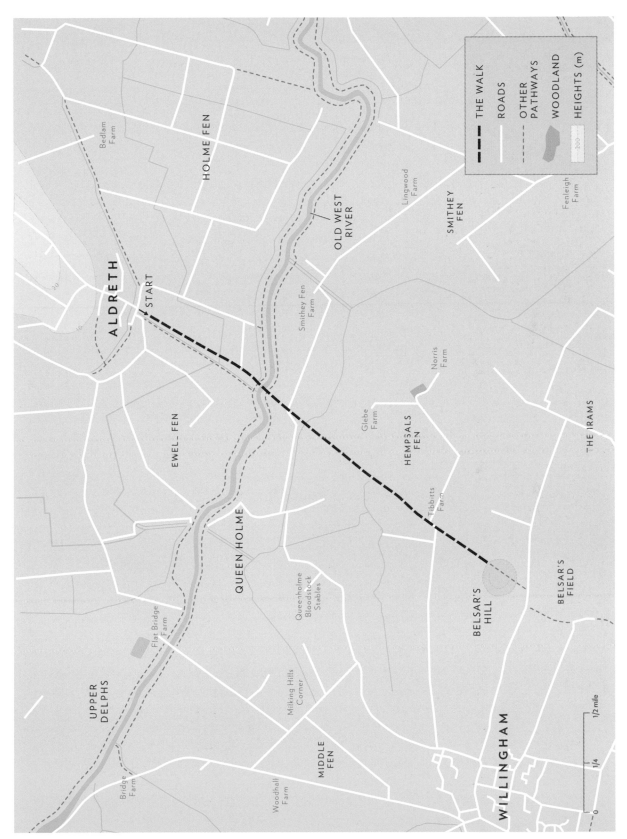

ALDRETH

START

HOLME FEN

Bedam
Farm

OLD WEST
RIVER

Smithey Fen
Farm

Lingwood
Farm

SMITHEY
FEN

Fenleigh
Farm

EWEL FEN

Glebe
Farm

Norris
Farm

HEMPSALS
FEN

THE IRAMS

QUEEN HOLME

Queenholme
Bloodstock
Stables

Tibbitts
Farm

UPPER
DELPHS

Flat Bridge
Farm

Milking Hills
Corner

BELSAR'S
HILL

BELSAR'S
FIELD

Bridge
Farm

Woodhall
Farm

MIDDLE
FEN

WILLINGHAM

THE WALK
ROADS
OTHER
PATHWAYS
WOODLAND
HEIGHTS (m)

200

0   1/4   1/2 mile

THE ROUTE | The causeway at Aldreth

Nicholas Rudd-Jones travels with Diana Rees, who has lived and worked in the fens, to explore an historic causeway leading to the Isle of Ely.

Before the Fens were drained the Isle of Ely was accessible only by river, or via the three causeways that reached across the swamp from the outlying hamlets of Stuntney, Earith and Aldreth. Of these, the Aldreth Causeway is probably the earliest, as well as the most important. It is part of the ancient road from Cambridge to Ely. It was made famous by the story of William the Conqueror and his attempts to oust the rebel Hereward the Wake and his men from Ely.

In 1071, in an attempt to reach Ely, the Normans built a causeway across the fens. However, during William's first attack, the weight of the troops in their armour was so great that the causeway sank and many soldiers drowned. William's second attempt to storm the island is recorded in the 12th-century Deeds of Hereward the Saxon. This time William's men built new defences and recruited a local witch to help them. In retaliation, Hereward's band set fire to the surrounding reeds. The flames and smoke drove off the king's men for a second time.

The village of Haddenham lies on the highest ridge in the Isle of Ely, at its western border. Its two spurs lead to the causeways at Aldreth and Earith. Parking the car at the south end of **Aldreth**, we spot the causeway immediately heading in a straight line south-west towards Cambridge. Nowadays it's a popular stroll out of the village for dog walkers.

It is at Aldreth that Hereward's band assembled (at four metres elevation!) and peered across the flat marsh anxiously to a point about two miles away where the ground begins to rise slightly again (to five metres) where William was assembling his troops on Belsar's Hill.

From Aldreth we walk less than a mile to the ford across the **Old West River**. The Old West probably originated from the abandonment of the Car Dyke and the flooding of the Earith area, which forced the creation of a new outlet for the Great Ouse. During the Middle Ages, the Old West was the main trade route from King's Lynn and Ely to the upper valley of the Great Ouse. Fuel, timber and other materials bound for the markets of Huntingdon, St Neot's and Bedford were brought upstream, while corn, hides and wool were sent to other markets in England and abroad.

The ugly concrete bridge here was built at the beginning of the

The Aldreth Causeway, alongside Catchwater Drain, heading south-west towards Cambridge, is now a popular stroll out of the village for dog walkers.

The history and wildlife of the causeway is recounted on an interpretation board.

20th century, when the road was still of some significance. There have been many previous structures, the first possibly dating back to the 12th century. When bridges collapsed through disrepair travellers had to cross by ferry. It could be dangerous. In the mid-17th century at least six people were recorded drowned at the crossing.

About a mile further on, we reach Willingham Field, on the edge of the fen, and **Belsar's Hill** settlement, which takes its name from the Norman commander who led the campaign against Hereward. About half of a circular bank-and-ditch entrenchment remains; when entire it would have contained about six acres. Although it is supposed to have been constructed by William when he besieged the Isle of Ely, it may originally have been a British work. If so, William probably made some alterations. It would always have offered an important strategic vantage point, controlling passage onto the Isle of Ely.

Here for the first time on this three-mile walk we get a real feel for the strategic significance of high ground in the Fens, and the inaccessibility and therefore defensibility of Ely. We are reminded that in the end it wasn't the geography that betrayed the city but its own inhabitants. The abbot and monks of Ely decided to side with William and guided the Normans safely onto the isle.

The causeway remained an important route right up to the 20th century, when it was superseded by surrounding roads. Alfred Watkins identified this route from Ely to Cambridge as part of an alignment that runs from Strethall Church to the Great Ouse. In his 1925 book *The Old Straight Track*, Watkins claimed that there was a network of lost ancient trackways criss-crossing the country in straight lines. These "ley lines" linked old earthworks and prehistoric sites.

The idea captured the popular imagination at a time when the Ordnance Survey maps were gaining widespread distribution, making the research straightforward and stimulating. The theory gave rise to a plethora of fanciful ideas about ancient – even alien – civilisations that Watkins himself would have found absurd. There have been plenty of critics of Watkins's methodology. Archaeologist Richard Atkinson demonstrated the point by taking the positions of telephone boxes and pointing out the existence of "telephone box leys". Whether it is an alignment or not, the path we are on is certainly an ancient and historic trading route.

Despite the flatness of the terrain and a rather dull grey sky, our short walk has been strangely evocative. The low clouds are whisked overhead on a brisk, chilly wind. We walk back the way we came, feeling the bleakness of the fen and its coldness towards an unfamiliar traveller. We cheer ourselves up with a rather fine pub lunch.

THE ANCIENT CAUSEWAY AT FLAG FEN

Flag Fen is a small area of wetland just to the south-east of Peterborough on the western edges of the Fens. To the east and west of it, where the ground is a few metres higher, there would have been fields, farms and settlements.

In about 1300 BC a line of posts arranged in five parallel rows was set in the ground, traversing the fen from the dry land shore of Peterborough at Fengate to a large island called Northey on the Whittlesey side, a distance of a little under a mile. Between these 60,000 uprights, nearly a million timbers were used to create a causeway that was about seven yards wide, lying in more or less a straight line. Partway across was a wider platform, like an artificial wooden island, the precise purpose of which is unknown.

As well as a practical thoroughfare to enable safe passage of man and beast over the boggy wetland, the causeway at Flag Fen would seem to be something more. Over 300 pieces of prehistoric metalwork and other apparently votive offerings have been found beside it. They include daggers that seem to have been deliberately broken and laid in the water, and beach pebbles that must have been carried from some distance away.

It is perhaps significant that the Flag Fen causeway was constructed at a time when the Fens were getting much wetter. The offerings may have been intended to summon up spiritual or ancestral support for an important boundary; the causeway may have been a symbolic defence against the rising waters.

The site was discovered in 1982 when Francis Pryor and a team of archaeologists carried out a survey of dykes in the area, funded by English Heritage. A section of the causeway has been excavated and can be viewed in the Preservation Hall, where the timbers are being slowly impregnated with wax. The dripping water, coolness and dark glistening timbers take one straight back in time. It is easy to imagine folk tramping home on this makeshift path after a day tending cattle in the low-lying fields.

Other wetland tracks to walk

The *Sweet Track* (named after the man who discovered it in 1970, Ray Sweet) is one of the oldest preserved timber trackways in the world. Dendrochronology, the study of tree ring dating, places its construction at around 3800 BC. The track runs across part of the Somerset Levels and its location on Shapwick Heath can be visited. As at Flag Fen, the track would have provided its Neolithic makers with access for fishing, hunting and foraging. The discovery of a jadeite axe head in perfect condition suggests that offerings may have been made.

A visit to the Stretham Old Engine, erected in 1831, is a good chance to look at a bit of Fenland history and industrial archaeology. Close to the village of Stretham near Ely, this land drainage pumping station (now disused) is scheduled as an ancient monument and has been restored by the Stretham Engine Trust. It contains a fine steam-powered double-acting rotative beam engine, and is the last surviving complete example of its kind in the Fens. Find out more at strethamoldengine.org.uk. Nearby *Wicken Fen* is a remnant of the once massive Cambridgeshire Fens kept close to its ancient state (wicken.org.uk). There is a short boardwalk (our modern take on a wooden trackway) taking you over the fenland habitat. You may be lucky enough to spot the rare swallowtail butterfly.

Further reading

To find out more about Flag Fen and to plan a visit, go to *flagfen.com*.

Flag Fen: Life and Death of a Prehistoric Landscape (Francis Pryor, The History Press) has all the detail you could wish for on one of Europe's most famous prehistoric sites.

From Punt to Plough: A History of the Fens (Rex Sly, Sutton Publishing) is by the leading authority on Fenland customs and farming. Sly himself comes from a long line of fen farmers.

East Anglia: Walking the Ancient Tracks (Shirley Toulson, Whittet Books) is hard to get hold of, but an invaluable starting-point for exploring the ancient tracks of this fascinating region. She was a follower of Alfred Watkins and many of these routes are inspired by a search for ley lines.

More walks, ideas and discussion can be found on the Walkingworld website at walkingworld.com

6 Monks' trods

The Norman conquest brought a new aristocracy to Britain. On their coat-tails, benefiting from the patronage of the powerful and wealthy, came the monks. In exchange for land and money, the inmates of monastic houses promised to pray for the souls of their benefactors and ease their way to heaven. In time they accumulated enormous wealth of their own. The Cistercian order, in particular, flourished on British soil. Its first British abbey was founded in Waverley, Surrey, in 1128; by 1152 Waverley had created five offshoots and some of these had daughter houses of their own. Before long the Cistercians had established more than 80 abbeys across England, Scotland and Wales.

The Monks' Trod near Rhayader in Wales has survived the damage caused by off-roading, which is now banned along most of the route.

The Cistercians were an offshoot of the Benedictine order. The new order was founded at Citeaux Abbey near Dijon in 1098, with the aim of following a more austere way of life, based on self-sufficiency, manual labour and prayer. Its members are often known as the White Monks, after the colour of their habit of undyed wool, worn in contrast to the black of the Benedictines. The Cistercian ideal took root rapidly, particularly under the control of Robert of Clairvaux, who joined the then modest order with 35 friends and family members in the early 1100s.

The Cistercians became an economic and political force from the 12th century to the time of the dissolution of the monasteries by Henry VIII. Their power was largely built on their extremely efficient and profitable farming of sheep. Fieldwork was an important component of the daily round for a Cistercian monk, so they were well placed to thrive as landowners. With their predilection for taking on unused and unwanted land, and relatively democratic monastic structure, the Cistercians were able to sidestep the normal feudal constraints on agriculture. Without the requirement to open their fields up for communal use by the local population, they were able to practise an early form of what was to become known as enclosure. Large tracts of land could be filled with sheep and cattle and tended by just a few herdsmen.

The Cistercians didn't invent the market for wool but they shrewdly built themselves a powerful niche within it, helped to an enormous degree by the fact that they didn't need to pay wages for their labour. Their sheep farmers were lay brothers, whose earthly reward was a roof over their heads, a secure source of food and clothing and a place to live when they grew old. The Cistercians also had the considerable advantage of not having to pay tax on their wool exports, a dispensation granted by the Pope and swallowed for several centuries by British rulers keen to keep God on their side.

From the start the Cistercian order was intensely practical. Robert of Clairvaux was canny in his support for the Knights Templar, a special order for fighting the Christian cause that was also intensely useful for trading the huge surpluses the Cistercian abbeys were able to produce. The Knights Templar had posts across medieval Europe, means of transport and even banks. They became a vital partner to the monks, whose vows prevented them from trading on their own behalf. It was similar to a modern charity setting up a separate commercial arm.

The rapid expansion of the Cistercian order called for efficient lines of communication. In terms of control, the Cistercians fell between the highly centralised rule of some orders and the almost autonomous abbeys of the Benedictines. In Cistercian houses the monks elected their own abbot and their abbey and all its property were their own. But the abbey was subject to the General Chapter, which maintained a vigilant hold over the order. The abbots were required to attend the Chapter once a year in September; failure to

turn up without proper cause brought severe penalties.

Throughout the rest of the year the abbeys kept in touch with each other. If a suitable connecting path did not already exist, a "trod" might well be created. Like the Roman roads but in a subtler way, the paths that linked the Cistercian monasteries were all about the maintenance of control and power. There would inevitably be traffic of goods and animals but also of important personages checking up on satellite institutions and making sure that they kept in line on religious matters, and up to date on commercial ones. The fact that the paths took an elevated and deliberately constructed route across the hills granted a measure of security from thieves and robbers, but there was also status to be gained from taking a "high road".

We can readily imagine monks and abbots journeying to outlying institutions to deliver the medieval equivalent of a PowerPoint presentation ("I have some illuminations here showing how our trade in Flanders is progressing..."). The trod was their channel of communication, their telephone line or internet, as much as it was the physical route for getting from one abbey to another.

The conditions enjoyed by the Cistercians laid the foundation for great power and wealth, and also for innovation. The White Monks had the time to acquire knowledge, not just in the theological sense but also in the fields of agriculture, technology and commerce. Remains found at Laskhill, an outpost of Rievaulx Abbey, suggest that they had developed a blast furnace for making large quantities of iron, several centuries before the technology became common.

But all this wealth inevitably led to strife, especially for a monastic order created specifically to counteract the excesses of the Benedictines. Everywhere the monks kept falling back into fervour for commercial success and the luxuries it could bring, rather than the austerities they had supposedly signed up for. As with an overblown modern-day conglomerate, there were repeated attempts to reform, to get "back to basics".

In Britain the job was eventually done by Henry VIII, who took the monasteries' land and other property for his depleted coffers. If the Cistercians were on the verge of building blast furnaces across Britain, kicking off an early industrial revolution, they never got the chance.

The oratory dedicated to Saint Guérin looks out across the Vallée d'Aulps, once entirely under the control of the Cistercian Abbey at St Jean d'Aulps.

THE CISTERCIANS IN EUROPE

The Cistercian order expanded right across Europe, into Spain, Portugal, Germany, Hungary, Italy, Poland, Sweden and Norway. By the end of the 13th century there were 300 houses; at the order's height in the 15th century, over 750. Everywhere you travel on the continent you are likely to come across its soaring architecture.

One Cistercian abbey sits just outside the village of St Jean d'Aulps in the Rhône-Alpes region of France. Leading from it and taking the high road along the Vallée d'Aulps is an ancient path towards Lake Geneva. We know it was used by the powerful of the order because just a mile or so beyond the abbey there is an oratory to the memory of Saint Guérin, second abbot of the abbey and bishop of Sion in the Rhone Valley. It is on a steep section of hill where the track cuts back and forth in a series of hairpin bends.

The unfortunate Guérin seems to have got this far and no further. The sign above the oratory tells us that he was "stopped here" by illness on his way to Sion in 1158 ("Ici la maladie arrêta St Guérin allant à Sion"). Of course it's possible he just had a tummy bug and had to return to the abbey for a few days before setting off again, but the implication is that the condition was terminal. The story is indicative of the way in which the order put out its tentacles into the remotest places and used the pathways to them to maintain control.

OUR WALK | The Mid Wales trod

The soaring architecture of the Cistercians is still in evidence in the ruins of Rievaulx Abbey

When Wales opened up to new Christian influences after the Norman invasion of 1066, its remoteness appealed to the solitude-seeking Cistercians. Thirteen monasteries had been founded there by 1226, the first being Tintern Abbey, nestled in a deep cut of the Wye valley. Strata Florida, Abbey Cwmhir and Strata Marcella were all daughter colonies of Whitland Abbey in south-west Carmathenshire, set up in the late 12th century.

The Monks' Trod in Mid Wales traces a lonely way across 24 miles of hills and moors, joining Strata Florida to Abbey Cwmhir to its east. A branch may have connected these two to Strata Marcella – travellers would have left the route at the Elan valley and struck off north. Like the earlier ridgeways and the Anglo-Saxon dykes, the trod hugs higher ground, though not necessarily on the very ridge.

This monks' trod is unusual in that it has not been overlain with a more recent track or road: it simply fell out of use after the dissolution of the monasteries. A typical section of it cuts across a slope heading towards a broad shoulder at Carn Ricet, around halfway between the two abbeys. It is clear that considerable work was done to cut the pathway into the slope: it wasn't just worn by many feet. All along the trod the builders used a cut-and-fill technique, piling the cut-away earth and rubble onto the downhill side to create a flat track. In places it looks like a rather narrow railway trackbed.

Elsewhere on the trod there is further evidence that the path was carefully constructed; in places it is metalled, and at one stream crossing (Nant y Sarn, visited during our walk) there appear to be the stone pedestals for a bridge, though it would be difficult to prove that these date from medieval times.

The obvious conclusion is that this path was not simply for walking, though this section at least was nowhere near wide enough to drive flocks of sheep or herds of cattle along. It was designed to be ridden by horse, and fast. Everything about it is fashioned to make the ride easy. And indeed accounts from the 12th century say that the journey from Strata Florida to Abbey Cwmhir could be undertaken in a single day.

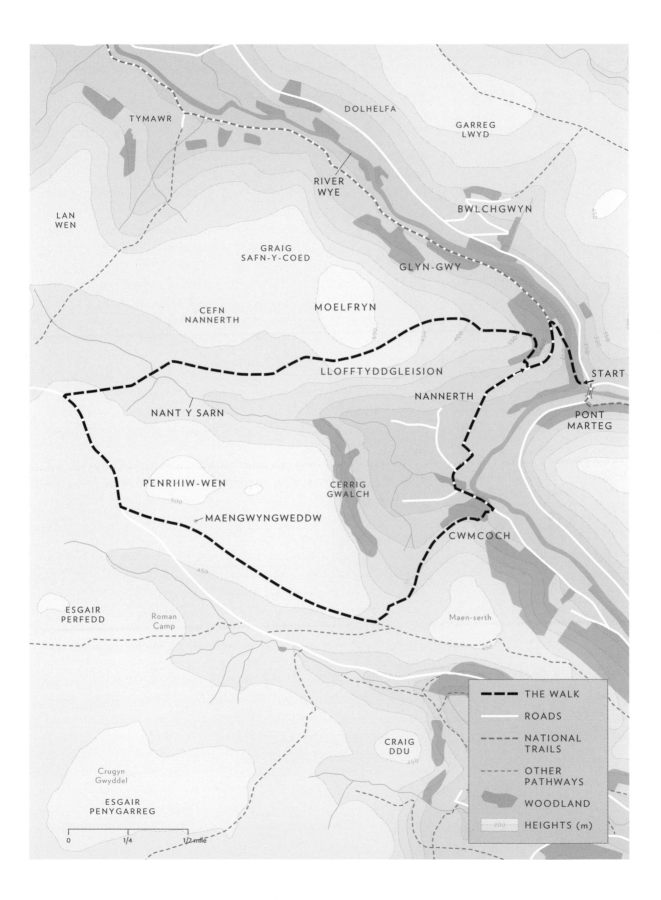

TYMAWR

DOLHELFA

GARREG
LWYD

LAN
WEN

RIVER
WYE

BWLCHGWYN

GRAIG
SAFN-Y-COED

GLYN-GWY

CEFN
NANNERTH

MOELFRYN

LLOFFTYDDGLEISION

START

NANT Y SARN

NANNERTH

PONT
MARTEG

PENRHIW-WEN

CERRIG
GWALCH

MAENGWYNGWEDDW

CWMCOCH

ESGAIR
PERFEDD

Roman
Camp

Maen-serth

CRAIG
DDU

Crugyn
Gwyddel

ESGAIR
PENYGARREG

	THE WALK
	ROADS
	NATIONAL TRAILS
	OTHER PATHWAYS
	WOODLAND
	HEIGHTS (m)

0   1/4   1/2 mile

THE ROUTE | The trod from Nannerth

A detail of the stonework from Rievaulx Abbey

David and Chris Stewart follow an ancient path that is almost completely deserted, even today.

We have been drawn to the Monks' Trod in Mid Wales by an article in *British Archaeology*. The magazine has a rough map of the trod, and from it we can see that there is a potentially interesting circuit in the vicinity of Rhayader. In the hope that we can experience two branches of this medieval track in one go, we drive down to Rhayader from our overnight stay near Oswestry, where we have been investigating Offa's Dyke.

We arrive in Rhayader in the afternoon, which gives us an opportunity to walk a section of the trod above Craig Goch Reservoir before the sun sets. Heading west away from the single-track road, the path immediately takes us into wide open grass and moorland. It is extraordinarily remote and beautiful, and almost completely treeless. We are accompanied only by a few birds drifting in as the shadows lengthen, a handful of sheep and cattle and a sole Tornado jet, which blasts across the big sky.

As we return from our short foray onto the trod and it begins to get dark, we become even more aware of how isolated this place is. A few pairs of headlights wind along the narrow roads but otherwise there is no sign of human life. For a monk and his companions walking this way it must have seemed even more distant from civilisation, and a bleak, desperate spot in bad weather. It may not have been quite as treeless then but that may have been seen as a disadvantage. In medieval times members of the ruling classes often ordered the cutting-down of woodland near their thoroughfares, to take away potential hiding places for robbers.

We head back to Rhayader and find ourselves a spot on the campsite beside the Wye. It's the very end of the season, so we are more or less on our own; the warden seems rather surprised to see anyone turning up. Wandering into town, we find the cattle market still in full swing, with the auctioneer singing through the numbers in a language that is totally incomprehensible to us (and not, as far as we can tell, because it is Welsh: it is just too fast to pick out the syllables). Opposite the market is a long queue at the fish and chip shop. We join the line.

The uniform of the sheep farmer must be the same across Britain: a collection of beige, moss green and brown, tweeds and waxed jackets

Large stone slaps mark out a single field above Nannerth. The trod passes along the boundary.

Running across the slope of the hill above Craig Goch Reservoir, the track has been constructed using a cut and fill technique.

and, more often than not, a flat cap. Perhaps it helps to merge into the landscape, or perhaps it's as well to be understated in one's dress, to blend in with the crowd. We've learned not to ask a farmer how well things are going – whether it's good or bad you'll get a pretty non-committal answer. The range goes from "It's not great right now" to "It could be worse, I suppose". Maybe the monks were as circumspect, keeping their business dealings under their hoods. These folk have good taste in fish and chips, though. These are some of the best we have had in years.

The next morning we park at Pont Marteg. Cwm Marteg is a nature reserve, with various circular routes along the disused railway track and along the continuation of the Monks' Trod to the east. We can see the path clearly as it rises diagonally up the opposite valley side, cut into the slope in its characteristic way. In the valley bottom at Gilfach lies a well-preserved 16th-century longhouse, now the education centre for the reserve.

Our seven-mile route, however, follows the trod to the west. We cross the busy main road and then the River Wye by a footbridge. The path leads up to a cluster of buildings at **Nannerth**. From here the public footpath zigzags up the western ridge of **Moelfryn**, the 500 metre-

The trod makes its way across rough moorland after crossing the stream at Nant y Sarn.

high hill that the Monks' Trod traverses, though it avoids the summit by passing through a narrow shoulder above some rocky outcrops. The zigzag path we take is not the original line of the trod, which dropped down half a mile further west to reach the former monastic grange at Nannerth Ganol. There is still a medieval longhouse there, dating from the mid-16th century. The path down to the grange descends in a series of hairpin bends, the only place along the whole trod that it does so.

Just beyond Moelfryn and as we start to cross the moorland, we reach an isolated and ruined farmstead, with a single field bounded by upended stone slabs. A path leading up from Nannerth Ganol suggests that it was part of the same property, perhaps an outlying gathering point for the sheep and cattle grazing on the moorland above. The trod becomes more indistinct as it crosses some boggier ground until it bears left to cross the stream at **Nant y Sarn** (which tellingly means "road brook"). Here the track cuts down between some rocky bumps and then climbs directly up the other side to a road, which it follows for a mile or more before joining the path we took the previous afternoon.

At the road, however, we turn left to join the ridge running down towards Rhayader. A branch of the trod follows this ridge, offering an alternative route via the town. Veering away from the road, we pass the site of a striking quartz standing stone, called **Maengwyngweddw** ("White widow's stone"). It may have marked the boundary point between two manors or simply been placed here to help travellers find their way.

A long-running battle over use of the trod for off-roading has been won by the conservationists for much of its length, at least for the time being. But not here. The track is deeply rutted and, where it isn't, it has been infilled with rubble. Channels have been cut to drain water from the roadway. Signs plead with drivers and bikers to keep to the track and not to diverge onto the grassy slopes either side. It seems an unsatisfactory solution for both parties. Driving along the heavily repaired trackway can be no more exciting than tackling a bumpy drive, albeit with better views. For the walker the repaired road service simply looks a mess, even on a day when no vehicles come along.

After a mile or so we cut left to drop into a curved valley. It's difficult to find the top of the path but once over the brow we can see it slashing a green gash through the bracken. Ahead is a patchwork of small fields in the fertile bend in the Wye Valley surrounding Nannerth Farm. The dog bounds ahead down the slope. We pass above a clump of trees and take a short steep path down to the single-track road leading back to our start point.

Brough follows in the footsteps of the medieval monks.

Rievaulx Abbey, now almost nine hundred years old, remains a magnificent sight.

RIEVAULX ABBEY

Rievaulx, in what is now the North Yorkshire Moors National Park, was the founding abbey for the Cistercian order in the north of England. It was established in 1132 with a group of just 12 monks arriving direct from France. It became the centre for the expansion of monasteries into this part of England and thence into Scotland.

As it grew in power and prominence, its buildings grew too. The original small church was replaced with a larger one in the late 1140s and then that was expanded again, with a magnificent new nave and crossing transepts in the early part of the 13th century. At its height the abbey had about 630 choir monks and lay brothers, and the magnificent church could hold them all, though the largely illiterate lay brothers were kept firmly separated from their superiors.

After the dissolution of the monasteries, the majority of abbeys fell into disrepair. Many of Rievaulx's buildings were deliberately destroyed by its new owner, Thomas Manners, Earl of Rutland, a man who was obviously keen to accentuate his reforming credentials. Fortunately much of the structure was beyond such vandalism, and substantial portions of the new church and of the refectory remain standing. The layout of the cloisters, infirmary and dormitories is still clearly visible.

Other places to follow the monks

It's always intriguing to look at a map of the countryside surrounding a Cistercian abbey, to try to figure out the paths leading out to the abbey granges (the usual term for an abbey farm) and beyond. Rievaulx Abbey, in north Yorkshire, had some 20 granges, all of which would have been in regular contact with the abbey and connected to it. Of course the majority of the major routes between the abbeys have been overlaid by modern roads.

On the North York Moors many miles of paved pathways have been found and attributed to the medieval monks. One well-known section, also called the *Monks' Trod*, leads to Whitby Abbey on the coast. There is no proof that these paved roads were built by the Cistercians, though it is possible, given their wealth, that they had a hand in some of them. Equally likely is that they were built as "pannier ways" joining the fishing ports with their markets, since it would have been important to make quick progress with cargoes of fish. They may also have been used to carry smuggled goods away from the coast during the 17th and 18th centuries.

Further reading

Andrew Fleming's article on the Monks' Trod is in *British Archaeology*, November/December 2009 (Council for British Archaeology). A more detailed article by Andrew Fleming, 'The Making of a Medieval Road', is available in *Landscapes Journal*, Volume 10.1 (Windgather Press).

English Heritage produces excellent guidebooks for the properties in its care. The best place to buy them is on a visit to the property itself, so you can immediately relate the story to the physical remains. The guidebook for *Rievaulx Abbey* (Peter Fergusson, Glyn Coppack and Stuart Harrison) can also be ordered from the English Heritage website at english-heritageshop.org.uk.

Sheep (Alan Butler, John Hunt Publishing) is a short and highly readable account of the economic importance of the sheep and its most important by-product, wool. The chapter on the Cistercians provides an insight into their role as innovators in medieval Britain.

7 Pilgrimage routes

Pilgrimage became a defining characteristic of the medieval church in Britain: it played an important role in placing the church at the centre of people's lives. A declaration of sainthood brought considerable advantages to the place in which a saint's relics were held. As well as conferring status on the establishment, the shrine would become a magnet for pilgrims. Pilgrims brought money, both in terms of offerings and the purchase of souvenirs and, more generally, to the businesses of the town. It is not altogether surprising that churches, cathedrals and abbeys went to great lengths to either get themselves a local saint or, at the very least, lay their hands on some notable relics.

We think of a pilgrimage as a journey lasting several days or even months, but the vast majority undertaken in Britain during the medieval ages were much shorter. A believer with a mental or physical malaise, or owing penance for some relatively minor sin, might be sent to a saint's shrine just an hour or two's walk away. Few people had the leisure and resources to undertake the longer journeys to the best-known shrines. The pilgrimage from London to Canterbury described in Chaucer's *Canterbury Tales* would be accessible only to those with adequate wealth and free time.

Despite the popularity of pilgrimage, first-hand accounts by pilgrims are few and far between. Records exist of the offerings made at shrines, but these are purely monetary accounts and tell nothing of the individuals who made them. The miracle stories that authenticated a saint's position in the eyes of the church are usually backed up with comprehensive details of the patient's condition and miraculous cure. But only a tiny proportion of pilgrims will have witnessed a miracle, let alone been the subject of one.

There are, however, some surviving personal documents that give a glimpse into the lives of real pilgrims. Wills occasionally set out bequests for pilgrimages to be undertaken on the deceased's behalf; in some cases these will have been fulfilled by a member of the family but there were also professional pilgrims who would undertake the journey for a fee. Some pilgrims were penitents, sent by their bishops to atone for their sins (adultery in particular required a long-distance journey, or sometimes a number of them). The penitent would often have to bring back a "certificate of performance".

Pilgrimages are also mentioned in evidence at inquests, for instance where a beneficiary's age needed to be proved. Witnesses would recall that they had seen a young person baptised, remembering the date because it matched a pilgrimage they were on at the time. In one example in 1373 a dozen men testified to being at the baptism of Walter fitz Waryn on the Feast of the Assumption in 1349. They knew they had the day right because, in their 20s at the time, they were in a company of pilgrims visiting Box that day.

One of the rare first-hand accounts comes from the remarkable Margery Kempe of Lynn, who like Chaucer's Wife of Bath travelled to some far-away shrines, abroad as well as in Britain. Her story suggests that it was normal for women to go on pilgrimage on their own, although at times she was asked for a letter of permission from her husband, rather to her indignation. She was enthusiastic in her devotions, being by her own admission somewhat prone to loud wailing and weeping. Her husband accompanied her on a few of her early trips but was clearly embarrassed by her over-egged

King's Wood, on the Pilgrims' Way near Canterbury, continues to be a worked woodland.

John Wycliffe was an early and vociferous Roman Catholic dissident.

performance, as indeed were some of the monks. On one visit to a shrine Mr Kempe made himself scarce and pretended not to know her. From then on, it seems, he decided to stay at home.

It is easy to be cynical about the role of the church authorities and of the keepers of the shrines, who found plentiful ways of parting the pilgrims from their money. From the middle of the 14th century, the Lollards (the followers of reformer John Wycliffe) argued that pilgrims were gullible fools being fleeced by the unscrupulous. The common practice of selling "indulgences" – reducing the time one would need to spend in Purgatory – did not help the image of the medieval Catholic church.

But in many respects the picture is more complex. The church did try to apply some level of proof to the claims of miracles, and we cannot expect the degree of scientific objectivity we would demand now. There's also reason to suppose that medieval pilgrims had mixed motives for their journeys: only one part may have been devotional. For a group of men in their 20s a pilgrimage may have been an opportunity to travel together and experience something new – not unlike a gap year now.

The church at Boughton Aluph on the Pilgrims' Way offered an unusual place of shelter for pilgrims on their way to Canterbury.

OUR WALK | The Pilgrims' Way

In recent years The Pilgrims' Way has become a popular waymarked trail.

The cult of St Thomas Becket was initially home-grown, encouraged by the Augustinian orders at both ends of the classic pilgrimage from Southwark in London to Canterbury, but it did not stay that way for long. The manner of Becket's death at the hands of four knights in Canterbury cathedral on December 29, 1170 caused outrage across the Christian world, and soon his shrine was drawing believers from every corner of Europe. Canterbury became a destination to rival Rome, Santiago and Jerusalem, bolstered by Becket's unusually swift canonisation in 1173.

With pilgrims coming from across the country and abroad, there would have been a network of routes radiating out from the city. A good proportion of European pilgrims will have landed in the south coast ports and made their way gradually north-east, possibly starting more than a hundred miles from Canterbury with a visit to the shrine of St Swithun in Winchester. A chapel dedicated to St Thomas Becket was set up in Portsmouth in 1181, suggesting that it was a starting point on a "Becket tour".

The so-called Pilgrims' Way, which runs from Farnham in Surrey to Canterbury, may have been used by pilgrims travelling this route. Most of the way it runs side by side with the North Downs Way, the modern long-distance path. The name first appears on 19th-century Ordnance Survey maps, put there, it is said, by an OS employee called Edward Renouard James. It surely cannot have come entirely from his over-active imagination. One can only assume that he put the name onto the map because it was in popular usage by those living on or near the track.

It is quite possible that pilgrims did use the ancient tracks running along the escarpments of the North Downs, though factual evidence is hard to come by. These higher routes would have been drier and slightly more passable in the spring, which was a popular time for making the trip to Canterbury, as recalled in the very opening lines of Chaucer's great work: "Whan that Aprill with his shoures soote, The droghte of March hath perced to the roote..."

But the North Downs route was by no means the only way to the martyr's shrine. The very busy pilgrimage route that opened up immediately following Becket's murder was directly from London, roughly following the modern A2 and therefore not quite as appealing to today's walkers. For a pilgrim, this route would have had special meaning, as it would match that made by Becket himself on his last journey from London to Canterbury. It was in fact the route that King Henry himself took in penance for his part in the saint's murder.

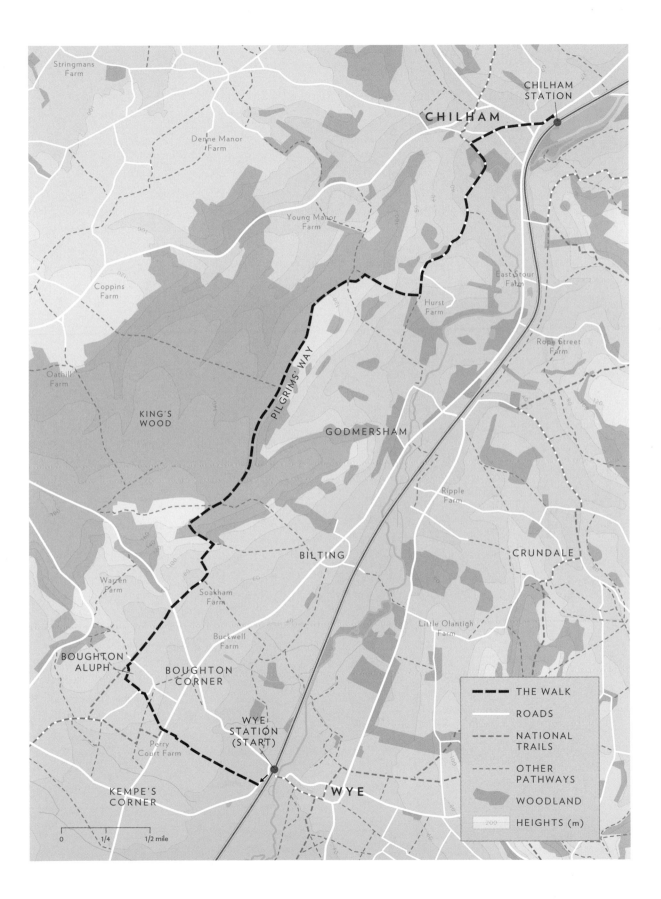

STRINGMANS FARM

DENNE MANOR FARM

CHILHAM
CHILHAM STATION

YOUNG MANOR FARM

EAST STOUR FARM

COPPINS FARM

HURST FARM

PILGRIMS' WAY

ROPE STREET FARM

OATHILL FARM

KING'S WOOD

GODMERSHAM

RIPPLE FARM

CRUNDALE

BILTING

WARREN FARM

SOAKHAM FARM

LITTLE OLANTIGH FARM

BUCKWELL FARM

BOUGHTON ALUPH
BOUGHTON CORNER

WYE STATION (START)

PERRY COURT FARM

KEMPE'S CORNER

WYE

	THE WALK
	ROADS
	NATIONAL TRAILS
	OTHER PATHWAYS
	WOODLAND
200	HEIGHTS (m)

0   1/4   1/2 mile

THE ROUTE | From Wye to Chilham

David and Chris Stewart seek out a winter pilgrimage route to Canterbury, the shrine of Britain's greatest saint, Thomas Becket.

Driving back to England after a trip to the French Alps, we emerge from the Channel Tunnel near Ashford in Kent. Looking at the map, we see a short section of what is known as the Pilgrims' Way running from Wye just north of Ashford to the village of Chilham, just short of Canterbury. There's a rail line linking the two villages, so we figure we can catch a train from Chilham to Wye and walk the section in one direction. Seven miles is all we have time for, as it's January, nearing lunchtime, and we'll be lucky to complete the walk in daylight.

We leave our car by the railway station at Chilham. On the short journey to Wye we discuss pedigree dogs with the guard, dwelling particularly on the iniquities of the Kennel Club breed standards that mean that our Jack Russell is a breeding reject, thanks to the patches of grey on his back. Throughout the conversation Brough gets a lot of petting, so he's happy enough. Getting off at Wye, we find an old-fashioned ticket office cum waiting room, complete with a bookcase of novels and a sturdy wooden bench on which we sit to adjust our laces.

Just outside Wye is **St Eustace's Well**. In 1200 Eustace, the abbot of a Cistercian monastery in Normandy, gave his blessing to a spring. The chronicler Roger of Hoveden reports that he sent a woman who was possessed by a demon and inflated by dropsy to the spring, where she vomited out two enormous black figures that turned first into dogs and finally into asses. For some reason the woman felt impelled to chase them but "a certain man who had been appointed to look after the spring sprinkled water from it between her and the monsters, which immediately rose into the air leaving behind them a foul smell".

The story is intriguing because it seems likely that the spring or well was already favoured as a site of worship or healing, and perhaps had been for centuries. Eustace may simply have been acting as a canny agent of the church in bringing it into the Christian fold. The church was usually at pains to outlaw unofficial shrines and to throw doubt on any claims of cures or other miracles taking place in those places. The blessing of an outdoor spring seems at odds with usual Catholic practice and more in keeping with older pagan rites.

Back at the station in Wye, we cross the railway lines at a gated level crossing and find our way onto a muddy path that rises gently towards the North Downs. The path is puddled and sticky with mud, thanks to recently melted snow, and strewn with shreds of plastic, broken crates

Coppiced sweet chestnut, found in King's Wood, took off in the 1800s as a source of long straight poles for the hop industry.

HOW DID YOU BECOME A SAINT?

The Catholic church has canonised more than 3,000 saints, canonisation being the official declaration that a person has joined the canon of saints in heaven. In the early years of the Christian religion martyrs and confessors (people who expressed their faith through their words and deeds) were venerated as saints in a somewhat haphazard way. In the late 12th century, however, the Catholic church announced that only the Pope had the authority to pronounce someone a saint and canonisation became increasingly complex and, some might say, political.

In medieval times there was a reasonably standard pattern to the process. It helped to have been martyred in some way rather than dying peacefully in one's bed (beheading was especially auspicious). Very often the body was found not to have decayed in the normal manner; if removed, the head might have mysteriously rejoined itself to the body. The body of Cuthbert, the bishop of Lindisfarne, was said to have been perfectly preserved when his tomb was opened 11 years after his death in 687 – a miracle that contributed greatly to the cult that was already growing around him.

The keepers of a prospective saint's shrine would hope to identify at least one miraculous cure that they could present to the papal authorities. This would be proof that the saint was interceding on behalf of his or her followers. If the miracle was found to be authentic – and the examination of the evidence was not unlike that of a court of law – then canonisation might ensue.

The size of the chimney at Boughton Aluph church is remarkable, filling the gap between porch and buttress.

and mounds of frozen carpet, the detritus of last season's picking and packing. The nearby farm is no tidier. We pass between some forlorn poly shelters, with dead fruit bushes, more shredded plastic and wooden pallets.

Crossing the main road, there's a straight path across an open field, with the church of **Boughton Aluph** standing clearly ahead of us. The name comes from the owner of the manor from 1210, Aluphus of Boctune. He is believed to have begun work on the present-day church, replacing an earlier Anglo-Saxon structure that would probably have been of wood. Construction continued in stages, with much completed in the 13th and 14th centuries. The church is much as it would have been in the heyday of the pilgrimage. One feature in particular draws our attention. The red brick south porch has a chimney and inside there is a large Tudor fireplace. The story goes that pilgrims waited here until there were enough of them to venture on through King's Wood without fear of being robbed.

That fear was not entirely unfounded. A group of pilgrims from Warwickshire reported being attacked and robbed at "la Bleo" on their way to Canterbury in 1332. The location is presumed to be Blean Wood on the London Road, just a few miles outside the city. People on pilgrimages would have been an attractive target. As well

The south porch at Boughton Aluph boasts a large Tudor fireplace, in front of which pilgrims could warm themselves before venturing into King's Wood.

as funds for eating, drinking and staying overnight on their journey, pilgrims would have the wherewithal to make offerings, buy souvenirs and give alms to poorer folk travelling the same route.

In Canterbury you could purchase small phials containing water in which there was, supposedly, a microscopic quantity of the martyr's blood. The liquid could be drunk in time of need or, more likely, hung around the neck as protection and as outward proof of your visit. Pilgrims could also purchase small pewter moulds, with images of the shrine or of Thomas Becket himself, which were perhaps pressed against the tomb before being taken away.

We walk round Boughton Aluph church, with its crumbly flint walls repaired here and there with red brick. There's a flying buttress at one corner, no doubt erected to forestall an imminent collapse. We try all the doors, including the oak door into the south porch, and find them all locked. The south side is covered with scaffolding: much-needed repairs are under way. It's mid-afternoon and threatening to rain, so we plod on across another field and along a farm track.

None of this seems authentically medieval, but now the path bears left and begins to climb up onto the escarpment. We pass a team of conservation trust volunteers planting a new hedgerow, and the incline increases. Finally we enter the woods and climb up to a path junction. Here we turn right onto a track that seems much more likely to be on the original ancient route. The going is difficult as the track is deeply rutted in places and very wet. It's easy to imagine it being much like this in medieval times during the winter months, with any carts passing along worsening the surface for those unfortunate enough to be on foot.

It's possible that those looking after St Thomas's shine were aware of the problem of marking the anniversary of his death at the end of December. In 1220 his relics were moved to a new shrine within Canterbury, the day of inauguration being a much sunnier July 7. The move set off a period of heightened promotion. There was a prescribed tour, taking in the place of the murder, the original tomb, the new shrine, a second shrine containing the saint's severed scalp, plus other churches in the city dedicated to St Martin and St Augustine. The midsummer date would have encouraged many more people to travel along the hopefully dry-baked trackways to the town.

The track runs close to the crest of the ridge but for the first couple of miles there is wood on either side. It is mainly coppiced hornbeam sweet chestnut but the stems have grown high from the ground-level stumps and on a dark afternoon it's hard to see far into the wood. At one point the dog spots or hears something in the undergrowth and disappears for a few minutes. Even with his white coat we cannot pick him out in the trees. We sit for a while and wait for him to return, a little impatiently as darkness is descending and we really want to be out of the wood while there is still some daylight.

A little further on a view opens out on our right-hand side and for the last mile or so on the ridge we have the wood only on our left. It brings a welcome evening glow onto the path. Finally, as it begins to get really gloomy, we start on the last slope down towards **Chilham Castle**. We feel some of the relief our pilgrims must have felt on leaving the enveloping trees behind. As we walk down the road into the village, we pass some timber-framed houses that may well have witnessed the traffic of real medieval pilgrims.

Arriving at the pub in Chilham, we can't help thinking that pilgrimage illuminates our relationship to walking more than following any other historical pathway. The notion that we are striving for something, even if it is no longer strictly religious, remains. For the pilgrim the act of walking – the journey itself – was a integral part of the experience, one that brought them to closer to Christ. It wasn't just a means of getting to one's destination. With that at least we modern walkers surely have something in common.

*Some unusual gravestones are
to be found in the churchyard
at Boughton Aluph.*

OLDER PILGRIMAGES

Pilgrimage is closely associated with the Catholic church but the notion of travelling to a special place to make offerings or appeal for help is very much older. The Romans built shrines to their gods: for instance there is a rock-cut shrine to the goddess Minerva in an old sandstone quarry at Handbridge near Chester. Travellers may have left offerings in the hope of a safe passage over the River Dee at that point.

Further afield, the Greek oracle at Delphi was famously visited by powerful rulers from right across the Mediterranean, searching for advice from the god Apollo on matters of state. The oracle could only be consulted at certain times of the year, as Apollo was said to reside elsewhere during the winter months. The utterings of the sybil or priestess, a carefully chosen local peasant woman, were translated by priests of the temple into elegant verse. The oracle fell into disfavour after various unreliable predictions. In 66 AD the Roman emperor Nero had some 500 of the best statues from the sanctuary removed to Rome.

Even older still is Paviland Cave, on the Gower Peninsula in South Wales. Here a corpse known as the "Red Lady" was buried some 27,000 years ago. The body is actually that of a young man; it is stained with red ochre and surrounded with grave goods, including ivory fragments and pierced periwinkle shells, also covered in ochre. Other finds from around the same date suggest that the site had special meaning and was visited regularly by people travelling from hundreds of miles away.

Other pilgrimages to make

The official *Pilgrims' Way* has many excellent sections, often on or close to the North Downs ridge. This National Trail of 120 miles follows ancient trackways that may or may not have been on the route used by medieval pilgrims travelling between Winchester and Canterbury. Much of the original route is probably under modern roads. Where ancient trackways were used by pilgrims, they are likely to be found lower down on the southern slopes, just above the sticky clay of the farmland, rather than on the more exposed ridge. The North Downs Trail, by contrast, often takes the ridge route with its better views. There are some sites, like St Martha's Hill near Guildford, that were certainly on the medieval pilgrims' itinerary.

Other trails have been set up with connections to saints and to pilgrimages. *St Cuthbert's Way* traces a route from Melrose Abbey, where he started his career, to Lindisfarne. There is no real evidence that the route was used in Cuthbert's time but the section leading to the Holy Island of Lindisfarne is evocative.

Further reading

Pilgrimage in Medieval England (Diana Webb, Hambledon and London) is sadly out of print but you may be able to find a second-hand copy on Amazon or in your local library. It is an academic book by a lecturer in medieval history, but full of interesting anecdotes and insights.

You can read *The Canterbury Tales* in the original Old English (Geoffrey Chaucer, Penguin Classics) in an edition with useful notes to guide you through the text. Alternatively there is another Penguin Classics edition with a translation by Nevill Coghill.

More walks, ideas and discussion can be found on the *Walkingworld* website at walkingworld.com

8 Forest tracks

In the century after the Norman invasion of 1066, a third of southern England was designated as royal forest. After the conquest William immediately asserted that he owned all the land of the vanquished country, and indeed the famous Domesday Book was an audit of what he regarded as his. The establishment of the royal forests was one of the key ways in which William and his descendants exerted control over the nobles and, within them, the monarchs indulged their passion for hunting. At the peak, there were 143 forests in all.

The word "forest" has come to mean a large tract of trees but its original meaning, as defined in John Manwood's Lawes of the Forrest (a legal treatise first published in 1598), was "a certain territorie of woody ground and fruitful pastures, privileged for wild beasts and foules of the forest, chase and warren to rest and abide there, in the safe protection of the King, for his princely delight and pleasure". As well as woodland, royal forests usually included large areas of heath, grassland and wetland – in fact anywhere that supported deer and other animals and fowl suitable for the hunt.

To protect his property and hunting activities William established a system of "forest law". Offences against this law were divided into two categories: trespass against the "vert" and trespass against the "venison". Trespass against the "vert" – the land and vegetation of the forest – included the enclosure of a pasture, erection of a building, clearing ground for agriculture, and felling trees. Trespass against the "venison" extended pretty much to every beast and fowl of the forest, including deer, boars, hares, wolves, foxes, martens, pheasants and partridges. Hunting or trapping of any form was prohibited. Ordinary folk were not allowed to carry hunting weapons and dogs were banned; mastiffs were permitted as watchdogs, but had to have their front claws removed to prevent them from hunting game. The only exception to the strict hunting laws was if a deer had escaped from the forest and was causing damage to agriculture, in which case it could be killed.

In villages and towns that suddenly found themselves inside a royal forest, people resented the restrictions placed on the environment in which they lived and on which they had relied for their living. Some common rights, however, such as access across the land, the gathering of firewood and mining rights, were not necessarily removed by the imposition of forest law, though they might be curtailed. This contrasts with the enclosure movement in

Woodlands were traditionally a rich resource for foraging.

A group of ancient chestnut trees run alongside Offa's Dyke.

England (see Chapter 13), which often resulted in the elimination of these rights altogether.

Forest law gave rise to a whole panoply of officers, charged with patrolling and protecting the forest. The chief royal official of the forest was the Warden. He supervised the foresters and under-foresters, whose job it was to maintain the forest environment and safeguard its game. The "agisters" supervised "pannage", the right to pasture swine in the forest, and collected the resulting fees. Another group, the "serjeants-in-fee", were allocated small estates in return for policing the forest and apprehending offenders.

Poaching was widespread in the royal forests, with dogs, bows and arrows, crossbows, nets and snares all being used to hunt and kill deer. The culprits were often otherwise law-abiding citizens. In the Middle Ages a large number of clergy were apparently involved. Among those charged with poaching or receiving venison from the Forest of Dean, for instance, were the Archdeacon and canons of Hereford, the Abbot of Augustine's, Bristol, and the monks of Tintern Abbey.

For the lower orders the penalties could be severe: for killing one of the king's deer, a serf could lose his life. Even apparently trivial offences prompted stiff fines. There is a record of a Blakeney man (on the eastern fringe of the Forest of Dean) being fined two shillings in the 17th century for beating down chestnuts. Chestnuts were a valuable natural crop, but the fine of two shillings would have been a week's wages for a skilled man. In the 1860s, a policeman called Bear came across a group of four poachers setting nets for game. The fracas that followed left him with a fractured skull and he died a few days later. All four men were found guilty of manslaughter and sentenced to 15 years' penal servitude.

From the death of Henry II in 1189, the control of the king over the royal forests began to wane. The Magna Carta of 1216 curbed the power of the monarch over the nobles, after which no new royal forests were designated. From this time onwards monarchs were increasingly willing to "abridge" their rights in the royal forests for a suitable payment; it proved a useful way of raising funds. Local nobles could, for example, be granted a royal licence to take a certain amount of game.

OUR WALK | The Forest of Dean

Trees have always set the Forest of Dean apart and been at the heart of its livelihood.

The Forest of Dean is set apart from the rest of the country, almost with an island feel about it. Bounded by the Severn on the south and east, and the Wye to the west and north, with the city of Gloucester providing the "plug" at the top, it has a history of non-conformism. The accent is also noticeably broader than in the surrounding areas.

Driving into the Forest of Dean, one is struck immediately by the sheer mass of trees in every direction: deciduous and coniferous, coppices and saplings, ancient woods and new plantations. Houses with views across the forest and valleys have evocative names such as Overdale and Great Gables.

Trees have always set the Forest of Dean apart and been at the heart of its livelihood. Woodland was typically more valuable than agricultural land because of all the resources that it offered, including timber, underwood, faggots and charcoal, minerals, game, wild swine, acorns and hazelnuts. Woodland areas were also hives of economic activity, attracting first craftsmen making hurdles, wheels and household goods, and subsequently charcoal burners, providing fuel for the iron-smelting furnaces that were key to the beginnings of the industrial revolution.

As England's naval strength grew, so the Forest of Dean became an important source of timber for shipbuilders. Oaks, with their short trunks and spreading branches, grew slowly on its poor soil and produced a strong, curved timber ideal for shipbuilding. By 1613 the forest was acknowledged as a "storehouse of naval timber". In fact, around the time of the Armada a few years earlier, the Spaniards were intent on destroying the Forest of Dean, regarding it as a key military asset. However the navy's demands and the production of charcoal meant that the forest was much degraded. It was the subject of a Re-Afforestation Act in 1667, probably the first of its kind anywhere in the world.

So since medieval times the Forest of Dean has been a worked landscape, rich in natural resources – trees and game above the ground, iron ore and coal beneath. The area is littered with old mines and tramroads (the forerunners of railways) designed to transport the mined materials from the steep valleys to the ports on the Severn. The complexity of the landscape and the early industrialisation set it apart from much of the British countryside.

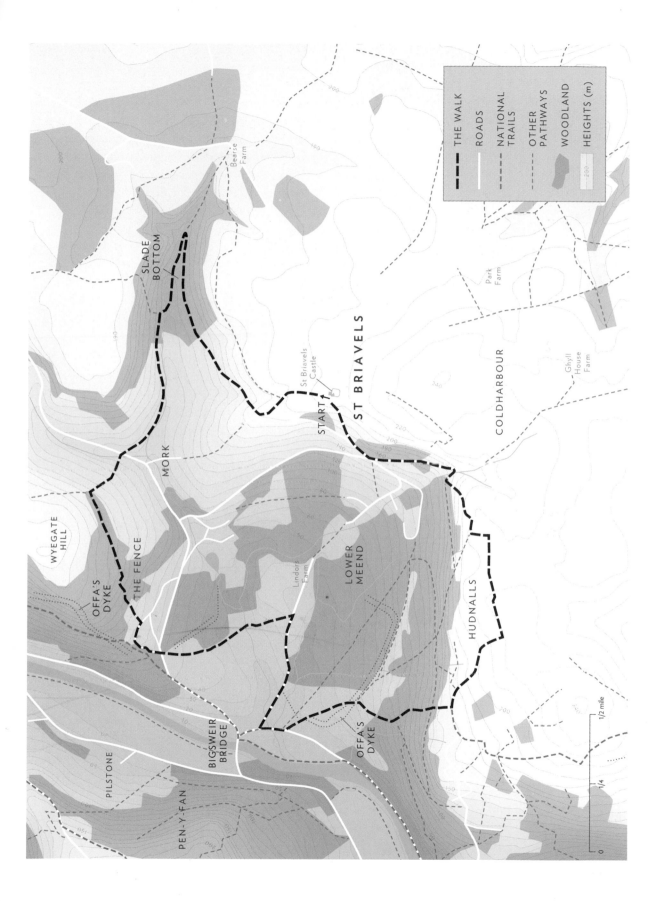

THE WALK
ROADS
NATIONAL
TRAILS
OTHER
PATHWAYS
WOODLAND
HEIGHTS (m)
200

Bearse
Farm

SLADE
BOTTOM

St Briavels
Castle

START

ST BRIAVELS

Park
Farm

COLDHARBOUR

Ghyll House
Farm

MORK

WYEGATE
HILL

THE FENCE

OFFA'S
DYKE

Lindors
Farm

LOWER
MEEND

HUDNALLS

PILSTONE

BIGSWEIR
BRIDGE

OFFA'S
DYKE

PEN-Y-FAN

1/2 mile

1/4

0

The lawyer Sir William Blackstone was unusual in being a member of the establishment who was critical of the game laws.

The relationship between the landowners and the common man has always been a bit different here, too. Despite the forest law laid down in 11th century, the common man in the Forest of Dean ended up with more rights to roam and forage than his counterpart in England's agricultural heartlands. There the precedent set by the king was taken up and expanded by the landed gentry into a much more draconian set of laws and punishments for anyone that poached on their land: the notorious Game Laws. As the lawyer Sir William Blackstone commented in the 18th century: "Though the Forest Laws are now... by degrees grown entirely obsolete, yet from this root has grown up a bastard slip, known by the name of the game law..."

There is a sense in the Forest of Dean that the common man has always stood up against authority. Forest dwellers challenged Charles I's annexation of large parts of the forest for timber for warships in the 17th century. In the 18th century locals appropriated land around the edge of the forest and built houses at places such as Berry Hill, Parkend and the Hudnalls. In the early 19th century a group organised the notorious Dean Forest Riots in an attempt to overturn the enclosure of Park Hill for navy timber. Perhaps it was another independent spirit who a few years ago reintroduced wild boars into the forest without the blessing of the Forestry Commission. They are by all accounts thriving, although there are reports of them attacking dogs during the mating season.

The result of all the different woodland activities, and the way that roughly built hamlets around the edge of the forest became established, is a complex landscape with many woods and coppices, irregular fields and smallholdings, twists and turns in the contours, and countless tiny pathways around and through the villages.

As for routes through the forest, it was always a pretty impenetrable place and often very muddy. The oldest highways were the rivers. We know that the Severn and Wye were used by Roman vessels and there is some archaeological evidence that there were trading routes even earlier, in prehistoric times. There was also a Roman road running between Ariconium (near Ross-on-Wye) to the Severn, near Lydney.

The hinterland remained extremely inaccessible until the arrival of the toll roads in the 18th century. The route between Monmouth and Chepstow, passing St Briavels, was turnpiked in 1755. In the early 19th century several tramroads were constructed that took the iron ore, coal, wood and stone from the mines and valleys to the ports in one easy movement.

The combination of impenetrability and complexity has led to myriad smaller paths, especially at the edges of the main forest.

The delightful Travertine Dams are naturally formed when spring water, saturated in lime, runs over an obstruction in the stream bed, resulting in the deposition of travertine, a porous, crumbly limestone.

Describing routes to other walkers is therefore much trickier than in parts of the country where the choices are limited. It seems likely also that fewer paths were blocked or closed by landowners, as there was limited enclosure for farming and fewer large estates. In the royal forests throughout the south of England there is a sense that, even if you can't quite roam at will, at least there's a path that can take you wherever you want to go.

THE ROUTE | Around St Briavels

Nicholas Rudd-Jones sets out with his old school friend Oliver Quick to explore an area neither has visited properly before.

We begin our seven-mile walk at the Norman St Briavels Castle, on a fabulous June morning. Peering inside before we set out, we discover it's now a youth hostel. A gaggle of walkers are just tying up their boots and getting ready for the off. It brought alive a comment I had read recently by a local author: "The Forest has changed over the centuries from a playground for kings to a playground for the masses."

Heading north out of St Briavels, we almost immediately get great views up the Wye Valley. The path turns east into **Slade Bottom**, and we walk along a typical forest track down which trees can easily be lugged by tractor. Heading back down Slade Brook and a much narrower path, we come across the remarkable **Travertine Dams**. It looks as if a zealous Victorian garden designer has been busy at work, but these are natural dams formed when spring water, saturated in lime, runs over an obstruction in the stream bed, resulting in the deposition of travertine, a porous, crumbly limestone. They are beautiful and mysterious, especially in the dappled morning light coming through the trees.

As we cross the road and start climbing again, we find ourselves on the broad **Weygate Lane**, which was part of the original 1755 toll road from Monmouth to Chepstow, superseded in 1828 by a lower, valley route.

Heading east again, we enter **Bigsweir Woods**, a beautiful mixture of ash, beech, lime and oak. The path runs along the edge of the wood. This would have been the route that the charcoal burners took as they travelled with their charcoal to the furnaces. The sites of charcoal platforms can still be seen in these woods, although we find them hard to distinguish from badger setts, which are also remarkably flat where the earth has been thrown up.

Bigsweir Bridge formed part of the toll road along the Wye Valley between Monmouth and Chepstow, and was opened in 1828, incorporating a toll house at the western (Welsh) end. In 1876 the Wye Valley railway opened, and St Briavels station was built near the western edge of the bridge, nearly two miles from the village that it served – and in another country! The line closed in 1964.

Moving away from the fast-flowing river and uphill again, we cross the impressive earthworks of **Offa's Dyke** and a delightful row

A typical forest track is flanked with ferns and wild garlic

ST BRIAVELS CASTLE

St Briavels Castle is said to have been built by Milo Fitz Walter in about 1130 to guard the Welsh border during the reign of Henry I. Milo became the first Constable of St Briavels and Warden of the Forest, guarding the king's rights and collecting taxes. The castle was used as a hunting lodge by succeeding monarchs.

In the 12th century the St Briavels Hundred was created and the castle became the administrative and judicial centre of the Forest of Dean. For centuries it was used for sittings of the verderers', miners' and manor courts. The verderers were responsible for preserving the vert and venison of the Forest, and "gavellers" were responsible for leasing "gales" (areas of ground) to "free miners" to work for iron ore, coal or stone.

During the 13th century, the castle was a major production centre for quarrels – the iron bolts fired from crossbows. There is a Quarrel Field south of the village, on the edge of the Common, and part of Hudnalls Wood was probably cut down to make charcoal for the forges.

St Briavels Castle, dating from the 12th century, became the administrative and judicial centre of the Forest of Dean. Today it's a Youth Hostel.

of ancient sweet chestnut trees. This would be a great place to hide. **Hudnalls Wood**, which we reach next, is an ancient semi-natural wood, which since the 13th century has been recorded as a place from which the men of St Briavels are allowed to cut wood by right. The Hudnalls enjoys some of the oldest commoners' rights in England, dating back to the 12th century, granting the men of St Briavels the right to take wood (estovers), graze animals (herbage) and turn out pigs for acorns (pannage).

We pick a path up through the trees in much the same way that gatherers of firewood and forest delicacies did hundreds of years ago. It's steep and slippy; it must have been tricky carrying a bundle of wood at the same time.

Coming out at the top of the woods, we arrive on **St Briavels Common**. In medieval times, most of the flatter uplands seem to have been relatively open woodlands, with grassy clearings used as pasture. Much of this was settled and enclosed by squatters between about 1750 and 1810. If a squatter was able to keep the chimney of his new cottage smoking from sunset to sunrise, his claim was thought to become legitimate. The result is a patchwork quilt of smallholdings, small fields, coppices, streams, winding lanes and footpaths, more recently peppered with newer houses and bungalows.

In 1296, during the Scottish wars of independence, Edward I used miners from the St Briavels Hundred to undermine Berwick-on-Tweed's defences and regain it from the Scots. As a result, the king granted them and their descendants free mining rights within the forest.

Many of the old forest rights remain in force today. True "Foresters" are those born within the hundred of St Briavels, an ancient administrative area taking in most of what is now considered the Forest of Dean. According to the statute, males who are over 21 and have worked in a mine for a year and a day can register as a "freeminer" and dig for minerals. In October 2010 a woman successfully claimed the right to be a freeminer. Residents of the hundred who are over 18 can also graze sheep in the forest, under an agreement between the Commoners' Association and the Forestry Commission. The sheep keepers, known locally as "sheep badgers", simply turn their flocks out to graze.

We shortly get back to **St Briavels** and repair immediately to the George pub beside the castle, where we enjoy a hearty Sunday lunch. It is one of those pubs that still has a vibrant local feel about it, and is packed with true Foresters enjoying their independence. But no sign of a riot!

⊕ Other royal forests to explore

Ashdown Forest is the largest public access space in the south-east. It has spectacular views over the Sussex countryside, and is famous as the "home" of Winnie-the-Pooh. Nearly two-thirds of its 6,500 acres are heathland.

Epping Forest straddles the border between Greater London and Essex. It has been in the care of the City of London Corporation since 1878, following unrest between landowners intent on enclosure and commoners defending their rights. Queen Victoria declared: "It gives me the greatest satisfaction to dedicate this beautiful forest to the use and enjoyment of my people for all time."

The *New Forest* in Hampshire retains much of its historic character and has numerous walking possibilities. It was protected by the New Forest Act of 1877 and in 2005 became a national park.

In the Midlands, there are still tracts of Rockingham Forest that can be visited, but they are only to be found in rather isolated parcels; likewise, *Sherwood Forest* near Nottingham has only a very limited area of wood remaining (which is perhaps why the recent BBC *Robin Hood* series was shot on the outskirts of Budapest, in Hungary).

Further reading

Exploring Historic Dean: Fourteen scenic walks in and around an ancient forest (John Sheraton and Rod Goodman, Fineleaf Editions) provides a cross-section of the many different aspects of the forest.

The Forest of Dean (Humphrey Phelps, Amberley) also covers every aspect of the area, including its customs and traditions.

A Right to Roam (Marion Shoard, OUP) goes into some detail on the battle between landowners and commoners for the royal forests. There is a particularly evocative passage on the fight for Epping Forest.

The History of the Countryside (Oliver Rackham, Phoenix) is the book for you if you want to dig a lot deeper into woodlands and royal forests. Meticulously researched, with strong opinions, it is one of the classics on the English landscape. Two chapters focus entirely on woodland and wood pasture.

More walks, ideas and discussion can be found on the *Walkingworld* website at walkingworld.com

9 The corpse road

You can come across a corpse road in any remote corner of Britain. On the map it might appear under any number of names: bier road, burial road, coffin road, coffin line, lyke or lych way, funeral road, procession way or corpse way. As funeral procession routes, the tracks date from late medieval times. As new chapels and churches were built to cope with an expanding population, the original mother churches strove to ensure that the dead from outlying settlements were still brought for burial, despite the hardship and risk involved in carrying a corpse for many miles. It shows a keeness to own the souls of the dead as much as those of the living. The burial fees no doubt played a part.

The corpse road crosses a broad saddle between Mardale and Swindale Head.

Of course there will have been plenty of routes to the churchyard that are not specifically named. The named roads may have been those for which there was no other major purpose. To some extent this was caused by a widespread belief that the carrying of corpses along a route made it a right of way. The belief probably had litle justification in law, but even so, landowners were keen that "church ways" did not become tracks for standard traffic and trade. So the paths ended up being routed through boggy and marshy patches and over other difficult terrain, to put off anyone thinking of taking a horse and cart along them in the course of their normal daily business.

This, of course, made the conveyance of a coffin in harsh winter or wet seasons extremely difficult. There are stories of coffin bearers mired in mud and mourners wading through bogs. It must have made the loss of a family member even more painful, unless it helped to take your mind off things. It certainly means that coffin roads go through some of the most desolate and remote parts of our fells, giving them an atmosphere appropriate to their role.

Corpse roads are, naturally enough, associated with spirits. Puck in *A Midsummer Night's Dream* talks of spirits following particular paths to and from their last resting places: "Now it is that time of night, That the graves all gaping wide, Every one lets forth his sprite, In the church-way paths to glide." No doubt the corpse road would be particularly appealing to a wandering ghost.

There seems to have been a particular risk, if you failed to deal with the body correctly on its way to the grave, that the deceased's spirit would make its way back home to haunt you. "Corpse candles" – balls of light or flame – were said to travel from the burial ground to the person's home and back again. Some traditions, such as always

High Street, an 800m Lake District peak, dominates the skyline, with just a faint glimpse of Haweswater Reservoir below.

keeping the feet of the corpse facing away from his or her old home, were supposed to help keep spirits firmly in the ground where they belonged. It was considered very bad luck to follow a route other than the designated corpse road to the cemetery.

There were often special rituals when the corpse was carried over water, such as a river or stream. On the corpse road leading through Swaledale in the Yorkshire Dales at Ivelet there is a stone by the bridge for resting the coffin, where the mourners could pause for a while before continuing the hard slog along the valley. A headless black dog is seen on occasions at the bridge, leaping into the water below. The phantom is considered a bad omen, even a portent of death.

The specialness of the river crossing seems to reflect a long-held belief that the spirits could not cross water and provides an interesting throwback to the obvious importance of water as a liminal place in Neolithic and Bronze Age times. Whether the Catholic church tacitly approved of all these pagan beliefs, knew nothing of them or quietly tolerated them is difficult to know.

Crossing water, even a mountain stream, was a significant moment on the journey.

Corpse roads were often deliberately routed over marshy difficult ground.

OUR WALK | The Old Corpse Road from Mardale

The Old Corpse Road on the eastern edges of the Lake District links the isolated hamlet of Swindale Head in Mosedale with Mardale. It's a bleak but beautiful crossing of a piece of sometimes boggy moorland, with views to High Street and Harter Fell.

Although there was a church in Mardale, it was only allowed its own cemetery in the 1700s. Until that time the bodies were carried all the way from Mardale, over the hill to Swindale Head and then a further trek of several miles over slightly less difficult ground to the church at Shap. Shap had its own abbey and so the church in the village no doubt assumed rightful dominance over all the surrounding valleys. Mardale was allowed to build a small oratory by the monks at Shap, later replaced by a tiny church with a steeple just 28ft high. Finally permission was granted for the church in Mardale to bury its own dead. The last body to be carried to Shap by the corpse road was that of John Holme on June 17, 1736.

The minuscule Mardale church has now disappeared under the waters of Haweswater. The whole valley was flooded in the mid-1930s after the building of a dam at the northern end. The existing lake grew over threefold in surface area, swallowing up the tiny church, several farms and the Dun Bull Hotel. Nowadays such a development in the national park would be met with an outcry; in the 1930s there was simply sadness and resignation. At the last service in the church on August 18, 1935 the Bishop of Carlisle spoke to the 72 people who could fit inside. Outside over 1,000 stood in the fields and listened as the service was relayed over loudspeakers. The church was dismantled before the flooding, with some of its stones and window lintels used to build the outflow tower that juts out into the reservoir. The bodies in the cemetery were disinterred and moved to Shap church, where they have their own corner near the railway line. So Shap church claimed them in the end.

If you are lucky you will see the one remaining golden eagle of the valley circling above. There used to be a breeding pair but the female was found dead several years ago. The failure of the male to attract a new partner may be down to lack of carrion. In the past the carcasses of sheep and deer were left to rot on the hillsides, providing a source of food capable of supporting two adults and their young. Now, mindful of the look of the environment and contamination of the drinking supplies in the reservoir, the landowners clear them away. It is difficult to imagine

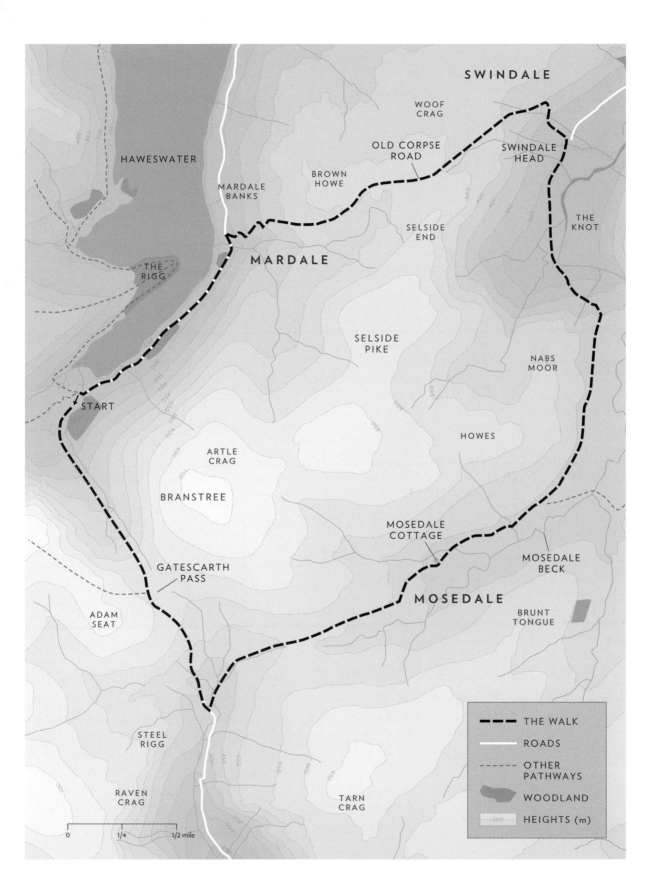

SWINDALE

WOOF
CRAG

OLD CORPSE
ROAD

SWINDALE
HEAD

HAWESWATER

MARDALE
BANKS

BROWN
HOWE

THE
KNOT

SELSIDE
END

THE
RIGG

MARDALE

SELSIDE
PIKE

NABS
MOOR

START

HOWES

ARTLE
CRAG

BRANSTREE

MOSEDALE
COTTAGE

MOSEDALE
BECK

GATESCARTH
PASS

MOSEDALE

ADAM
SEAT

BRUNT
TONGUE

STEEL
RIGG

RAVEN
CRAG

TARN
CRAG

	THE WALK
	ROADS
	OTHER PATHWAYS
	WOODLAND
200	HEIGHTS (m)

0   1/4   1/2 mile

The Old Corpse Road drops down to the old farm at Swindale Head.

that the occasional dead animal could have much effect on the water or that tourists would care more about an unsightly carcass than about the glorious sight of a family of golden eagles soaring on the updrafts, scanning the ground below for a meal.

THE ROUTE | Swindale Head to Mardale

David Stewart retraces a route he has walked many times, along an ancient corpse road on the outlying hills of the Lake District.

We discovered this nine-mile walk more or less by accident while looking for a decent circular route from Haweswater that did not reach right up to the higher fells. It was mid-winter, we had four young children and the weather forecast did not look too promising. It's a fabulous walk and we have done it many times since, in all weathers.

On that first walk three of our children opted out before we even started – a sensible choice, as it turned out. It was left to the three blokes – old colleague Warren Baxter, our teenage son Greg and me – to complete the route we had traced out on the map. We took the more obvious path out of the head of the valley, a track leading over Gatescarth Pass towards Longsleddale. This would have been a standard packhorse trail heading south from Mardale towards the market town of Kendal, a route for the living rather than the dead. From the southern tip of Haweswater it climbs steadily towards the pass, the dark crags of Harter Fell dominating on the right and a tumbling stream on your left.

The track down from **Gatescarth Pass** is easy going. Then we turn left to navigate through a wide valley, heading slightly upwards to an indistinct shoulder leading into **Mosedale**. Walking through here on that winter day, our prospects began to darken, literally. It started to rain. The valley is deserted at the best of times and on a poor day you are unlikely to meet another traveller. The path is easily lost in the grass and reeds; it needs more feet to keep it well marked.

Eventually an unlikely-looking property comes into sight, the single-storied **Mosedale Cottage**. No doubt at one time a shooting lodge – it is difficult to imagine any other purpose for it – it is now a bothy under the protection of the Mountain Bothies Association. As such it can be used by anyone passing by who needs shelter or a place to stop for the night, free of charge. We stay in one on our walk tracing stalking tracks in Scotland (chapter 14).

We clamber down a steep escarpment into Swindale. Mosedale Beck transforms into Swindale Beck as it enters the valley and meanders towards the few buildings of **Swindale Head**. Over the centuries the river has thrown up high banks of sediment, providing a welcome dry parapet along which to walk above the wetter ground. Fifteen years ago the three of us managed to find an open barn in which to shelter from

Brough surveys the path down to Swindale Head.

THE LOST CORPSE

A ghostly tale from the Lake District highlights the risk of using horses rather than human bearers for carrying the dead. A young man had died and his body was being taken from Wasdale Head to Eskdale on the remote corpse road over Burnmoor. It was a misty winter's day and some way into the journey the horse took fright and bolted. The party of mourners searched for hours but the horse and its grisly cargo had vanished.

Returning home, the young man's mother, in despair at losing first her only son and then his body, collapsed and died. During her own funeral procession, on the same path and at the same place, her horse too took fright and ran off into a snowstorm. In the desperate search that ensued the son's horse and corpse were discovered but the mother's had disappeared for good. The ghostly horse and coffin that appear from time to time on the lonely fell is assumed to be hers.

the downpour. We were cold and wet, with just a few biscuits to cheer us up, and the day was fast fading. All that lay between us and the car and the rest of the family was the Old Corpse Road.

Swindale Head remains delightfully remote. With no parking for walkers – cars have to be left more than a mile further up the valley – the farmhouse is as isolated as it has been for centuries. The path to Mardale is signed directly opposite the house. It climbs directly up the hillside for a couple of hundred yards and then, crossing a stream, does a single long zigzag to cross the same stream again 50 yards or so higher up. Until the descent into Mardale this is the last time the path looks constructed, cut into the slope of the hill.

After the stream it is simply a faint line trodden into the grass. Behind, on a good day, the valley is a patchwork of colours, from the green fields by the river, to the greys of Outhlaw and Gouther Crags on the opposite flank and the darker hues of heather between.

On that day with Warren and Greg, the skies darkened here and it began to snow, but not in a picturesque, delicate way. The wind picked up as we clambered onto the open moor and battered the sleet directly into our faces. It was hard to tell if the stuff was solid or if it just felt that way as it stung our eyes and faces. Dropping our heads, we stumbled forward, stopping now and then to check the compass and make sure our direction was more or less right. We were following a boggy track; but beyond it there was very little to see. Every now and then I looked back to young Greg with his arm across his face, lurching forward as best he could. I am sure it was a formative experience for him.

After a mile or so on a fairly featureless felltop, the path begins its steep descent back to **Haweswater**, in a series of hairpin bends. A spectacular waterfall crashes down the hillside on the left. For years we had wrongly assumed that corpses were taken from the tiny settlement of Swindale Head to the church in Mardale, which seemed logical enough. But we were mistaken: the corpse route went the other way, out of the Mardale valley, through Swindale Head and on to Shap. Climbing these bends complete with corpse must have been hard work at the best of times. This maybe explains why the practice here was to strap the body onto a pony, encased in a simple shroud rather than a coffin.

Sometimes, in periods of drought, it's possible to look down to Haweswater and see lines of walling just below the surface. Very occasionally the reservoir drains to such an extent that the walls and the remains of a few houses, including the old inn, resurface and it's possible to walk the field paths again. It is, of course, a stony experience as there is never time for any vegetation to grow. It is almost like walking through the skeleton of the place.

Coming down the zigzag path we reach the road, newly constructed in the 1930s along with the dam. To our right is the **Haweswater Hotel**, built to replace the drowned Dun Bull Inn. Voices at the time pointed out that, as a hotel, it was misplaced; that it should have been built on the other side of the reservoir so visitors could walk straight out onto the Lakeland Fells. There's no doubt that the hotel has a magnificent view but there are no footpaths directly from its door. Instead there is the road, which some also complained was too wide for its setting. Aesthetically they were absolutely right: it should by rights be no more than a country lane or track, as it leads to no settlement, just the head of the valley. But at least it means you can walk along it with plenty of room for the cars to pass on their way to and from the crowded car park.

A few posts mark out dangerous pits in the ground. The path could be easily missed in poor weather.

Other corpse roads to walk

Every now and then you will see "corpse road" marked on an Ordnance Survey map. It is usually easy to trace the way to the mother church. The *Lych Way* is a track lying to the south-west of Devil's Tor on Dartmoor. The dead from remote moorland homesteads were taken along this track to Lydford church for burial. There have been reports of monks in white and ghostly funeral processions along the path.

In the Yorkshire Dales the village of *Feetham* was a traditional stopping place for the corpse-bearers taking bodies from Keld and Muker to the burial ground at Grinton, further down the Swale valley. The Punchbowl Inn at Feetham had a "dead house" where the corpse could be left while the funeral procession took an overnight break. The story goes that on one occasion two processions stopped at the inn to refresh themselves, their drinks paid for in the traditional way by members of the deceased's family. The following morning, still somewhat the worse for wear, the parties picked up the wrong wicker coffins. The error was, one assumes, finally spotted when they got to Grinton church.

Further reading

Most stories about corpse roads, and particularly tales of supernatural happenings, are to be found in local histories and guidebooks. The tale of the mother and son lost on the path to Eskdale featured in *The Folklore of the Lake District* (Marjorie Rowling, HarperCollins) and much of the information about Mardale in a local pamphlet, *Mardale Revisited* (Geoffrey Berry, Westmorland Gazette). Such publications are often out of print but can be found in secondhand bookshops or from Amazon. *The Penguin Guide to the Superstitions of Britain and Ireland* (Steven Roud, Penguin Books) is a good reference book if you are interested in folklore generally.

More walks, ideas and discussion can be found on the *Walkingworld* website at walkingworld.com

10 Packhorse routes

Before the improvements to the road network in the 18th century, which allowed wheeled vehicles to reach the major points of population for the first time, most goods were carried by packhorse. In the Lake District, for example, no wheeled vehicles could travel west of Keswick until after 1750. The packhorse train was as vital to the economy of the 18th century as the HGV lorry is to today's. It was a common sight, especially in mountainous areas.

Packhorses were a flexible and reliable means of transport, able to carry up to about 400lb (180kg) each. Goods were carried in panniers slung on either side of the horse from wooden pack frames. To allow clearance for these panniers, the parapets of the bridges were very low, often alarmingly so to a modern walker.

Various breeds of horse were used. One favourite was a sturdy animal derived from a German hunter called a Jaeger; another was the Galloway from south-west Scotland. In the hill districts of Dartmoor, the Yorkshire Dales and the Lake District, locally bred ponies were used. They travelled in trains of up to 40 animals. Thomas Bewick, in his *General History of Quadrupeds* (1790), commented: "In their journies over the trackless moors, they strictly adhere to the line of order and regularity custom has taught them to observe: the leading horse, which is always chosen for his sagacity and steadiness, being furnished with bells, gives notice to the rest, which follow the sound, and generally without much deviation, though sometimes at a considerable distance."

The packhorsemen were given the name "jaggers"; the name deriving either from "jag", meaning "a load" in old English, or from the breed of horse. Jaggers often did the packhorse work as a sideline to earn extra money, seasonally or when times were tough. Many jaggers were farmers who depended on this contribution to their income; they seldom travelled beyond the market town a day or two away. Much short-distance carrying was undertaken in the slack spells before and after the hay harvest when the tracks were normally dry and firm.

Packhorse trains were rather slow, travelling perhaps 15 miles a day in hilly country and 25 miles on the flat. Thus the journey from Manchester to Sheffield, about 37 miles, probably took a couple of days with an overnight stop in Edale, roughly in the middle.

Many packhorse routes survive. They are easier to trace in hilly areas, notably in the Pennines and the Lake District, as they

Crowden Tower on the edge of Kinder Scout provides a fine view into the Vale of Edale

are mostly on the higher ground and are less likely to have been overlaid by turnpike or metalled roads. These newer roads tended to follow the valley bottoms, where they called for more frequent and substantial bridges.

Packhorse routes sometimes overlapped with drovers' roads. However while a drovers' road required a broad swath to allow the passage of a large herd, packhorse routes were generally narrow, just one horse wide. Consequently, many packhorse routes have happily transitioned into leisure paths across the moors and fells.

For those path detectives who are less perambulatory, another way of hunting down an old packhorse route is by the names of pubs: Packhorse Inn, Bay Horse, String of Horses, Nag's Head and Woolpack are all pub names that suggest you should take a closer look at the contours, bridges and paths to see if there is an old packhorse route running close by.

OUR WALK | The Peak District

The packhorse bridge at the foot of Jacob's Ladder is a popular stopping point for walkers.

The major era of the packhorse in the Peak District was the 1650s to the 1750s. Of the dated packhorse bridges in Derbyshire, the earliest is from 1664 and the latest from 1734. Packhorse business was at its busiest when the towns and cities that surrounded the Peak District were beginning their expansion as industrial centres. Significant cargoes included lead and tobacco from Liverpool heading east; corn, textiles, cloth, salt and Sheffield cutlery heading west.

The woollen industry on both sides of the Pennines generated a large amount of packhorse traffic, with raw wool, yarns and woven pieces all being carried this way. Many of the first textile mills, sited in the hills to take advantage of water power, could receive and dispatch goods only by horse.

Edale, today a popular walkers' destination, was a convenient stopping point on two significant packhorse routes. It would have provided an overnight break for packhorsemen and their horses, with accommodation and a smithy.

One packhorse route headed south towards Casterton, with one fork then veering west at Mam Tor towards Chapel-en-le-Frith. The other packhorse route made for Manchester to the west and Sheffield to the east, running along the contour of the valley. As well as taking materials and finished products from the larger conurbations, it served cotton mills along the way. The nearest was Nether Booth, a couple of miles east of Edale, built in 1790 on a site originally occupied by a corn mill and tannery.

It is on this second packhorse route, just to the west of Edale, that a classic and very picturesque packhorse bridge is to be found. When you first spot it in the distance you imagine it will get bigger as it gets closer, but it never does. With a modest span of only 12 feet and a width no greater than a narrow footpath it is typical in scale for a packhorse bridge. It is situated at the foot of Jacob's Ladder, a fabulous example of the use of zigzags to navigate a steep slope. This bridge and zigzag climb epitomise the era of the packhorse.

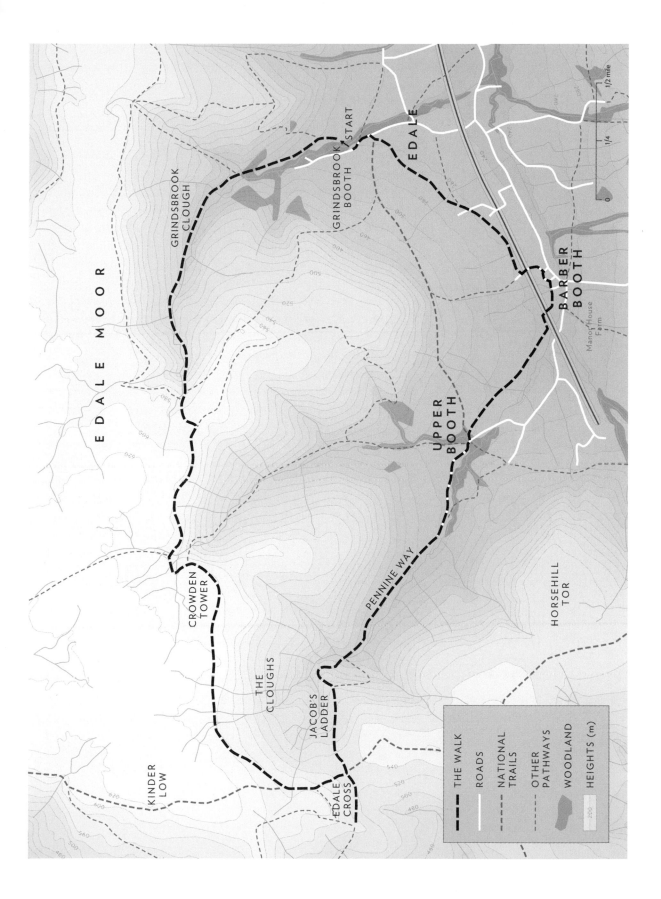

EDALE MOOR

GRINDSBROOK CLOUGH

GRINDSBROOK BOOTH / START

EDALE

BARBER BOOTH

Manor House Farm

UPPER BOOTH

HORSEHILL TOR

PENNINE WAY

CROWDEN TOWER

THE CLOUGHS

JACOB'S LADDER

EDALE CROSS

KINDER LOW

1/2 mile

1/4

0

THE WALK

ROADS

NATIONAL TRAILS

OTHER PATHWAYS

WOODLAND

HEIGHTS (m)

200

THE ROUTE | The Peak District

The single arch of the standard packhorse bridge made it sturdy and straightforward to construct.

Nicholas Rudd-Jones and Peter Raffan, a friend from Stamford, walk this route on a glorious May day.

Not surprisingly perhaps, our walk begins at a packhorse pub, the Nag's Head Inn in Edale, which is on the packhorse route that runs east to west, and also on the start of the Pennine Way running north. Today the back yard is full of backpackers enjoying a pint and some pub grub, about to set out on their journey or just returned. The scene must have been pretty similar 300 or so years ago when it was the "jaggers" taking a break. The Nag's Head, built originally in 1577, was formerly the village blacksmith as well. It would have been ideally placed to serve the packhorse trains as they passed through the village.

Before exploring the packhorse route itself, our path takes us up the delightful **Grindsbrook Clough**, clough being the local term for a small valley. Throughout the Pennines it was streams such as this, feeding the mills situated at the foot of the valleys, that helped create the products that were transported out by the packhorse trains.

After a steady climb along the valley bottom, we come out onto the moor, where large stone slabs have been laid in the past few years to make the going better underfoot and to limit erosion. These are similar to the slabs that were used on packhorse routes back in the 18th century to make it easier to traverse wetter land: a large stone slab was just wide enough to allow passage for a horse. A notable surviving example of these packhorse "causeys" or causeways is Reddystore Scoutgate from Littleborough to Todmorden, which has large stone flags for much of its length.

Our route soon reaches **Crowden Tower**, the first of a series of impressively large and fantastically shaped gritstone outcrops: the Wool Packs (with echoes of the packhorse loads), the Pagoda Rocks (resembling a Chinese pagoda), the Pym Chair (looking like a seat) and the distinctive Noel Stool (anvil-shaped and near a large cairn). To the north of these stones is Kinder Scout, scene of the mass 1932 trespass to campaign for the right of access to moorlands (see Chapter 19).

The path swings back to the top of **Jacob's Ladder** and joins the packhorse route running from Hayfield to Edale. We take a short detour here to the **Edale Cross**, an ancient monument that once marked a boundary of land ownership and is one of the many guide stones on the packhorse routes of the region.

In the drive to improve communications, a 1702 act of parliament

Jacob's Ladder was on a key route across the Pennines

required such stones to be erected. The 1709 Derbyshire Order Book for Quarter Sessions (county courts held four times a year to hear criminal cases) includes the following entry: "It is herein Enacted for the better convenience of travelling in such parts of the Kingdome which are remote from the townes... that there shall be in every Parish or place where two or more Cross Highwayes Meet, Erected or fixed by the Surveyors of the highwayes... a Stone or Post, with an inscription thereon in large Letters, containinge the name of the next Markett Towne to which each of the said Joyning highways Leads..."

One cannot but think of the similarities to the government edict in the late 1960s that highway authorities should signpost paths where they left metalled roads, and waymark rights of way along routes. This was in recognition, as would have been the case with jaggers passing through a region, that paths were not used only by locals with intimate knowledge of the way.

If you have the time you can follow the packhorse route east from Edale Cross to Bowden Bridge on the edge of Hayfield and stop at the Packhorse Inn in the middle of the village. Staying on our planned route, however, we descend Jacob's Ladder and reach the picturesque Jacob's Ladder packhorse bridge.

In the later 18th century a man called Jacob Marshall occupied Edale Head Farm, the ruins of which are just up from the bridge along a track heading west. He kept a small enclosure for packhorses to graze in and is credited with constructing the steep direct path up the hillside to give the jaggers a respite while their horses took the longer zigzag route; hence the Jacob's Ladder name.

The path then continues along the contour of the valley, through **Lee Farm** where the National Trust has an interesting interpretation centre and a wood-turning workshop. Here there is a delightful water trough, now a haven for ferns but in former days no doubt a much-needed refreshment stop for the horses.

The path undulates only slightly as it progresses along the side of the valley back to Edale, with glorious views south towards the Iron Age hill fort of Mam Tor, and an ancient ridgeway track running east-west. Looking west, we spot the entrance to the Cowburn rail tunnel, over two miles long and connecting Manchester and Sheffield. When it was opened in 1891 it would have made Jacob's Ladder redundant at a stroke.

Shortly before reaching **Edale**, the path becomes a sunken holloway – a pathway worn down over the centuries by animals' hooves or water erosion so that it is lower than the surrounding land. Imagine

This beautiful packhorse bridge is found at the foot of Jacob's Ladder.

THE CONSTRUCTION OF PACKHORSE BRIDGES

A frequently surviving part of a packhorse route is the packhorse bridge. They were built because it was unsafe to drive a heavily laden horse with a valuable load across a stream. Packhorse bridges are easily recognisable, being narrow (one horse at a time) and having low parapets to accommodate the loads slung on each side of the horse, although higher parapets might subsequently have been added (which a close inspection of the stonework might reveal).

A single arch is the basic building block of a packhorse bridge: it is a simple and strong structure. If held between immovable abutments it is virtually indestructible and is capable of carrying enormous weights. It is also relatively straightforward to construct, and is usually of "rustic" construction, probably built by a farmer with a knowledge of dry stone walling rather than a professional stonemason.

The only danger to the bridge is a lateral force from an abnormal flood, especially if an obstruction develops across the arch from an uprooted tree. Of course there are limits to how far a single arch can span, usually not more than 20 feet, so the bridges tend to be over smaller mountain streams.

145

Jacob's Ladder lies at the very head of the valley, with the route climbing up past Kinder Low in the far distance.

the impact of 160 or so horses' hooves tramping down the ground every time a packhorse train passed. Holloways are a feature of many packhorse routes for that reason.

The path disgorges us in front of the Nag's Head Inn and the end of our seven-and-a-half-mile walk. But before we pop in for liquid revival, we take the few extra steps to another packhorse bridge, this one across Grindsbrook. It's an evocative spot to dwell a while and imagine the clattering of horses' hooves as they hurry up in anticipation of fodder or a rest.

Again, if you have time, you can continue on the packhorse route east, reaching Jagger's Clough after a couple of miles. There are also packhorse routes connecting south – one heading for Castleton via Hollins Cross and the other via Mam Tor due south, where another east-west track is joined.

Sipping our pints, we reflect on a fabulous walk and take our hats off to the jaggers who blazed these trails across the peaks, expertly choosing the most efficient route to minimise the gradient and make the passage as easy as possible for their beasts.

The path undulates along the valley side on the return to Edale.

A trough provides a welcome drinks break for the horses after their exertions over the hills.

147

The bridge across Grindsbrook in Edale is a classic packhorse bridge.

Other packhorse routes to explore

Packhorse routes can be found wherever the terrain was too hilly for wheeled carts to transport goods. Today they are most easily traced in the Lake District and the Peak District, as well as on the chalk uplands that straddle Somerset, Wiltshire and Dorset, and on Exmoor and Dartmoor.

In the Yorkshire Dales the main packhorse routes run east to west, bringing staples like salt in from the north-east and carrying out coal, wool and lead. The *Craven Way* can be traced along the side of Whernside (one of the Yorkshire "Three Peaks"), joining Dent and Ingleton. This route is unusual in that it is oriented north to south and so may also have been used by drovers bringing animals down from Scotland.

Reddystore Scoutgate from Littleborough to Todmorden is a good example of a "causey", having large stone flags for much of its length. Other flagged pathways (referred to in Chapter 6) are found across the North Yorkshire Moors, mostly likely used by packhorse trains carrying fish from port to market (quite possibly along with a bit of contraband).

On Dartmoor, there would have been several packhorse routes for transporting peat, minerals or stones. One, the *Blackwood Path*, is located on Ugborough Moor, three miles north-east of Ivybridge, and once used by peat cutters for the carrying of peat. The remote routes across Dartmoor were first marked by stone crosses, and later by wayside stones, many of which still survive. On this route you can see the granite Spurrells Cross, dating back to the 14th century and notable for its spurred arms (only one of which survives).

Visiting many parts of the world without a developed road network you can still see goods delivered on packhorse trains. Most of the trekking routes in Nepal, for instance, double as packhorse routes and give a glimpse into what it must have been like in much of Britain a few centuries ago.

Further reading

Packhorse Bridges of England (Ernest Hinchcliffe, Cicerone Guides) is an ambitious work that aims to list every packhorse bridge surviving. A helpful starting point for planning a route.

Packmen, Carriers & Packhorse Roads (David Hey, Landmark Collector's Library) is probably the most detailed book on packhorse roads, full of economic analysis. An excellent chapter on the different type of carriers.

Peakland Roads and Trackways (A.E. and E.M. Dodd, Moorland Publishing) gives lots of ideas for specific walks along packhorse routes in the Peak District.

Walking on Bridges in Cumbria (Robin Bray, Hayloft Publishing) does the same for Cumbria, but with much more detailed maps that mean you can set out with little other research. There are 24 routes described in total.

More walks, ideas and discussion can be found on the *Walkingworld* website at walkingworld.com

1762
H E^d
SAER

11 Drovers'
roads

From the time of the Norman Conquest to the middle of the 19th century when the railways arrived, any traveller in Wales might find his way blocked by hundreds of cattle, sheep, pigs or even flocks of geese, on the way east to the markets in England. This same pattern was repeated across mainland Britain, as animals were moved from highland areas to lowland markets, towns and cities. The high point of activity was in the 18th century, with the growth of demand from the cities and the lack of alternative transportation, and it is from this period that we have the most substantive records.

These herds were controlled by drovers, the cowboys of yesteryear – tough men who knew their minds and were well rewarded for their efforts. Their status in society was enhanced because their role went well beyond the droving of animals. They were relied on as news-carriers between farms, were often asked to take on financial commissions and were sometimes even requested to chaperone youngsters down to London, making the journey safer for the sons and daughters of well-to-do families.

To reconstruct the network of drovers' routes is something of a detective task today, since many of them are now metalled roads. Often the easiest clues to find lie in the overnight stays. In the open country a farmer who wanted to let the drovers know he was willing to provide food, accommodation and grazing planted three Scots pines. These were visible at a great distance, and the drovers used them as waymarks. Field names are also a useful way of tracking down old inns. A halfpenny a night per beast was the standard charge for grazing in the 18th century, so Halfpenny fields are likely candidates, sometimes found behind a building that served the double purpose of inn and smithy.

A traveller would not come on droves unexpectedly. They would be heard long before they could be seen, from two miles or more away. It was a deliberately noisy cavalcade. The drovers, walking or riding horses at the side of the cattle, would give warning of their coming with cries of "Heiptro Ho!" When the farmers of the neighbourhood heard that shout, they rushed to pen up their cattle, to prevent any beasts from joining the drove.

Corgis were often used to keep the herds together. These dogs are so low on the ground that they can snap at the heels of a beast, and be well out of the way of the ensuing kick. There are stories that, on arrival at the drove's destination, the dogs were sent back home

alone, stopping at pre-arranged places where their food was paid for. Evidence for this practice is scant, but it makes a good tale.

At the end of a droving season, the men's journey home was liable to be more leisurely, with or without their dogs. Usually they formed groups of two or three and rode back the way they had come. Sometimes they sold their ponies at their final destination and walked back. One imagines they had a lot of fun on the way home and arrived back somewhat the worse for wear.

The droving culture began to fade with the onset of the railways and of refrigeration, which meant that animals could be butchered before being transported, but lasted in a few places until the early years of the 20th century.

OUR WALK | Snowdonia in North Wales

The bridge stone at Pont Fadog.

The Welsh network of drovers' roads has three main strands. The northern roads typically started on the fertile plains of the coast, which were well suited to cattle breeding, and headed towards markets in Wrexham and Shrewsbury. The central strand led to Birmingham. The southern strand, passing just north of Llandovery, headed towards the towns of central and southern England, notably Hereford and Banbury.

The drovers' route that we explore is exceptional because the route is largely intact, and has many interesting features including a packhorse bridge and in several places stone slabs underfoot. It is the old road from Harlech to Dolgellau over the hills, which became disused when the marshland around the estuary was drained to provide a better route, so it was never obliterated by a made-up road. It takes a neat line through a mountain pass. It is easy to imagine the drovers looking down on the Mawddach estuary and calculating the hours remaining in the day before they stopped for the night.

The area is a magical combination of seascape and hillscape, with the wide Mawddach estuary leading down to Barmouth and the sandy beaches, and hills to the north and the south, including the impressive Cadair Idris on the south side. Today the area is a haven for outdoor activities, with the disused railway line on the south side of the estuary converted into a cycle track (the Mawddach Trail), and a circular walking route taking in all the hills around (the Mawddach Way, a 27-mile route taking three days). There are also plenty of bucket-and-spade activities down on the beach, and in the summer it has the feel of old-fashioned family holidays.

But in the past the area must have seemed very different. Alison Gilbert, who contributed this walk to the Walkingworld website, writes: "Standing on the main A496 road in the village of Bontddu, it is hard to imagine that this was, not so long ago, marshland. If you wanted to travel from here to the west coast, you had to take to the uplands – and that is exactly what you're going to do now. This route, in 1800 a modest turnpike road, was used even before that by the drovers, herding their vast flocks of lowing, bleating, squealing stock from the west coast to Dolgellau and beyond. Today this is a journey into the peace and silence of the mountains, where skylarks trill and a glimpse of the occasional soaring buzzard is not unknown."

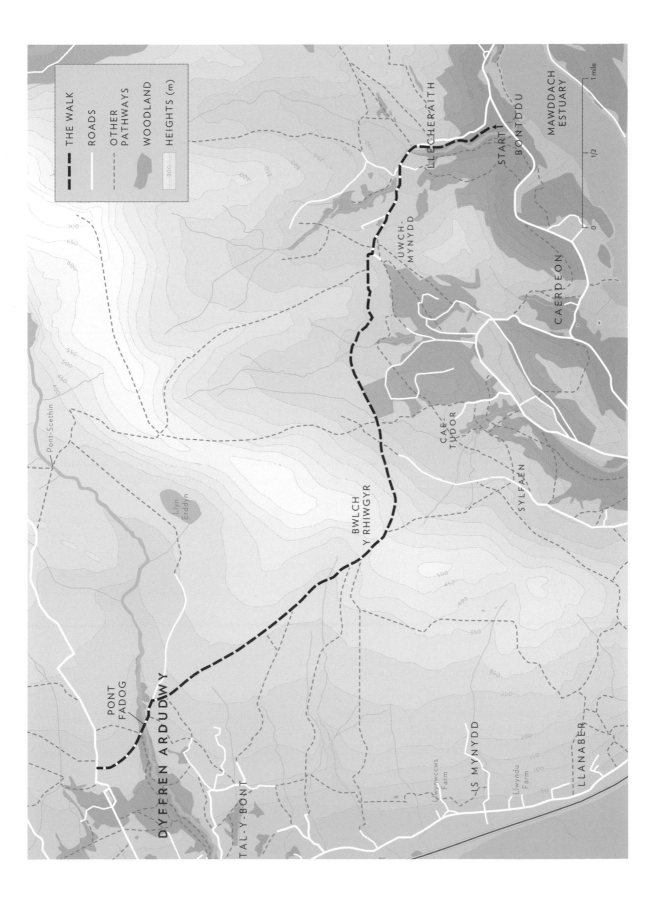

THE WALK
ROADS
OTHER PATHWAYS
WOODLAND
HEIGHTS (m)
200

DYFFRYN ARDUDWY

PONT FADOG

BWLCH Y RHIWGYR

Pont-Scethin

Llyn Erddyn

TAL-Y-BONT

Llwyncwws Farm

IS MYNYDD

Llwyndu Farm

LLANABER

CAE TUDOR

SYLFAEN

UWCH-MYNYDD

LLECHERAITH

START

BONTDDU

CAERDEON

MAWDDACH ESTUARY

1 mile
1/2
0

THE ROUTE | The Harlech to Dolgellau road

Nicholas Rudd-Jones and an old school friend, Oliver Quick, do this walk on a (you guessed it) very wet and windy Welsh day.

If we had been drovers waking up on the morning of this eight-mile walk we would have been decidedly disgruntled. The rain is lashing down, visibility is poor and I have a slight head from the excellent hospitality of the night before. Still, we shouldn't complain. After all, we don't have a herd of animals to feed and are almost certainly better protected from the weather than our drover forebears.

Shirley Toulson, an expert on drovers' roads, writes: "Drovers wore the traditional farm labourer's smock, which, even in high summer, was likely to be perpetually sodden at the hem. To protect their trousers from the wet, they covered them with knee-length woollen stockings. These were knitted during the winter evenings in the farm kitchens. The stocking was protected, in its turn, by leggings, which in the 19th century were made of good stout Bristol brown paper, made somewhat waterproof by being rubbed with soap."

Clad in our technically advanced waterproof layers and boots, we climb up from Bontddu alongside a deep ravine through woodland. We are still very grateful for the protection it provides from the elements. As we come out on a track higher up the valley, we are surprised to see what look like miniature rails in the ground. We follow them along to discover a series of dilapidated workings, which we subsequently learn were once **a small gold mine**. Gold was apparently first mined here in Roman times. The mine was developed again in the 1862 "gold rush" and continued as a major operator until 1911, producing nearly 80,000 troy ounces of gold in total. Since 1911 the mine has been reopened several times for smaller-scale operations. It last closed in 1998, but is still owned by a local exploration company, no doubt with half an eye on the ever-increasing price of gold. When in production the mine used the 2ft-gauge railway that we had stumbled across.

Climbing gently from here to the end of the made road, we imagine ourselves slipping back into the past, for at the top of this road is an ancient milestone. The faded inscription marks a divergence of the ways. One side indicates the route north to Harlech, while the other shows the path for Tal-y-Bont, five miles away.

We have read that in the 17th century this route north to Harlech via Pont Scethin was the scene of many highway robberies. Our walking poles would have provided little defence, but our drover forebears

It is easy to imagine the drovers looking down on the Mawddach estuary and calculating the hours remaining in the day before they stopped for the night.

would have carried weapons if the route held any dangers from man or beast. There might be as many as a dozen drovers in a drove with 400 head of cattle, and they would be armed if there was a chance of attack. They received an exemption from the Disarming Acts of 1716 and 1748. Occasionally, they employed armed escorts, particularly in the Scottish Highlands.

As for ourselves, we decide on the safer option and take the left track towards Tal-y-bont. As we follow the well-marked track towards the airy heights, we realise that we are walking on stone paving slabs sunk deep into the ground – a legacy of the days when this road was better used. Before too long we spy, on the horizon, the deep notch of **Bwlch y Rhiwgyr**, marking the pass through the upper reaches of Llawlech. And the weather, which up until now has been foul, starts to improve and we glimpse a dash of blue sky.

A drover at this point must have felt a burst of elation as the weather became more agreeable and the high point was attained, particularly if he was coming towards the end of his day. A drove typically proceeded at about two miles an hour and covered 15–20 miles a day: it was important throughout to keep the beasts in good condition, so it was not a journey that could be rushed.

The view from the Bwlch itself is a mountain dreamscape. Looking back towards the south, the Mawddach estuary twists and shines between its sandbanks. Beyond it is the dark, rounded, hunched-up shape of the great throne of the giant Idris, and over to the west are the pale sand dunes between Barmouth and Harlech.

Beyond the pass you might find further inspiration in the wealth of ancient settlements scattered on the high ground. As we enter civilisation again, to a huddle of stone cottages and farmhouses among the trees, we cross **Pont Fadog**, an old packhorse bridge whose worn inscription you just might be able to decipher, though we could not. One of the cottages here was probably an emergency stop-off for re-shoeing the drovers' horses.

Just beyond the bridge, we come across a well-preserved stone

A toll bridge crosses the Mawddach Estuary at Penmaenpool.

The Gors-y-Gedol Neolithic burial chamber

THE MANY ROLES OF A DROVER

From the 1700s onwards a man could only apply for a droving licence if he was over 30, married and a householder. Drovers were well rewarded for their skill, typically being paid two or three times as a much as a humbler labourer.. They appear to have had several roles beyond transporting animals.

Until the 19th century the few roads that existed in Wales were impassable for most of the year, so there was very little communication between the scattered hamlets, and the drovers were relied on as news carriers between the farms. Legend has it that it was from drovers returning from London that the Welsh learned of the victory at Waterloo in 1815.

Drovers also often acted as bankers. Well-to-do families regularly asked drovers to undertake financial commissions in London; and many a rich man's son, making his way to a career in law at the Temple or the Inns of Court, would rely on money brought by the cattle men to settle his lodgings account. Yet movement of cash is always a risky business in wild country. To avoid the risk of loss, the drovers started an effective banking system at the end of the 18th century. Anyone wanting a drover to deal with a financial transaction in London put the money into the drover's Welsh bank. The drover then paid the London bills in cash out of the sums he realised on the sale of the cattle.

The drovers' road makes its way across the moors.

chamber right beside the road (Gors-y-Gedol Neolithic burial chamber) and there are other rather less obvious cairns and circles to explore if you have the archaeology bug.

There are a couple of options from here. If you have done enough walking, head down to Llanbedr for train or buses back to Barmouth. Alternatively, take the bridleway right shortly after the burial chamber and head to the Standing Stones and the isolated Pont Scethin, and then along another old Harlech-to-Dolgellau route. Watch out for the brigands! If you want to make a weekend of it, stay in the George III Inn at Penmaenpool on the south side of the magnificent Mawddach estuary and on the second day climb Cadair Idris (893m) just to the south for spectacular views in all directions.

Other drovers' roads to walk

Drovers' routes are spread throughout Britain, heading generally from hilly regions in the north or the west towards a market or a large conurbation, especially London. There are many to be found in Wales and Scotland, as these were the most concentrated cattle-rearing regions of the country. And they are often easier to trace than those in the lowlands which have been built over or become part of a larger, metalled road.

The *Scottish network* extended from the Highlands and Islands with a multitude of tracks heading across the hills, aiming for various cattle markets. There were essentially two main streams: one from the west coast and Skye, and the other from the far north. In the early days, these streams converged on Crieff, where the most important cattle fair was held in the early autumn each year; after 1770 it was transferred to Falkirk. At these Trysts many of the cattle were bought by English dealers, and then driven southwards. Defoe, writing in 1726, noted that some cattle were driven all the way from Caithness to East Anglia, a distance of around 600 miles.

In *England,* the Hambleton drove road in Yorkshire is one of the best-preserved lengths still to be seen. It is part of the route from Durham to York and passes over the western end of the Cleveland Hills, reaching a height of over 300 metres. It is a good example of the drovers' use of a hill track rather than the turnpiked road in the vale below.

Northern Ireland is also dotted with drovers' roads in its many upland areas; an especially good place to look is the Antrim Hills, where the tracks lead down the valleys to Antrim, then south to Belfast.

Further reading

The Drovers' Roads of Wales (Fay Goodwin and Shirley Toulson, Whittet Books) is superbly researched and written. The introductory chapters are highly recommended. Specific drovers' routes are then analysed in detail and will give you walk ideas, although not all make great routes nowadays as there can be long stretches of road-walking.

Welsh Cattle Drovers (Richard Moore-Colyer, Landmark Collectors Library) is a data-rich book that is invaluable if you are interested in the logistics and economics of a vast trade.

More walks, ideas and discussion can be found on the *Walkingworld* website at walkingworld.com

12 Village walks

For more than a thousand years, the commonest form of path in this country has been the one linking farm to village, village to village, village to town. These are the paths that have been used by countless generations moving from their homes to work in the fields, to visit friends and relations, to carry out the everyday business of a community where most people had nothing more than their own legs to take them from place to place.

Almost all the villages that we see on the map today were already firmly established by the 11th century. Many are mentioned in the Domesday Book, William the Conqueror's survey of his kingdom completed two decades after his triumph at the Battle of Hastings in 1066. It is thought that some date back as far as the fifth or sixth centuries. It was in the following 500 or so years that the "nucleated" village emerged, with households brought together from their scattered farmsteads into a cluster of houses, typically around a green, with a church and a well, and paths and lanes leading into the central space from all points of the compass.

The nucleated village coincided with the adoption of the open-field system, whereby land was parcelled out in strips to each householder. The system became the primary method of land management in a vast swath of lowland England from Yorkshire and Lincolnshire, through the Midlands to most of south-central England. It coincided with a rise in population and allowed the villagers to have shared use of the more efficient heavy ploughs. The method of ploughing gave rise to the characteristic landscape feature of "ridge and furrow", where the fields are corrugated into ridges between five and 20 yards wide, sometimes with a slight curve at each end to make a long reverse S shape (an effect of the way the team of oxen and plough had to turn round at the end of each furrow). A similar pattern called "run rig" can be found in Scotland. Both features can still be seen today, hundreds of years after the open-field system was abandoned, especially at dawn or dusk when the sun is low.

In many upland regions, where the land was not suitable for arable farming, the model remained that of the scattered farmstead, with a network of paths joining them together and to the villages in the valley. In other parts of the country, such as Kent and Essex, land continued in the more ancient configuration of small squarish fields.

Back in these early medieval times, the notion of trespassing on

Now a pleasant green lane, this was originally the main route from Helpston to Peterborough.

land belonging to another person seems to have been unknown. The open-field system meant that everyone had a reason to have access to the land. Folk could pretty much wander around the countryside as they pleased, although if you were a stranger to a region and travelling through a wood you were expected to sound your hunting horn to indicate that you were not a poacher or a thief.

With the Norman Conquest there was a profound change in the structure of land ownership. William made all land the property of the Crown, and then parcelled it out to his barons, who in return were required to contribute troops on demand. There may well have been a continuation in the formation of nucleated villages and open fields, under the direction of new lords of the manor. However, even under Norman rule paths remained generally accessible, as they were vital to the commerce and communications of the countryside.

There are many examples of paths being protected in court in medieval times. Rowland Parker wrote in his book *The Common Stream*: "The manorial court looked after all matters relating to the village, and was the place to register transactions relating to the sale, lease, sub-letting and inheritance of land. It also exercised the right to fine villagers for misdemeanours, including many relating to paths: 'Henry Atthil ploughed a public way to the width of half a foot; fined 2d.' Much of the stuff bought up in court was about the encroachment of one man on another's land. Obstruction of roads and paths was a frequent reason for being in court." Likewise there is a record from 1320 of a route to Canterbury Cathedral that was arbitrarily closed. Users of the path, mainly monks at a local monastery, took the case to court. The sheriff ordered that the path be kept open as he judged it to be an "ancient and allowed highway".

From this period until the parliamentary enclosures of the 18th and 19th centuries, paths traced the movements of labourers and farmers between fields, commons, villages and homes. Although there were well-beaten tracks linking regular destinations, one might still wander at will through common or uncultivated land and by a variety of ways along the unploughed "balks" that divided the narrow strips where crops were grown.

The Parliamentary Enclosure Acts of 1750–1850 changed all this. The purpose was to increase farming productivity and consequently the value of the land. Where heathland had been broadly accessible to everyone, with only loosely defined paths, now there was no entry unless there was a "right of way" as laid down by the enclosure map. Access to the countryside became much more restricted.

Enclosure meant the extinction of common rights that people held over the farm lands and commons of the parish – the abolition of the scattered holdings in the open fields and a re-allocation of holdings in compact blocks, accompanied usually by the physical separation of the newly created fields by the planting of hedges. Thereafter each field was reserved for the sole use of the individual owners or their tenants. It is from this time that those forbidding signs start to appear: "Private property – trespassers will be prosecuted."

And indeed most landowners were keen to curtail any footpath they could that ran across their land. Until 1815 they could simply put up barriers or "no trespassing" signs to discourage the use of paths across their lands. In 1815 an act of parliament – the Act as to Closing Footpaths – was passed, requiring two justices of the peace to close a public right of way. But this power was widely abused. It was recorded in *Hansard* that one magistrate would commonly say to another, "Come and dine with me: I shall expect you an hour earlier as I want to stop up a footpath."

Enclosure changed the number and type of paths in a variety of ways, as Anne Wallace describes in *Walking, Literature and English Culture*: "Some of the footpaths which followed the old field boundaries simply vanished under the new cultivation, obliterated by the plough. Other paths, curiously enough, achieved their first legal status as public ways across private lands because they appeared on the maps which accompanied awards of enclosure."

New enclosure roads were generally built straight and at a stipulated width of 40 feet to enable animal droving and carts to manoeuvre around potholes and puddles.

OUR WALK | Helpston in Cambridgeshire

*A statue of the poet stands
in the yard of the John Clare
centre in Helpston.*

The enclosure act covering Helpston in Cambridgeshire was enacted in 1809 and, as elsewhere in the country where enclosure had taken place, dramatically altered the landscape. At the time of the Helpston enclosure the justices of the peace needed little encouragement to side with the landowners in the closure of a path. This improved slightly after an act of 1835 that transferred the power of closing paths to juries.

Where there had been heaths and fields, typically over 1,000 acres apiece, now there was a neat patchwork of much smaller fields, typically 10–20 acres, separated by thick hawthorn hedges. New roads were built (another major economic benefit of enclosure since it expedited the time to market) at a stipulated width of 40 feet to enable animal droving and to allow carts to manoeuvre around potholes and puddles.

Helpston is the birthplace of the poet John Clare (1793–1864). It is a classic English village, with footpaths going through it, others leading to the neighbouring villages of Marholm and Ashton, and a green lane that was originally the main route to the neighbouring town of Peterborough.

Clare's popularity has steadily grown as environmental issues have come to the fore. His poetry is characterised by an affinity with nature, captured in a fresh and vivid tone. He stands apart from other 19th-century romantic pets in that he was a labourer on the land rather than an intellectual. He loved nothing more than to ramble along his native paths, and his best poems record the impressions of those hours in simple and direct language:

And then I walk and swing my stick for joy
And catch at little pictures passing bye
A gate whose posts are two old dotterel trees
A close with molehills sprinkled oer its leas
A little footbrig with its crossing rail
A wood gap stopt with ivy wreathing pale
A crooked stile each path crossed spinney owns
A brooklet forded by its stepping stones

THE MOOREHENS NEST, 1820

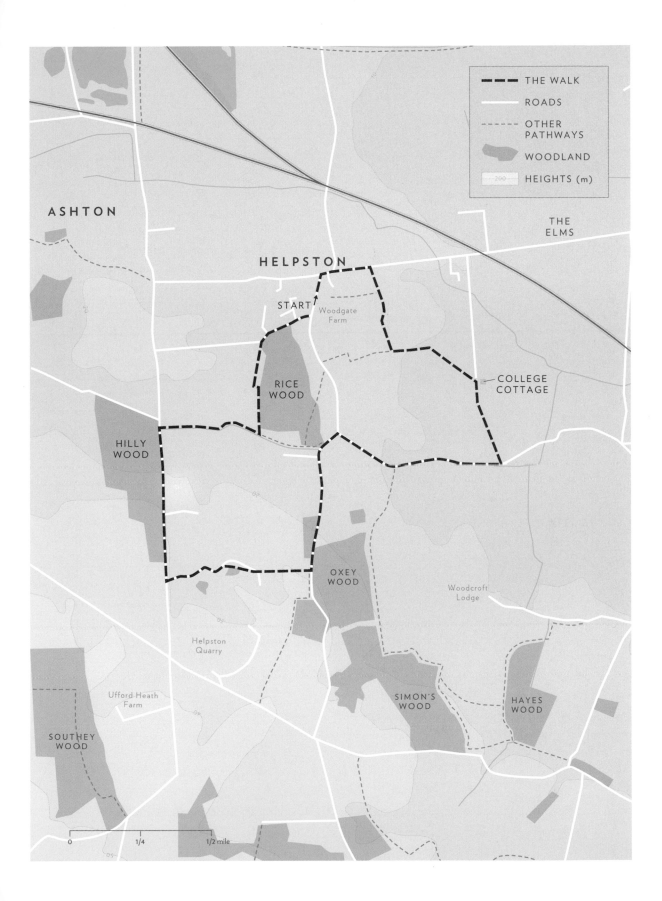

ASHTON

HELPSTON

START

Woodgate Farm

RICE WOOD

HILLY WOOD

COLLEGE COTTAGE

THE ELMS

OXEY WOOD

Woodcroft Lodge

Helpston Quarry

Ufford Heath Farm

SIMON'S WOOD

HAYES WOOD

SOUTHEY WOOD

THE WALK

ROADS

OTHER PATHWAYS

WOODLAND

200 HEIGHTS (m)

0   1/4   1/2 mile

In Clare's early childhood, the heaths of Helpston, Ailsworth, Ufford, Southorpe and Wittering were almost continuous, apart from small wooded areas and parts of the villages' open fields. This heath was a level area of limestone, which was maintained as grassland by the grazing of the villagers' sheep and cattle.

At the time of the Helpston enclosure in 1809, Clare, by then 16, looked after flocks of sheep and geese on the heath, so he was directly and detrimentally affected by the change as the heathland was enclosed. John Barrell, in his classic book on Clare, *The Idea of Landscape and the Sense of Place* 1730-1840, describes how devastating the effect of enclosure could be:

"Everything about the place, in fact, which made it precisely this place, and not that one, was forgotten; the map was drawn blank, except for the village itself, the parish boundary, and perhaps woodland too extensive or too valuable to be cleared, and streams too large to be diverted. The enclosure commissioner would then mark in the new roads he was to cause to have made to the neighbouring villages, running as straight as the contours of the land would allow... The effect of enclosure was of course to destroy the sense of place which the old topography expressed, as it destroyed the topography itself."

Clare's journal from September 1824 records:

"Took a walk in the woods saw an old wood stile taken away from a favourite spot which it had occupied all my life – the posts were overgrown with ivy and it seemed so akin to nature and the spot where it stood as tho it had taken on a lease for an undisturbed existence it hurt me to see it was gone for my affections claim a friendship with such things..."

And in his poem 'The Village Minstrel' (1821) he was in no doubt about the negative impact of enclosures upon paths:

There once were lanes in nature's freedom dropt,
There once were paths that every valley wound,
– Inclosure came, and every path was stopt;
Each tyrant fix'd his sign where paths were found,
To hint a trespass now who cross'd the ground:
Justice is made to speak as they command;
The high road now must be each stinted bound:
Inclosure, thou'rt a curse upon the land,
And tasteless was the wretch who thy existence plann'd.

John Clare's birthplace, in the centre of the village, is now open to the public.

THE GAME LAWS

The game laws were another way in which landowners took control of the English countryside and denied rights and access to the common man wherever possible. They were relatively benign when first conceived in the 12th century to protect royal forests – they conceded, for example, that no man was to lose life or limb for poaching the king's deer (see Chapter 8). But they were ratcheted up at the same time as the enclosure movement gripped the countryside. Hanging, deportation and flogging became commonplace punishments for poaching.

In the last 60 years of the 18th century only five acts were passed dealing with the poaching of small game: in the next 50 years there were well over 50. The period saw a steady process of punitive escalation as the landed gentry tried to take complete control of the countryside in pursuit of their grand obsession, the shooting of pheasants. Their stubbornness also arose from fear that, if they didn't keep the common people firmly in their place, they would rise up as their French counterparts had done.

But despite the increasing severity of the punishments, poaching remained endemic in Britain. The general population often sided with the poachers, who were frequently otherwise stalwart members of the local community.

Straight lines and thick hawthorn hedges are tell-tale signs of the enclosure movement.

While enclosure undoubtedly improved agricultural productivity, it also profoundly changed the relationship between the villagers and the countryside around them. What had been part of their existence became a place of work that was at other times inaccessible.

Helpston today remains the classic English village, with old cottages along the main street, a church, a pub and a village shop struggling to survive. The routes around the village are not much altered since Clare's days, but very few inhabitants make their living from the land today. Many people commute into Peterborough or even London to work, although in many homes you will now find at least one of the partners working from home. It is this trend to homeworking, along with the growing popularity of moving to a village on retirement, that has done so much to keep the English village alive. It has also meant that the paths are more likely to be kept open, as many of these newcomers enjoy walking or have dogs, and are willing to defend and maintain "their" public rights of way.

THE ROUTE | The country paths around Helpston

Nicholas Rudd-Jones sets out with David Stewart and the good dog Brough, eager to understand why today's footpaths take the routes they do.

Our five-mile walk begins at John Clare's birthplace, in the centre of **Helpston**. It is a quaint old village cottage that has been transformed by the John Clare Trust into an environmental and educational centre designed to raise awareness of the poet and to "explore and look after the world in which we live today".

Leaving the village, we immediately sense the change that must have occurred to path directions at the onset of enclosure. The path hugs a field edge and then, without warning, plunges diagonally across a field to **College Cottage**. It is not particularly logical for a path to cut across a field, and we can only assume that it existed before the enclosure field, at which time it would have fallen on the balk or uncultivated area between crops.

South of College Cottage the path soon reaches **Maxham's Green Lane**. Before the fields were enclosed, this was the most direct route from Helpston to Peterborough. The field to the north of Oxey Wood was the site of a Roman villa. In the 1820s Clare apparently helped with an archaeological dig here, during which Roman pottery and a mosaic floor were unearthed.

Coming out onto the road, we encounter an S bend. This is a classic example of the joining-up of an old village road (to the north) and a new enclosure road (to the south). The field layouts were typically planned first, then the roads to provide access to them. Almost as an afterthought the village and its existing main street had to be slotted in; hence you often come across a sharp bend to join the new with the old. Walking along this road we note classic enclosure road features – a wide 40ft carriageway between robust hawthorn hedges, well-dug ditches and a straight trajectory.

We leave the road and head towards **Swaddywell Pit**, which is now a nature reserve, after a recent history of light industrial use. This was a great haunt for Clare as a boy, and he called it Swordy Well. In his poem 'The Lament of Swordy Well' he bemoans the loss of this wild space to enclosure and to the plough. Swaddywell is steadily being returned to the state of natural glory that he would have known (you can find out more at botolphsbarn.org.uk). It probably most merits a visit in early summer, when you will be rewarded with an array of wild

Helpston today remains the classic English village, with old cottages along the main street, a church and a pub.

The most popular use of village paths nowadays is walking the dog.

The country stile is perhaps the archetypal feature of the enclosed British landscape.

flowers, including the pyramidal and bee orchids, and numerous birds and insects. Out of season it is rather forlorn.

Emerging from the bridleway that runs from east to west above the pit, we soon reach **King Street**, formerly a Roman road linking Water Newton with Bourne and Lincoln. Slightly raised as it is, you can easily visualise a Roman legion marching along it.

On the other side of the road is **Hilly Wood**, another of Clare's favourite haunts. On one of his visits he records in his diary that he found five types of fern in this wood. On another, he was accosted by one of Sir John Trollope's "meddlesome and consieted" gamekeepers and accused of being a poacher. He was indignant because he had "never shot so much as a sparrow in my life".

Hilly Wood is all of 30 metres above sea level and pretty much the highest point of the walk. David, the Cumbrian hill dweller, is looking positively twitchy about the lack of contours, but these things are all relative – Clare pined for the rolling landscape of Helpston Heath when he moved for a while to the truly fen-encircled Northborough just up the road.

Coming back through **Rice Wood**, it is worth recalling that it used to be called Royce Wood after a family who lived in the nearby village of Alwalton, one of whose descendants was the Royce in Rolls Royce. And that is a reminder of what a throughway this part of the country has always been: the East Coast rail line passing just to the north-east of Helpston and visible for much of the walk, the Roman road almost touching the village, and a few miles west the Great North Road (now the A1) carrying coaches from London to York.

In the past 50 years village footpaths have become almost exclusively used for leisure purposes, especially dog walking. During our walk we encounter a group of horse-riders, in whom Brough takes rather too much interest. In this period local paths have been increasingly well protected and looked after by walking groups and residents. Indeed, the walk we have taken today is available in Clare Cottage and is called "John Clare Country: the poet's favourite places". What would he have made of that?

The John Clare centre is open 10.30am–3pm each day.

Check opening times on 01733 253330 or visit clarecottage.org.

⊕ Other village walks

Take a curious eye to just about any village in England and you will find something of interest footpath-wise. It's worth noting that while the enclosure acts changed vast tracts of countryside in the Midlands, they hardly affected upland areas or the south-west. So this is a key consideration as you set about your detective work.

Laxton, 25 miles north east of Nottingham, merits a visit as it has the last remaining open-field system in the UK. Fields, divided into strips, are farmed in common between the landowners of the village. Although the village is now recognised as an important heritage site, it is home to working farmers who rely on the land for their income. The Old Fosse Way also runs across this medieval field system.

Further reading

The Enclosure Movement (W.E. Tate, Walker & Co) is a classic of its kind, always quoted when enclosures are mentioned. A thorough analysis of what turns out to be a complex process, carried out through several centuries and varying in its extent in different parts of the country

Parliamentary Enclosure in England (G.E. Mingay, Pearson Education) concentrates on the main period of parliamentary enclosures, from 1750-1850.

The English Path (Kim Taplin, Perry Green Press) takes a delightful look at the changing role and meaning of paths through the medium of English literature. It has a good chapter on John Clare and his poetry.

For a book on poaching, *The Long Affray: the Poaching Wars in Britain* (Harry Hopkins, Faber Finds) is a joy to read, using the story of one poacher's fate to illustrate the whole history of poaching from both sides of the fence.

The Lost Village: in Search of a Forgotten Rural England (Richard Askwith, Ebury Press) takes a firsthand look at how the English village has fared in the past few generations.

The Common Stream: a Portrait of an English village through 2,000 years (Rowland Parker, Holt Rinehart Winston) is an outstanding evocation of the development of one village through the ages – a brilliant combination of fact and supposition.

13 Smugglers' trails

Smuggling flourished throughout Great Britain in the 18th and early 19th centuries, encouraged by the punitive taxes that were levied not just on luxury products but even, as the desperate need to finance various wars ratcheted up, on staples such as salt, leather and soap. The taxes were made up of two components, customs and excise, though for the consumer the distinction was largely immaterial.

At the height of the smuggling era the price of tea was as much as four-fifths tax (as some might ruefully point out, not so very different from the situation with petrol or alcohol today). During the Napoleonic wars (1799–1815) the tax on soap went up to three pennies a pound (a quarter of a day's wages for many workers of the time); the tax was not repealed until 1835. So the demand for contraband was huge. On some islands, like the Scillies and the Isle of Man, smuggling supported the economies so completely that when proper enforcement was instituted they virtually collapsed.

The trade in contraband permeated every level of society: those who were not actually moving contraband were providing a ready market for it. A successful run of luxury items could drain a whole region of cash. This meant that public attitudes to "free trade", as some preferred to call it, were equivocal at least. It was notoriously difficult to gain a conviction even if smugglers were caught red-handed.

In the south-east of England, smuggling was a well-organised, properly funded, quasi-capitalist venture. With a huge market in London waiting to be satisfied, investors included established retailers, who could mix a bit of contraband with their legitimate stock. Finance sometimes came from pure speculators who simply looked for their money back with a hefty interest payment. Huge gangs could be mustered, bribes paid and large shipments purchased.

In more remote areas, such as Cornwall, smuggling was mixed with more legitimate ways of earning a living, either trading or fishing. Attempts to control the illegal trade would be left to small numbers of enforcement officers, whose job was difficult if not impossible. It is likely that many took backhanders to turn a blind eye or, as stories tell, were simply lured to a public house and got drunk on the night that a shipment was due to arrive.

The riskiest time for the smuggling crew and the land party was the moment of landing. Smugglers developed quite sophisticated methods of signalling, as sending any sort of message to a smuggling

*The rugged Cornish coast,
epitomised by Piskies Cove,
was not suitable for large-
scale smuggling but ideal for
clandestine landings.*

vessel was itself an illegal activity. A classic ploy would be a light placed in a tiny window, known as a squint, carefully placed so that it could only be spied out at sea. With nights much darker than they are now, a single match or flash from a flintlock pistol could be enough to tell a ship that the coast was clear.

Sympathetic locals could be very helpful. One Cornish farmer would ride his white horse conspicuously across his land if he knew that the customs officers were either absent or otherwise employed. Elsewhere the sails of a mill were said to indicate the safety or not of making a landing.

After landfall most loads were initially carried away by hand, by gangs of "tubmen". Containers were constructed for ease of carrying, the best-known being the half-anker, a small barrel with one flat side used for over-proof alcoholic liquor (which would be

watered down and coloured before resale). Two half-ankers could be strapped together and carried one on the chest and one on the back. It must have been hard and bruising work, with the weight of the liquid crushing the air out of your lungs. Even so, a labourer or miner could make as much in a night as during a whole week in his normal employ, so no doubt there were plenty of folk willing to get involved.

Ponies may have been used, though smugglers had to be careful not to have beasts for whom there was no ostensible legal purpose. Tales abound of animals being "borrowed" in the night with the owner's tacit consent. The horse or pony would be found back in its stable the next day, wet and exhausted, and there would be a "present" hidden in a locker or under some hay nearby.

OUR WALK | Cornwall

An old ship's timber stands between Bessy's and Piskies Coves.

Cornwall was not particularly well placed for smuggling operations, even though for centuries it was at the centre of the major Atlantic trading routes. It was backward, out of touch and not that close to the continent, and landing places were difficult. Unlike in the prosperous south-east, runs would be financed by individual families or by small groups.

The Carter brothers, John, Harry and Charles, ran a profitable family "firm" from around 1770 to the early 1800s. John was clearly the prime mover. His nickname was the King of Prussia (a title he apparently gave himself during childhood games) and it is indicative of his influence that the centre of operations, Portleah Cove, came to be known as King of Prussia's Cove, or Prussia Cove or King's Cove for short. He is said to have developed the slipways, harbours and roadways and adapted the caves in nearby Bessy's Cove.

Harry is one of the few smugglers to leave a firsthand account of his life and activities. Many smugglers, judging from the professions given in court records, would have been illiterate. Of those who could put pen to paper, few would have been inclined to put a confession into writing. Harry Carter's memoir, first printed in the *Wesley-Methodist Magazine* of October 1831, is a confession of sorts, written after he had "seen the Light" and when he was old enough to not care about the consequences. It is sometimes rather heavy going. However, sections are lucidly descriptive and give a rare insight into a man caught up in a complicated and morally ambiguous profession.

Harry was one of 10 children – two daughters and eight sons. Carter is not a Cornish name and there is some suggestion that the family came from Shropshire, perhaps relocating in an attempt to better themselves. Although Harry's father was a miner, he was also able to rent a small farm and two of his sons, the eldest and youngest, were educated as "good country scholars" – the only two for whom this privilege could be afforded. Harry refers to their upbringing as "decent poverty". In his teens he joined two older brothers, presumably John and Charles, fishing and smuggling to bring in money to help support the large family. The smuggling part of the business was clearly a success and, as a "speculating family", they kept moving on to bigger and better ventures.

Harry taught himself to read and, more importantly for a smuggler perhaps, to keep his own accounts. Boat owners were known to keep

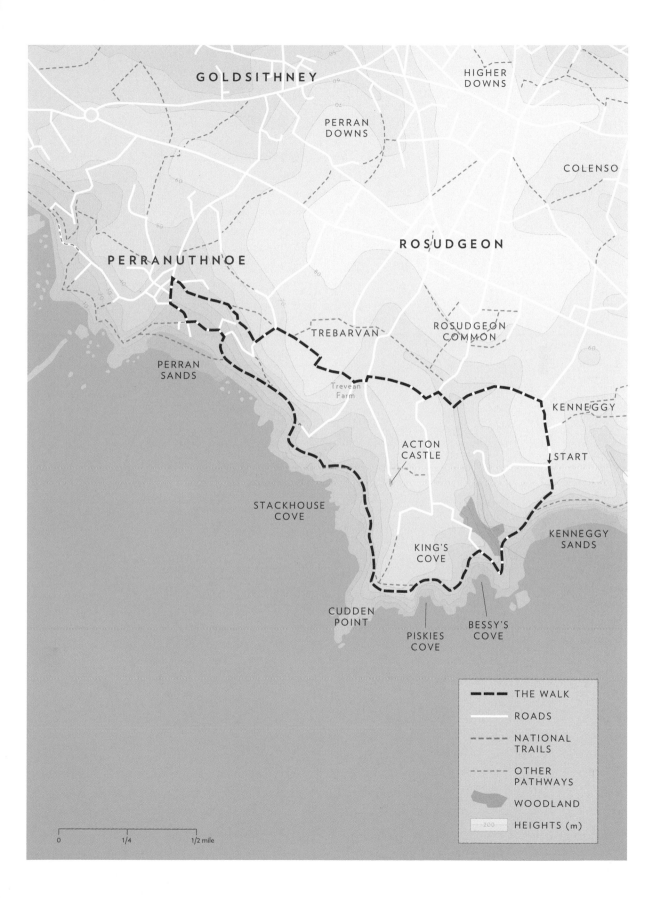

GOLDSITHNEY

HIGHER
DOWNS

PERRAN
DOWNS

COLENSO

ROSUDGEON

PERRANUTHNOE

TREBARVAN

ROSUDGEON
COMMON

PERRAN
SANDS

Trevean Farm

KENNEGGY

START

ACTON
CASTLE

STACKHOUSE
COVE

KENNEGGY
SANDS

KING'S
COVE

CUDDEN
POINT

PISKIES
COVE

BESSY'S
COVE

THE WALK

ROADS

NATIONAL
TRAILS

OTHER
PATHWAYS

WOODLAND

200   HEIGHTS (m)

0   1/4   1/2 mile

two sets of books, one for the above-board business and one for private perusal only, which must have made accounting pretty complicated. By his mid-20s Harry was ordering his own vessel, a sloop, followed quickly by a bigger cutter, both of which did good service for him. "By this time I began to think something of myself," he says.

The cost of getting caught would have been high. Smugglers frequently went to jail; those who had been implicated in violence could be sentenced to death or, if they were lucky, to transportation. On one occasion Harry was tipped off that things were getting too hot for him to remain in the area, as a bounty of £300 had been put on his head. It is an astonishingly high sum for the time. For the brothers to be able to run their smuggling business over such a long period without being caught, there must have been some intimidation of the local populace.

However, if the popular image of the smuggler as a lovable rogue is just a myth, the Carter brothers must come as close to it as is humanly possible. Certainly they operated by codes of decency that were unlikely to be matched elsewhere. Harry is at pains to point out that he hated swearing and punished anyone he heard blaspheming on his boats. There's also a story, not in Harry's account but quite possibly accurate, that John Carter and his men once broke into a revenue store to retrieve a shipment that had been snatched. John's men argued that it was too risky, but John insisted on their retrieving the goods on the basis that he had promised them to someone and he couldn't let them down. Returning the next day, the revenue men commented that it must have been John Carter's doing because he had taken only his own goods and left everything else.

Approaching Perran Sands, with St Michael's Mount behind.

THE BRUTAL SIDE OF SMUGGLING

In many parts of the country, and particularly in the south-east of England, there are records of smugglers' brutality, with informants and revenue officers menaced, battered and killed without a second thought. In a case that became famous at the time, a minor customs official called William Galley and a prospective witness, Daniel Chater, were viciously murdered by members of the notorious Hawkhurst Gang. On Valentine's Day 1748 Chater was being escorted by Galley to Chichester to identify his friend John Diamond, a member of the gang. Chater had made the mistake of mentioning Diamond's name to his neighbours after seeing him on a smuggling run.

The two men unluckily found themselves at an inn in Rowland's Castle whose landlady was sympathetic to the smugglers. Members of the gang turned up and by morning had resolved to kidnap the pair. Galley and Chater were tied to ponies and beaten severely as they travelled along. They were taken to Harris' Well in Lady Hope Park with the initial plan of killing them and throwing them down. However, the leader of the gang, William Jackson, changed his mind and they headed for another inn, the Red Lion at Rake.

Galley tumbled off his pony on the way to the inn. He was apparently lifeless when the gang dug up a fox hole less than a mile from the inn and dumped him in it, but judging by the state of his body when it was found, he later regained consciousness and made some attempt to escape. Chater was taken back to Harris' Well and there the gang first tried to hang him with a rope that was too short. Having failed, they dumped him down the well and threw down rocks until his cries were silenced.

Seven members of the gang were tried and convicted at Chichester Assizes, after two others had turned King's evidence. Six were hanged. Jackson died in jail before the sentence could be carried out.

THE ROUTE | Kenneggy Sands and Perran Sands

Wooden posts near Cudden Point are covered with lichen.

David and Chris Stewart, accompanied by the dog, take a seven-and-a-half-mile walk through the haunts of one of Cornwall's most famous smuggling families.

We drive from Bristol to Cornwall in just a few hours, reminding us that Cornwall has become close enough for city types to weekend in their cottages and get back in time for work on Monday – a far cry from the days the journey must have taken in Harry Carter's time. It's late when we get near to Penzance, having stopped midway in Bovey Tracey to have a side window fitted in the camper van. We are hoping that there will be space for a small van at the campsite at Kenneggy, once the home hamlet of Charles Carter. We're in luck: there's just one pitch left, right up against a hedge so we don't have to improvise a curtain for the new window. For the past couple of hours our terrier Brough has been stretched out in the footwell silently farting. So after a quick mug of tea we set off in the dark towards **Kenneggy Sands**, in the hope that the dog will empty before we are condemned to spending a confined and smelly night with him.

The first part of the track is wide enough, leading down to a circle of field gates. Here the path continuing down to the sea becomes little more than an enclosed ditch, with uneven stone and a lot of mud underfoot. On either side are traditional Cornish "hedges", enclosing the path in deep darkness. The name is most likely derived from the Anglo-Saxon word "hecg" for a territorial boundary and so is not related to the planted hedges seen elsewhere.

Cornish hedges are similar to dry-stone walls but with a wider earth core between the stone sides and a wide concave top, or "batter". Some survive from prehistoric times – it has been argued that they are some of the oldest manmade artefacts in the world still fulfilling their original purpose – while many are medieval or date from early industrial ages. With the earth core kept at a fairly constant level of dampness by water running off the batter in winter and foliage growing on the top in summer, and plenty of crevices in the stone wall sides, the Cornish hedge becomes a true mini-ecosystem. Various plants and flowers spring up through the seasons, while small animals, insects and reptiles house themselves in the stone walls.

The hedges must also have been fundamental to local smuggling operations. It's easy to imagine such a path providing perfect cover for troops of tubmen, and possibly even ponies, spiriting their loads away

*Old fishermen's huts near
Bessy's Cove evoke a past era.*

into the hinterland. With these sunken paths an integral part of the landscape, there's little need for the specially constructed tunnels so often talked about in relation to smuggling but so seldom found.

The next morning we take the same path down to the beach, following a family with windbreaks and buckets and spades. It's much easier to negotiate in daylight. At the coastal path the family peel off left to climb down the ladder to the sand. We bear right. Above us is a terrace of coastguard cottages built in 1826 in a bid to put an end to illegal goings-on in the area – a case, one feels, of shutting the stable door after the horse has bolted. We pass by the Arts and Crafts-style house of Porth-en-Alls, designed in 1911, with its unusual high-walled circular turning space.

Soon the track opens out onto a terrace overlooking **Bessy's Cove**. Clambering over a gate, we walk down onto the sloping rocks, joining a fisherman casting his line into the sea. **King's Cove** is on our left; it's now a private beach preserved for those renting the flats in the Porth-en-Alls property. On this promontory the Carters had the temerity to mount a battery of guns, used at least once to fire on a revenue cutter (which returned fire, though without loss on either side). King's Cove is open to the seas and could only have been used for landing if conditions were absolutely right. Harry Carter reports using it once as his launching spot on one of his enforced flights into exile, fleeing to Roscoff in France in an open boat. It was an unlucky choice of destination, as he was promptly captured and held prisoner during France's Reign of Terror.

As far as landing places were concerned, two strategies were available to smugglers. By landing on a wide open beach you would be in full view of any revenue men, but then equally they would be on full view to you. Open beach landings were, in the main, the preferred method for smugglers on the east coast. The incoming boats would be beached at low tide, giving plenty of room to arrange the unloading into waiting carts ostensibly there to collect kelp. With such landings the chief issue was how to avoid having a large gaggle of tubmen hanging around on the beach waiting for the boats to come in. In some places the waiting men were said to bury themselves in the sand, with only their heads sticking out. On the signal the beach would erupt with men ready to get on with the unloading. It must have been a bizarre sight.

Where open beaches were lacking or unsuitable, the alternative strategy for smugglers was to sneak into a hidden cove, well away from prying eyes. Bessy's Cove, on our right, is a sheltered bay, hemmed in by rocks, and ideal for a bit of smuggling. From whichever angle you approach, it is completely hidden until you are right upon it. With some

Cliff Cottage, which sits above Bessy's Cove, may have been used in the Carter's smuggling operations.

careful watch-keeping and a bit of judicious signalling, a ship anchored offshore could be warned off if revenue men were sniffing around.

It didn't always go to plan, of course. Harry Carter tells of an attempted drop-off at Cawsand, further east on the Cornish coast. Seeing two boats heading out to his ship, he assumes they belong to his colleagues. Too late he realises that they are full of revenue officers. His crew panic and dart below before the ship is boarded, leaving Harry the only man prepared to put up a defence. He is overpowered and knocked down onto the deck. Twice the revenue men discuss putting him down below with the others and twice they don't bother, on the assumption that he is either dead or nearly dead. With his skull "shot to atoms", Harry manages to clamber over the side and tries to swim ashore. Rather unsurprisingly, he finds that his strength fails him. Luck must be on his side, however, as by hauling his way along some ropes he finds himself in shallow water at the bow of the ship. After some further painful hauling he meets some friends, presumably those who were supposed to be helping to unload the contraband. He is whisked across country to his brother Charles's house.

As we look into Bessy's Cove we can see the bricked-up caves, steep footsteps cut into the rocks leading down to a tiny pebble beach, and the slipway running diagonally up the further side of the cove. We climb down the steps to find a few parties of swimmers, mostly encased in black wetsuits, and family groups making the best of a rather weak sun. There are no visible entrances to the caves, forestalling our desire to search for smuggling tunnels. A brightly coloured dinghy bobs on a mooring at the foot of the slipway, right at the point where the unloading of contraband would be easiest.

Climbing back up the steps and continuing westwards, we find some tumbledown shacks at the top of the path leading onto the slipway. The shacks themselves may not date from the Carter brothers' time but from this vantage point we can see a thatched cottage and the property now called Cliff Cottage, both of which are certainly contemporary. Cliff Cottage is thought to have started life as a fish cellar. Its over-large proportions and extreme proximity to the cove suggest that it owes a debt to the Carter's smuggling operations. If, as some stories relate, John Carter did construct a tunnel from the cove, this house would seem a likely destination.

The coastal path continues to the west, skirting around **Piskies Cove**, a tiny natural beach without the obvious advantages of Bessy's Cove but no doubt useful in emergencies. The footpath passes above a huge gaping cave and then on to **Cudden Point**, owned by the National Trust. Cudden Point splits the more populous part of the coast to the west, to Marazion and beyond to Penzance, from the rocky coastline we have just traversed. From the sea cliffs the ground slopes gently upwards towards the main road between Helston and Penzance, although it would have been little more than a track in Harry Carter's time.

In between are tiny hamlets and isolated farmsteads. Harry and his brothers would have known every home and every person in this strip of land. Just above Piskies Cove is Acton Castle, a grand private residence owned by the Praed family. John Carter rented the farm at Acton Castle and, while the owners of Acton Castle were away, he was able to hide his brother in the house after his escape at Cawsand. Harry writes that he only dared to light a fire at night, for fear of the smoke giving away his position. It must have been a chilly and lonely hideaway. It seems he filled his hours there "improving his navigation" – keeping up his theoretical skills while he couldn't put them into practice. He still went down to Bessy's Cove at night to join his brothers and companions for a drink of grog and some banter. In the end lying low became too

John Carter is said to have built the slipway at Bessy's Cove

difficult for Harry and he was forced into exile in New York.

Our path continues beyond Cudden Point, past Stackhouse Cove, and St Michael's Mount comes into view. **Perran Sands**, by the village of Perranuthnoe, are dotted with bathers and surfers. We stop at the café by the path to the beach for a late lunch, and just beyond the car park stop again for ice cream. Then it's time to return across the fields, following field boundaries and sunken lanes connecting the dispersed farmsteads and hamlets. It's been a wet summer and the tracks are filled with mud, so we try various routes. It's indicative of the many choices our smugglers would have had in spreading their goods across the countryside, and we are only attempting paths that are marked as rights of way so there must have been many more. Eventually we find our way back to Kenneggy, where the dog collapses on the front seat and we can put the kettle on.

That night we tuck into fish and chips accompanied by a glass of red wine, surrounded by families chatting away happily in their tents and caravans. We realise that the sheer struggle to survive in those times – of which smuggling was just one small but indicative part – is so alien to us that it is almost impossible to imagine.

All the fields are bounded by traditional Cornish 'hedges'.

⊖ Other smuggling routes to follow

The Peddars Way in Norfolk runs along the line of a Roman road, although the name was most likely given during the Middle Ages. Smugglers favoured ancient tracks and green lanes as they could pass largely unnoticed. The section of the Peddars Way north of Massingham to Hunstanton became known as the *Smugglers' Way*, though this title was accorded to a number of other tracks in the region.

The sites of the grisly deaths of Daniel Chater and William Galley can still be visited. You can follow the Sussex Border Path from Rowland's Castle, near Portsmouth, to Lady Holt Park and on to Rake. Harris' Well, where Chater was murdered, is just off a footpath in the wood at OS grid reference SU753172. Harting Combe, where Galley was buried in a fox hole, is a mile south of Rake, and is crossed by a public footpath.

Culver Hole (SS405929) on the Gower Peninsula is a dramatic hiding place supposedly used by smuggler John Lucas. It can be reached by the cliff path from the public car park beyond Llangennith.

St Peter's Chapel sits at the mouth of the River Blackwater in Essex and, thanks to its remote position, was used for the storage of smuggled goods. You can walk there from Bradwell Waterside, where smugglers used to frequent a 16th-century inn, the Green Man.

Further reading

Smuggling in the British Isles (Richard Platt, Tempus Publishing) is full of fascinating information about the era, as well as the characters involved in smuggling. Platt's website smuggling. co.uk has further background information, including terrible tales of violence and intimidation. The website includes a guide to hundreds of smuggling haunts you can visit.

Harry Carter's memoir can be read in its entirety online; you can find links from Platt's website. Although some of the language takes a bit of deciphering, the account is worth reading. As well as the smuggling stories, Harry tells movingly of tough times working as a labourer near New York and of his experiences as a prisoner in France.

More walks, ideas and discussion can be found on the *Walkingworld* website at walkingworld.com

14 Stalkers' tracks

Looking at aerial photographs of lowland Great Britain, we expect to see the countryside parcelled into neat fields and pastures, separated by fences, hedges and walls. The organised patchwork pattern stretches, almost without break, from coast to coast. Rather more surprising is to find precise rectangles of black, brown and purple spread over the upland moors of Scotland and northern and south-western England. These are places we expect to be wild and untamed, but they are not.

Management, or mismanagement, of Britain's uplands goes back to the earliest prehistoric farmers. By the Bronze Age a growing population had cleared much of the higher ground and was farming it. But climate change, over-intensive grazing or over-enthusiastic clearance of the ground with fire – or a combination of all three – led to vital minerals being leached from the soil. Before long the peaty, boggy ground was suitable only for the heathers and brackens we see on the moors today.

For over two centuries heather has been carefully managed to support a new upland land use, the sport of shooting. With the steady development of ever more powerful and accurate shotguns during the 18th and 19th centuries there was a surge in the popularity of game hunting within the upper classes. In lowland areas hunting parties could fire off at the slower-moving pheasant, a bird imported to the British Isles and specifically reared for the purpose. On the moors the target was the grouse, a wild bird that flew faster and was therefore more of a challenge for the competitive shot.

Being wild, the grouse population could only be brought up to a level appropriate for large-scale shooting through management of its habitat. Selective burning on a cycle of between seven and 25 years removes the old heather, which, while suitable for cover and nesting, is sterile as a foodstuff for the grouse. Providing the burning is done when the heather is dry but the ground is damp, the fire shocks the seed lying dormant in the ground into germinating. Within a year or so a new carpet of heather appears, with succulent young shoots for all manner of wildlife to feed upon.

People who shoot for sport pay a disproportionately high price for the animals they slay. Deer stalking parties pay handsomely for the privilege of taking part in a cull that would have to be done anyway, simply to keep the population of deer manageable and healthy. Today, to shoot a pheasant on a driven shoot – in which the birds are flushed towards a line of guns by beaters waving white flags

Eis a' Chual Aluinn, with its 200m drop, is Britain's highest waterfall. It looks out over Loch Glencoul.

– can cost £25 or more, and to shoot a grouse two or three times that. At market a shot grouse or pheasant may fetch a couple of pounds.

The difference pays for the team of beaters and pickers-up on the day and for the year-long employment of gamekeepers to manage the moor. As well as maintaining the variety of heather cover, gamekeepers control the bird's natural predators: foxes, stoats and crows are all legally killed, to the benefit of the grouse and other birds that nest on the moors, such as curlew. The Game Act 1831 stipulates when the season for particular game is open or closed. The "Glorious 12th" (of August) marks the start of the red grouse shooting season, a day on which large numbers of birds may be slaughtered.

There is still great potential for mismanagement of the land and its ecosystem. Heather needs to be burned in relatively small patches, so that the landscape retains a variety of habitats. There is a temptation for moor managers to create much wider areas of new heather, in effect farming grouse and further elevating the population for those lucrative shooting parties. Over-efficient drainage, to make the land suitable for sheep, can make the peat crumble away as it loses its essential bogginess. The occasional illegal shooting or poisoning of birds of prey continues to be reported.

OUR WALK | The Highlands

Where rivers carve through rocks the geology is revealed.

Geologically the highlands and islands of Scotland are complex. Driving north across the desolate and hauntingly beautiful Rannoch Moor towards the great mass of Buachaille Etive Moor standing sentinel at the entrance to Glencoe, the red rhyolite is a marked contrast to the summits of the Trossachs left a few miles behind, where metamorphic rocks known as schists predominate. The Cuillins on Skye have two different rock formations within a single mountain range: basalt and gabbro in the group called the Black Cuillin and granite forming the basis of the Red Cuillin to the east. Further north still, in the north-west Highlands, the Moine Thrust Zone denotes an area where younger rocks have been forced over older ones, creating a landscape of extraordinary diversity. Mountains within the belt have complicated layers of rock and continue to attract geologists deepening their understanding of the powerful forces that created them.

Despite this great variety in geology, one factor is common: these places are depopulated. Vast tracts of land, from deep glen to barren mountaintop, are without habitation, and where settlements do exist they are small and remote. In so much of the Highlands the air is one of true wilderness, of a landscape untouched by human hand. But the impression is misleading, as it has been shaped by human intervention as much as any part of the British Isles. It's just that the people are now missing. In large part this is down to the fact that while England and the central belt of Scotland were in the throes of an industrial revolution, a combination of geographical, political and economic factors meant that the Highlands failed to develop a significant manufacturing or trading base. The result was a steady stream of Highlanders emigrating from their homeland. The most notorious episode of this long-term exodus became known as the Highland clearances.

The Highland clearances have been elevated through song, poetry and story-telling to mythical status, fuelling resentment that has been sustained through generations of "dispossessed" Scottish people. The true story is rather more complex. Even before the rout of the Jacobite clans at Culloden in 1746, the old social system was beginning to break down, although at a considerably slower pace than had been happening through the enclosure movement in England and in Wales. Landowners were already following a more capitalist approach to their assets, taking advantage of the increased rents that could be charged by having

KYLESTROME

GLENDHU FOREST

GLENDHU

Maldie
Burn

LOCH GLENDHU

AIRD DA LOCH

GLENCOUL

LOCH
BEAG

EIS A' CHUAL
ALUINN

LOCH GLENCOUL

LOCH A'
CHÀIRN BHÀIN

KYLESKU
(START)

UNAPOOL

LOCH NA
GAINMHICH

THE WALK
ROADS
OTHER
PATHWAYS
WOODLAND
HEIGHTS (m)

200

0   1/2   1 mile

the land grazed by cattle and sheep rather than occupied by people scratching a living from subsistence farming.

The collapse of the old clan order after Culloden increased the pace of change, as confiscated Jacobite landholdings were earmarked for "improvement". Removals gathered pace after 1780 and continued into the early 19th century. Many of the contemporary accounts of the clearances are harrowing and there's no doubt that some evictions were cruel and at best terribly mishandled. In the worst examples whole communities were uprooted in a single brutal eviction, assisted by the military, with families forced to put their few belongings into carts to be taken off to a "new life". Often they ended up on poor crofts by the sea, where surviving would have been tough even if they had the requisite skills, or they were given tickets for ships to Canada.

But such mass evictions were avoided if at all possible by landlords, who feared the publicity they attracted. In many more places the process was gradual, with the slow dispersal of the population by attrition rather than by forceful removal. For all of the popular image of the old Scottish clan as a stable and secure existence, tenancies were actually very short-term: many were simply not renewed and the people just moved on. Indeed, some of the "tacksmen", the second-rank clansmen who rented land from the laird and sublet it to smaller tenants, emigrated of their own accord, taking some pleasure in the discomfort of their landlords who genuinely wanted them to stay. Often, ironically, emigrating Scots dispossessed the indigenous people of the New World in their quest for land of their own. They even moved down into England: many farms in Essex, for instance, were taken over by ambitious Scots whose efficient farming methods were widely acknowledged.

Far from being mad keen to clear the land of their people, many lairds tried desperately to maintain the status quo, despite their growing debts. One of the most eloquent was David Stewart of Garth (no relation to the author of this book). Stewart was a man revered for his support for the common Highlander, thanks to the observational "sketches" he published extolling the virtues of the Highland people. However, his own bold attempt to maintain the old system was doomed, despite his shoring up his Highland estates with profits from his slave plantations in the West Indies. In the end even he begged his tenants to emigrate, essentially in order to achieve the rents needed to re-establish his solvency.

The reality was that the difficult terrain of the Highlands and its remoteness from the burgeoning industrial centres to the south could not sustain a rapidly rising population and something had to give.

The bothy at Glendhu is a simple dwelling, with no power or running water.

While a few Scottish landowners were fabulously rich and could make choices, vast numbers with smaller holdings were either bankrupt or on the verge of bankruptcy. It was the agents employed to straighten out their accounts who had the job of shifting the small-scale tenants and their dependants from the land, so that it could be brought back into some kind of profit.

In the end sheep and cattle farming, even in its supposedly efficient new form, was not particularly lucrative in many parts of the Highland landscape. Landowners often spent more on the process of "improvement" than they could gain from the stock imported to graze on their newly enclosed lands or the rents they could achieve from incoming tenants. A lifeline for many estates was thrown in the form of grouse shooting and deer stalking, turning the Scottish Highlands into a playground for the wealthy. Their passion for everything Scottish helped to kickstart wider tourism to the Highlands and Islands, making a benefit of a countryside largely denuded of its populace.

THE ROUTE | Glendhu and Glencoul

Small clumps of birch manage to get a grip on the hillside above Loch Glendhu.

David and Chris Stewart, accompanied by David's brother Ian and their dog Brough, visit two stalkers' cottages on a two-day trek through a Highland shooting estate.

We have decided to tread some proper Highland ground on a walk through one of the Duke of Westminster's estates just to the north of the small coastal town of Ullapool. The Reay estate is just outside the parish of Assynt, which became one of the best documented of the Countess of Sutherland's clearances. At the beginning of the 19th century the Reay estate was also owned by her and it was in fact "cleared" at around the same time. We passed through the area a year before on our way to Orkney and walked a short way along the lochside near the tiny village of Kylesku. The track along the loch was stunning even on that rainy day but our walk was cut short as a bridge over a raging mountain stream was down and only half-repaired.

The map shows an intriguing potential route along Loch Glendhu, followed by a hop over a ridge to Loch Glencoul, at the head of which is Britain's highest waterfall, Eis a' Chual Aluinn. Climbing up by the waterfall, it should be possible to continue back to Kylesku over a moorland track. Even better, there are two bothies, owned by the estate but run by the Mountain Bothies Association, allowing the 15-mile walk to be broken into two days with the prospect of a decent night's rest in the middle.

We stop off for the night in Edinburgh to pick up my brother Ian, who is joining us for the escapade. We share the driving, a good four hours, to arrive in Kylesku in time for a late lunch at the Kylesku Inn, overlooking **Loch Glendhu**. As we tuck into fish pie and fish cakes it clouds over and begins to rain. The loch turns dark in that quintessentially Scottish way as we watch two kayakers slip their vessels into the water from the slipway and disappear from view. We linger over a cup of tea and hope for the rain to ease. It doesn't. Eventually we pack our rucksacks and head off towards the elegant bridge just north of the village, opened in 1984, that now takes the main road soaring over the mouth of the loch. On a rocky ledge a few hundred yards away the hulk of the old ferry sits rusting away.

Across the bridge and up the road we turn right onto the lane leading back to the lochside and the main estate properties. It is clear that there is no shortage of money here for maintaining the cottages and the grand estate house. The walls and even the drainage ditches are beautifully restored. Behind the stable the vehicles are spotlessly clean and parked nose outwards, in good regimental order.

Even in the rain the walk along the lochside track is breathtaking. Out in the loch are lines of buoys, which we assume are for farming the mussels we saw being devoured by other diners in the inn. A pair of oystercatchers chase us along. At one point we disturb a seal stretched out on a rock jutting up from the loch; he arches his back for a moment and slips into the water, disappearing into the blackness. Brough scampers ahead, possibly remembering the track from a year ago and maybe hoping to see the courteous young gamekeepers we met that day returning from the hills in their all-terrain buggy. But today the path is deserted and before long we cross the brand new bridge below the waterfall of **Maldie Burn**.

Our original plan was to bypass the bothy at **Glendhu** and continue on around the loch and over the ridge to the one at Glencoul. But we have dithered so long in the warmth of Kylesku Inn, and the weather is so dismal, that we decide to cut our day short and stop over at Glendhu. The bothy is tiny – just two simple rooms downstairs and two bare bunkrooms in the loft, all four with fireplaces. The toilet is a spade, accompanied by a sign telling you to dig your hole as far away from the bothy as possible and nowhere near a water course.

One of the downstairs rooms is already occupied by a couple with a sheepdog called Molly, so we strip out of our dripping wet-weather gear in the other and get out the stove to make tea. Shortly afterwards we are joined by a Mountain Bothies Association member called Gus. Gus is determined to light the fire. He drops his bag, grabs a saw and handaxe and goes out hunting for wood. Given that there is hardly a tree in sight, finding firewood seems an unlikely prospect but he returns with news that there are some logs washed down by the river a few hundred yards away. Ian and I go to collect the ones he couldn't carry himself, while Gus sets to chopping them into fire-sized lengths.

Gus is definitely good value, we decide, and should be a standard feature of every bothy. After knocking up a half-decent tuna and sweetcorn kedgeree and all six of us, plus the two dogs, gazing contentedly at the fire burning away in the grate for an hour or so, we disperse to sleep. Our party of three plus dog settles down in one of the loft rooms. Even with a sleeping mat, the wooden floor is hard and we spend a chilly night trying to get comfortable. The dog decides it's too cold to sleep on his own so he clambers his way down into our double sleeping bag and snuggles down between us. We can't be bothered to throw him out and, besides, he's acting as a bit of a hot water bottle.

The stalker's cottage at
Glendhu catches the early
morning sun.

The next morning we are up early as the sun streams through the skylight; apparently there are three months in the winter when sunlight never touches the cottages at all. We make some porridge and cups of tea, pack up and set off towards the head of the loch. Next to the bothy is a larger cottage built by the Duke of Westminster around 1880 for his estate workers. Peering through the windows, we can see that it has been renovated. The kitchen is equipped with an Aga cooker, one of the downstairs rooms has new bunk beds with comfy-looking mattresses and the new lid of a buried septic tank in the garden tells us that it has proper toilet facilities. We learn later that the cottage has been renovated by the estate and put back to use as a bunkhouse for disadvantaged children.

At the head of the loch we are able to cross the river swollen from yesterday's rain by a footbridge. Whatever you think of the rights and wrongs of this land being taken over for hunting and fishing by the fabulously wealthy, it's difficult to imagine the footbridges and tracks being kept in good repair for any other reason. We're certainly pleased to have a dry, safe way over this particular torrent.

We pick our way through a large boulder field under some spectacular waterfalls. The path gradually rises away from Loch Glendhu, passing through some stunted birch woods. The trail, no doubt used for centuries by stalkers and their parties between Glendhu and Glencoul, is faint and hard to follow. Every now and then a small pile of stones acts as a marker to guide the way. Crossing the ridge at **Aird da Loch**, we gain our first glimpse of **Loch Glencoul**. The path continues above the crags, which sheer down to the loch, so for a mile or more we contour through the heather. Finally the cottages of **Glencoul** appear directly below us and a few zig-zags of rough track take us down to them.

In this tiny settlement there are the remains of some older dwellings near the loch shore. The Glencoul bothy is a near replica of the one at Glendhu. The estate cottage, built around 1885, is attached like an odd extension to it. Unlike the Glendhu cottage, this one remains boarded up. Despite being abandoned in the 1950s, it is remarkably intact. We learn later that it is due to be renovated and used as an outdoor activity centre as well.

As a home it must have been incredibly isolated. But with supplies brought by estate boat it was, according to Ishbel Mackay, who lived there with her parents until 1953, perfectly comfortable and a great place to grow up. When the house was built it was occupied by John Elliot, who worked as a stalker for the Duke of Westminster (who at

THE ASSYNT ESTATE

The Assynt area north of Ullapool was one of the first of Elizabeth Gordon, Countess of Sutherland's, estates to be "improved" through the removal of its residents. In the early 1800s the countess was able to draw on the vast inheritance of her husband, the Duke of Stafford, to finally get her own loss-making lands into order. The couple and their factor, Patrick Sellar, who was given charge of the removals, have become three of the most vilified actors in the story of the Highland clearances.

In Assynt itself the process appears to have gone reasonably smoothly. Many of the people were rehoused in the enlarged seaside settlement of Lochinver. For her part the Countess of Sutherland seems to have genuinely believed that the change was for the long-term benefit of all the parties. But underlying resentments must have simmered away. Across the Highlands the better life promised in crofts on the coast failed to materialise. The collection and treatment of kelp, a seaweed that could be burned to create chemicals for soap and glass-making, provided valuable extra income for a short while, but then cheaper supplies from the continent crippled the industry.

As the countess moved on to her other estates things became much more difficult. Sellar made a tactical mistake in catching the main law agent for Sutherland, Robert Mackid, in the act of poaching, causing embarrassment all round. Later, as reports came in of the mismanagement of clearances on the Sutherland properties, Mackid used his position to have Sellar arrested on a series of counts, including one of culpable homicide. One of the most serious accusations was that Sellar had ordered a dwelling to be burned down with a sick old woman still inside. The burning of cottage timbers was a common occurrence during the clearances, designed to prevent the inhabitants from walking away and then returning a few weeks later. The sight of burning homes must have made the act of removal particularly hard to bear.

At court the accounts proved to be conflicting and Sellar was acquitted. His reputation never recovered, however, and while he continued as a sheep farmer in his own right, he was relieved of responsibility for the continuing Sutherland removals.

Now Assynt has become the location for a new experiment in Scottish land ownership and management. After much lobbying, a major part of the Assynt Estate, some 44,000 acres, has been passed into the hands of a community collective, the Assynt Foundation. The foundation promotes a whole range of activities, including fishing and stalking.

this point was renting the estate from the Duke of Sutherland). Elliot's eldest two sons were killed during the first world war; a white cross erected to their memory by the Duke of Westminster stands on a small hillock above the cottage. John and his wife Margaret moved out of Glencoul in 1917 and retired to live with a member of the family, another stalker, at Glendhu.

We stop at the bothy to brew a cup of tea and have some cereal bars for lunch. Then we take the track up the valley towards the great white spout of Eis a' Chual Aluinn, with its 200m drop. The track peters out at the slipway in **Loch Beag**, a small extension to Loch Glencoul. From here what path there is turns out to be intermittent and indistinct. We follow the river up towards the waterfall. There's plenty of water to make it a real spectacle and also to swell the river, which we are beginning to regret not crossing at its widest point at the outflow into the loch. At some point we know we are going to have get across if we are to climb up to the top of the waterfall and from there take the "tourist route" back to the road. The alternative, which is considerably less attractive, is to retrace our steps all the way back to Kylesku via Glendhu. We figure that if we walk beyond the waterfall there will be that much less water in the river and it may just be possible to wade through. But before we get much further the river bends and we can step from submerged rock to submerged rock to make a tentative crossing, in my case once with my rucksack on and once carrying a worried-looking dog.

Again there are no clear pathways, just the occasional tantalising stretch of track trodden by deer through the heather and rocks. We work our way round beneath the rounded buttress from which the waterfall is spouting and then upwards in the general direction of its top. It's brutally hard work climbing up through the heather, hoping for some bare rock to make the going easier. Finally we come out on a rocky platform to the east of the fall. There's a magnificent view of the waterfall and beyond it to the loch.

From the **head of the waterfall** we need to climb another 200 metres to reach a ridge, first alongside the feeder river for the fall and then across barren ground studded with rocks. The route is marked with small cairns so navigation now is much easier, but we are quite worn out from our battle through the undergrowth earlier in the day. Beyond the ridge the path drops down to the high **Loch Bealach a' Bhuirich**, skirting it and then descending further through boggy ground to **Loch na Gainmhich**.

At the road we stretch out in the warm sunshine. Ian volunteers to walk the four miles to Kylesku to fetch the car. Blaming the dog for our own inability to continue, we accept his offer. We watch him through the binoculars to make sure he keeps up a decent pace until he disappears from sight. The three of us doze contentedly on a sleeping mat. In the end it takes Ian a very reasonable 65 minutes to get to Kylesku and return with the car.

With the sun setting, we drive back through the Highlands in search of a good dinner. All the pubs and hotels are packed with tourists for the bank holiday weekend and it is hard to find a table. Hundreds of thousands of visitors, like ourselves, seek out this wilderness every year precisely because in its depopulated state it seems utterly wild. Today it is very difficult to separate ourselves from the romanticisation of the Highlands and harder still to regret the way the Highland landscape has turned out. We may feel a deep empathy for the people forcibly removed from the land, but the tracks we follow, the bridges we cross, the inns we eat in and the wide-open landscapes we gaze across are in a large part the end product of a century and a half of Highland clearances.

Our return path leads down to Loch na Gainmhich

⊕ Other shooting tracks to follow

Scotland has in effect "right to roam", so there are many places where you can strike off onto heather-covered moorland. The *Cairngorm* mountains encompass several old hunting estates and deer are still stalked, though the level of culling is controversial. The National Park Authority would like to see the numbers closely managed as the deer damage the vegetation, particularly new woodland. The 20-mile walk through the Lairig Ghru, the high-level pass that provides north-south access right through the Cairngorm range, is a superb way to experience the environment without tackling the summits.

Access legislation in Scotland requires estates involved in deer-stalking to advertise the days on which walking should be avoided. The busiest period for deer stalking is June to October. The Hillphones service (snh.org.uk/hillphones) can be used to find out if stalking is taking place on your planned route.

In northern England, particularly on the *Pennines*, there are vast tracts of moorland, much of which is covered by the new access legislation. Typical moorlands can be crossed on the Pennine Way, on the sections from Keld in the Yorkshire Dales to Bowes in Country Durham, Middleton-in-Teesdale to Dufton in the Eden Valley, or from Dufton over Cross Fell to Alston. In access areas it is possible to walk where you like, but often landowners have been given dispensation to ban dogs at any time. Grouse moors can be restricted for short periods by giving at least one month's notice. Maps with up-to-date restrictions can be found on the Natural England website (naturalengland.org.uk)

Further reading

The story of the Highland clearances and their aftermath has been told many times, with varying degrees of objectivity. *The Highland Clearances* (Eric Richards, Birlinn) is a balanced account tracing the origins of the clearances from the 18th century to their culmination in the crofting legislation of the 1880s.

More walks, ideas and discussion can be found on the *Walkingworld* website at walkingworld.com

15 Miners' tracks

Mining shaped the development of transport and communication in Britain, perhaps more so than any other industry, including wool. Not only did the miners have to be able to get to the mines, but the valuable materials that they brought up needed to be carried away to the places where they were worked and consumed. Mines also needed tools, equipment and supplies; in many areas and for many decades these were brought in from further afield on the packhorse roads. During the 18th and 19th centuries, coal and iron fuelled and enabled the creation of new methods of transport, including the canals and the railway. Mining, technology and transport came together during the industrial revolution to create a "perfect storm" in which parts of the British landscape and way of life changed utterly.

Trade in metals, fine stone implements and salt helped to create the first long-distance trading routes, many no doubt following the ridgeway paths encountered in Chapter 1. Stone axe heads gathered, hewn and polished at Great Langdale in the Lake District have been found, carefully interred as valued funerary objects, in prehistoric burials many hundreds of miles away. British tin, mined in Cornwall or on Dartmoor, found its way into the Mediterranean during the Bronze Age, probably travelling much of the way by sea.

Britain has a very varied geology and a wealth of valuable metals and ores beneath its surface. Copper ore is found in huge quantities in parts of Wales and Anglesey, and has been mined there for centuries. Mining for iron and lead goes back to the Romans and quite possibly before. We have seen how mining areas were connected into the Roman road network. The monks of various orders, between the Norman Conquest and the dissolution of the monasteries, ran mines and built smelting mills. The metals were traded far and wide.

Because of its bulk and weight, most quarried stone is used locally but where it is particularly fine it has been transported in large quantities for many miles. Some 70,000 tons of Purbeck stone, a shelly limestone from the Jurassic coast that can be polished like marble, was used in the building of Salisbury Cathedral. A great deal more Portland stone made its way to London, where it is found in many magnificent buildings, including St Paul's Cathedral.

But, without doubt, it was coal mining that transformed the country and changed its transport network for ever. Rich coal measures, laid down in the Carboniferous Period some 300–400 million years ago, were found in South Wales, the Midlands, the

A track leads up to the Old Gang smelting mill in the Yorkshire Dales.

north-east of England and in the central belt of Scotland. It was in precisely those places that the great new manufacturing towns and cities sprang up during a period of rapid industrialisation. Canals, railways and a properly maintained road system developed to satisfy their transport needs, supplanting the packhorse and drovers' roads of a previous era.

In many parts of the country, however, mining still relied on a local workforce, not just of men but of women and children too, making their way to remote places in order to earn a few pennies. In some cases the track would be walked just twice a week, to the mine on Sunday afternoon after chapel and back again on Saturday morning, with the miners sleeping and eating together during the week in barracks and bunkhouses. Each miner would take his own food and make it last the week. The "mine shop", as it was sometimes called, must have been crowded, smelly, raucous and a test of anyone's patience. Fights were common, though balanced by the common ability among mining communities to entertain themselves with music and song.

OUR WALK | The lead mines of the Yorkshire Dales

Some rusting mineral extraction equipment sits in the Old Gang smelting mill.

In the Yorkshire Dales mineral deposits are found in the alternating layers of limestone, shale and sandstone that make up the Yordale series. These layers were laid down as the landmass that is now Great Britain passed through the equatorial zone in its long, lazy drift north from near the Antarctic, travelling at a few centimetres a year. Scotland had already joined England and Wales after starting off several thousand miles away. The Pennines were being created layer by layer in a vast delta in which the sea level fluctuated, so that the deposits of animals, coral and sediment varied.

Crushed down under the weight of later deposits, the layers all became rock, to be finally topped off with millstone grit, created from eroded material from a huge mountain range that had risen up over the landmass that would become Scotland. In some areas the sea receded enough from time to time for a marshy landscape to develop in which lush forests sprang up. The decaying plant material from this forest was laid down to eventually form coal – there is a narrow band at Tan Hill that provided coal for the mining industry.

After the rocks had become hardened, a granite core below them, centred on Wensleydale, reheated, filling the crevices with hot brines that hardened into baryte, fluorite, witherite, calcite – and galena, which was the lead ore targeted by generations of miners. There was no telling how these seams of lead ore would turn out until you dug along them: they might be very thin, they might widen out or they might pinch out to nothing. Most ran through vertical crevices in the rock, which meant that the miners had to work downwards or upwards to keep following the seam. The preferred method was to work upwards, with waste material stored on platforms as it was cut or blasted out, rather than having to be lifted out of a deepening shaft. The ideal, though, was to find a "flat", a wider, thicker horizontal band of ore that could be mined much more easily.

Mining in the Dales started way back in Roman times, or possibly even earlier. The earliest miners worked on the surface, venturing into the rock only as far as natural ventilation and drainage would allow. If evidence of a workable vein were found, a dam with a sluice gate would be built on the hillside above. The sudden release of stored water stripped off a layer of topsoil and rock, exposing more of the seam to be worked. Men would pick at the vein with pickaxes and a second flush of water would take the ore down into a pit dug below. These "hush gullies"

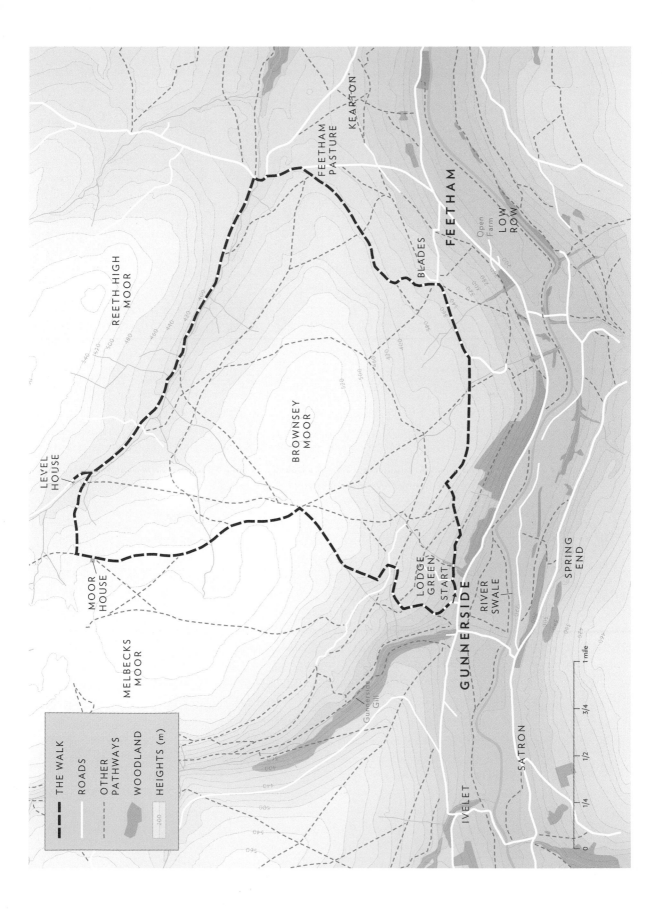

THE WALK
ROADS
OTHER PATHWAYS
WOODLAND
HEIGHTS (m)

200

FEETHAM PASTURE

KEARTON

FEETHAM

Open Farm

LOW ROW

BLADES

REETH HIGH MOOR

LEVEL HOUSE

BROWNSEY MOOR

MOOR HOUSE

MELBECKS MOOR

LODGE GREEN

START

GUNNERSIDE

RIVER SWALE

SPRING END

Gunnerside Gill

IVELET

SATRON

0   1/4   1/2   3/4   1 mile

can be seen across the Dales, artificial rockfalls that gash the sides of the hills. The real mining revolution began around 1700, with the advent of gunpowder. It was a major industry in the Dales for nearly 200 years.

Working deeper into the hillside, the two key requirements are to be able to provide air to breathe and to stop the mine from filling up with water. Being in hilly country, the Dales lead mines could generally be drained by cutting "levels" into the hillside. From these, shafts could be taken up or down, either in pursuit of ore or to create ventilation, or both. The Dales mines did not generally need pumping engines, in contrast to the vast majority of coal mines, although from time to time these were used if drainage became tricky. The larger levels would be laid with tracks so tubs of ore could be taken out, pushed or pulled along by men or ponies.

The extent of the levels, cross-cuts, shafts and adits cutting through the hills meant that they often joined up with the workings of other companies. By taking circuitous routes through the shafts and levels it was possible to go from the Swaledale mines right through to Arkengarthdale on the other side of the hill. There was no knowing when you would come across an old working – when they did miners referred to it as "t'Old Man". There were, of course, few written records or maps of where mining had taken place in the distant past.

Mining was an unhealthy occupation, with life expectancy among the men during the mid-19th century being as low as 46. An accident or early death could leave a whole family destitute and help for those on the breadline was basic, to say the least. In an infamous ruling in 1831 in Muker, the administrators of the parish funds ruled that a pauper's pension could only be paid once all the family's "unnecessary" possessions had been taken away and sold. Items deemed to be superfluous included bibles, clocks, frying pans, cupboards, even the kitchen table. The Poor Law Amendment Act of a few years later made matters even worse, with the destitute being forced out of their homes and into the workhouse.

Despite this, men looked to the mines to make extra provision for their families alongside small-scale farming, but the income was uncertain. Miners formed partnerships of four to eight men and made a bargain with the mine owners to work particular seams. The price paid for the lead ore varied according to how much they were able to extract from the seam. If it was hard going, the price would be many times that of an easy seam. The system was susceptible to creative accounting, of course. Managers were suspected of favouritism towards their relatives and friends. Miners who had struck lucky were known to eke out their

The 'Hard Level' of Old Gang lead mine must have been completed in a hurry, as it is not cut to the standard height.

output so that the price remained high, unless their agreement was running out, in which case they worked like fury.

One Swaledale miner, "Captain" Jammy Harker, was famous for having hit a rich flat just four months before the end of his tenure. He worked day and night extracting every ounce of ore he could, having his meals taken up to him as he picked away. His good fortune and tenacious attitude earned him a comfortable retirement. On his death a friend asked to be left his Bible to remember him by: a touching and pious request, it seemed, until it was discovered that the insides of the pages had been cut away. It was one of the hiding places in which Captain Jammy stored his £1 notes.

Captain Jammy did well, but for most it was a hard way to earn a few shillings. Payouts for the partnerships came only once every six months. The value of ore would be calculated at the appropriate price and deductions taken for equipment, candles and gunpowder (dynamite was used instead in the late 19th century and considered to be much easier to work with), as well as any food loans made by the company shop. If the partnership had driven a particularly hard bargain, it might be made a special payment or excused the loan payments. If things had gone well enough the group would move swiftly from indebtedness to solvency. The reckoning was often made at a local inn and inevitably some of the income was converted into liquid form. The Temperance movement did quite well in the Dales, no doubt heavily supported by the miners' wives.

One of the Old Gang Mine levels drains into the gill.

Despite its beauty Swaledale is very much an industrial landscape.

THE RISKS OF OWNING A MINE

Life was exceptionally tough for the miners but being a mine owner was not without risk. There were endless disputes over drainage of the mines and who should contribute to it, and even over ownership of the ore seams themselves. George Fermor, the 2nd Lord Pomfret, who owned Old Gang Mine in Swaledale in the late 18th and early 19th centuries, had a stubborn turn of mind that did him no favours. In 1770, he joined in a bitter dispute with Thomas Smith, the new Lord of the Manor at Crackpot Hall, over mining rights on the land. Miners from both sides supported their masters with more enthusiasm than was seemly, getting involved in underground fights, theft of ore and deliberate disruption of the mine drainage systems. The court found in Smith's favour, much to Lord Pomfret's outrage. Saddled with £400 compensation to Smith and lawyers' fees amounting to many hundreds more, he found himself committed to a debtors' prison in London, where he had to remain until he had paid off his creditors.

Lord Pomfret also had little luck with one of his employees, John Davies, whom he hired at the turn of the century to oversee the Old Gang Mine. Very likely a rogue and certainly incompetent, Davies messed up the surveying of one of the levels, which caused huge expense as the ore had to be dressed away from the smelt mill. He later delayed the start of another level, perhaps knowing that he wasn't up to it. Pomfret stuck with Davies in spite of his failures, which were partly offset by the high price of lead at the time. The shareholders of the company that took over the mine after Pomfret, however, refused to accept the accumulating losses and Davies was finally sacked.

Lord Pomfret's final error of judgement was to lease out two other mines, at Lownathwaite and Blakethwaite, far too generously. The leaseholders took out vast quantities of lead, to the value of tens of millions of pounds in today's money. It was all too much for Lord Pomfret: the frustration and disappointment was said to have contributed to his death.

THE ROUTE | Old Gang lead mine

David and Chris Stewart follow in the footsteps of the subsistence farmers who supplemented their family income in the Old Gang lead mine.

We start another seven-and-half-mile walk from Lodge Green on the outskirts of the tiny village of **Gunnerside** in Swaledale. Gunnerside sits in a typical Dales landscape. The pretty walled-off fields, many with a fieldhouse to store winter feed, look quaint and timeless. However, the long lines of stone that divide the landscape reveal how the enclosure movement affected these remote valleys. Acts of parliament forced those grazing the land to erect these walls at their own expense. This provided some labour for the subsistence farmers of the Dales and added to a portfolio of work that included working in the mines. But it was a financial hardship for the larger tenant farmers, who under their agreements were liable for the upkeep of the property, and many decided to leave the valley rather than shoulder the expense. The consolidation of landholding that ensued will have been of considerable advantage to the owners and their subsequent tenants, but much of the population would have resented the dry-stone walling that we now consider so emblematic of the Dales landscape.

We climb away from the **River Swale** to walk along one of the characteristic limestone shelves, here several hundred yards wide, the result of differing erosion of the rock layers. This feels like an ancient track, joining farmsteads on a contour at a little over 300 metres above sea level. Heading along to work on such tracks, many miners made good use of their time by knitting, just like the drovers. In fact whole families were involved in knitting, including the young children. It all added pennies to a precarious existence. Today it is a dry although somewhat chilly June evening. The walk would have a completely different character on a wintry night after working the usual eight hours in a damp mine. On freezing nights miners would arrive back with their leggings frozen like boards.

At the hamlet of **Blades** we bear left onto a track climbing to the edge of the fell. John Wesley preached at Blades in 1761 and commented that it was a lively church community. Methodism took a strong hold in Swaledale during the mining years, playing a key role in binding the community together and helping the people to make some sense of their hard lives.

Crossing over Feetham Pasture (the same Feetham encountered

Only the columns remain of the peat store at Old Gang lead mine, where fuel for the smelting mill was kept under a thatched roof.

THE PROBLEM OF DRAINAGE

In order to extract ever-greater quantities of coal and other materials from ever-greater depths, miners must be able to pump out the water that would otherwise flood their workings. Initially water was taken out in buckets lifted up as if from a well, in an endless and laborious process, often using horses strapped to a winding wheel. The depth to which satisfactory drainage could be achieved was limited. What was desperately needed to open up the riches below was a mechanical method that enabled water to be brought up consistently from much greater depths.

Thomas Newcomen (1663–1729) made a massive leap forward with his invention of an atmospheric steam engine. His machine generated considerable force from a piston alternately raised up by steam and coming down under the weight of atmospheric pressure, as the steam was suddenly cooled with water to create a near vacuum. Successive inventors improved on his original design, but it was the Newcomen engine that set the ball rolling.

Newcomen's lack of formal status and education, however, meant that his achievement was played down by the men of science of his day. He was forced into a partnership with an English gent, Thomas Savery, who, without inventing anything that really worked, still registered a patent on any engine designed to pump water out of mines. Newcomen spent a lifetime installing his machines in mines across the country, but failed to receive the recognition or financial reward that his invention merited.

in Chapter 9), we join the road and come down towards **Surrender Bridge**. On our right are the ruins of Surrender Smelt Mill. We turn left to follow the beck on the old miners' track, kept in good repair with the help of crushed spoil from the mines. After a mile the imposing remains of **Old Gang Smelt Mill** come into view, with one chimney still intact. This isn't the chimney for the main smelting furnaces: the flue for these ran up the hill to a prominent stone structure on the ridge, where it turned and continued on up the fell.

These massive flues made the fires in the furnaces hot enough to process tons of lead ore and, just as importantly, took away the poisonous sulphurous fumes. Every now and then youngsters would be sent up the flues to scrape out any lead and lead oxide that had condensed on the sides, which could be recovered for reprocessing. In the Dales the smelting mills are always found by rivers, as water wheels were used to power the bellows for the furnaces. Old Gang had four running side by side. Much of the main furnace building still stands, with the channel for the waterwheel separated by a wall at the northern end. A few bits of rusting equipment lie around: these are from attempts in the mid-20th century to process minerals from the mining spoil, not from the original smelting process.

Ore brought out of the mine was sorted and crushed on the dressing floor by gangs of women and children, using flat hammers called buckers. We watched women and children doing much the same in the Annapurna region of Nepal, breaking up fist-sized rocks by trapping them in a metal ring held in one hand and hitting them with the hammer with the other – though in this case it was to make gravel for a new road. The pieces of broken ore and rock were sieved in water, with the heavier lead ore falling to the bottom. The smelting process burned off the sulphur in the lead sulphide ore to make lead oxide, which was then reduced to produce molten lead. This was poured into "pigs" to make solid blocks.

With no train, tramway or canal to transport the lead, it was carried by horse or pony to Richmond along the track we have just walked, the pigs being slotted into sleeves on a specially made leather pannier. From there it most likely made its way to Hull for delivery to London or abroad.

We climb a rough path up the slope above the mill and just beyond it find the stone columns of the **peat store**, stretched out in pairs around 20 feet apart and some 390 feet from end to end, looking for all the world like a ceremonial monument. The store had a thatched heather roof and was used to dry the peat used in the smelting furnace, mixed

The flue for the smelting mill stretched hundreds of yards up the hillside.

with a small amount of Tan Hill coal. May and June were peat cutting time, with all the families coming out to load a dozen carts with peat that would be deposited in the store. Once dried out, it would be fetched down as required to fuel the smelting mill. The collection and storing of the peat were all completed in little more than a week.

The exit of **Hard Level** into the gill can be found a few hundred yards beyond the remains of Old Gang Mill, just beyond a bridge over the gill. Even on a summer's day after a long dry spell, the rust-coloured stream pouring out is over a foot deep. Clambering through its entrance and shining a powerful torch into the darkness, a few wooden props can be picked out. The mine owner Lord Pomfret brought about the cutting-through of Hard Level some time around 1799. Originally called Force Level, it was renamed by popular consent thanks to the sheer effort that went into the construction of its 1,150-yard length.

The level is certainly lower here than the standard six feet from floor to ceiling; we have to stoop right down to enter it. This last section of the level is also at a kink from the planned line and has all the characteristics of being cut as quickly and cheaply as possible. The original design would surely have brought it out, at full height, somewhat nearer to the mill. Also, the first air shaft is some 300 yards in from this point, considerably further than would normally be considered safe. It seems that Lord Pomfret was running out of money and needed it completed even if it was less than perfect. It was certainly a bold piece of work and contributed greatly to the mine's future profits, although sadly for Lord Pomfret most of the benefits accrued after his death.

Walking further up the gill, we come to another bridge. Just a short way up the track to the right we find the remnants of **Level House**, the home of Adam Barker, Lord Wharton's mine manager in the late 17th and early 18th centuries. The Whartons were a well-established and wealthy family of the area but lost their grip on the dale when the last Lord Wharton made the grave error of supporting the Jacobite cause and then in joining the Spanish in an expedition against Gibraltar. He died in exile in a Spanish convent. The property sits in a hollow, sheltered from almost every angle by mounds of spoil. Adam Barker used the house as a chapel as well as his residence. The last known occupant was "Splitmate Meg", who lived there alone with her big black dog and worked on the Old Gang dressing floor. There is very little of the house left and none of the large smithy that supposedly stood nearby. The corner stones of Level House that remain are substantial; it must have been tempting to rob abandoned houses for building material. A good deal of stone from the Old Gang Smelt Mill was transported to Muker to build the Methodist Chapel there in the 1930s.

Returning to the bridge, we take a well-surfaced track further up onto the moor. The spoil heaps from the mines provide perfect gravel for these tracks, kept in good shape for shooting parties. All along the tracks are lines of shooting butts. As we walk up, a gamekeeper drives by in his Land Rover, no doubt happy to see the dog dutifully trotting along on his lead.

The path takes us between the sheep folds and the large walled enclosure of **Moor House**. The walls are massive, a good foot or more higher than the average dry-stone wall and no doubt designed to provide some shelter from bitter winds. Like Level House, the property

Moor House once housed a large family.

has been reduced to a couple of standing walls and looks rather forlorn standing in the middle of an enclosed field surrounded by munching sheep. At one time it was home to a farmer-cum-miner who lived here with his wife and 21 children. Even with these large families cottage owners were known to take in lodgers, incomers to the Dales enticed by work in the mines during the boom years. It must have been a bit of a squash, but the extra income was sorely needed.

The track takes us on over the moors. Here the millstone grit that sits as the final layer on top of the Yoredale series has encouraged the growth of heather, ideal for grouse. Every now and then we startle a group of the birds hunkered down by the track side, and with much squawking and flapping they take to the air. In a few months this will be the prelude to their being blasted with a battery of modern non-lead shot; for the moment they simply fly to another patch of heather and settle down again. Their ancestors might well have been dodging shot from the neighbouring mines, though that wouldn't have made the experience any better for them. The tiny balls of lead were made by dropping molten metal from a "shot tower" into water, taking advantage of the natural propensity of liquids to form into perfect spheres when in

Rusting pieces of equipment left in Old Gang Smelt Mill are from more recent attempts to extract minerals from the spoil.

freefall. Quite a lot of the Dales' lead went into making other forms of ammunition, much of it for loosing off at humans rather than wildfowl.

Some of the heather has been burned back recently, making that typical patchwork of grouse moor, with the older heather for the birds to nest and rest in and the newer shoots better for eating. From time to time we are joined by other fowl. A golden plover darts across and a couple of curlews bat their way overhead. Later, on the edge between moor and farmland, we encounter dozens of lapwing, circling overhead and peewitting in a noble attempt to distract us from their nesting sites.

The track crests the ridge and, just as the final shafts of sunlight break through the gathering clouds, we get a superb view of Swaledale ahead and the deep valley cut by Gunnerside Gill reaching up into Melbecks Moor to the right. Turning a corner, we are confronted by great mounds of mining spoil, refuse on a truly industrial scale. Even after many years of exposure, not a single tuft of grass has grown upon them. It's our cue to turn left and begin our descent back down to Gunnerside. A couple of hundred yards and we are back in a world of green grass and dry-stone wall.

Other places to follow the miners

Wherever you find an old mine working on the map there is likely to be a pathway along which the miners came and went. Unless there was a tramway – the earliest had wooden rails along which horse-drawn carts could be pulled – the mined materials would be carried out the same way. But it's also worth remembering that, in deep mines, the miners would have walked many miles underground, often in wet, dangerous and uncomfortable conditions. The trudge to and from the mine above ground was just part of their day's walking.

The well-known *Miners' Track* runs into the heart of the Snowdon (Yr Wyddfa) Horseshoe in Wales. The old copper mines can be seen but not entered, though you get a good sense of the hardship of mining in such a remote and mountainous region.

The Lake District has a rich mining history. *Greenside* is a few miles walk from Glenridding towards Helvellyn. It was the largest lead mine in the Lake District. Lead ore was discovered there in the 1650s and mined until 1962. On the northern side of the Lake District you can walk through the remains of rich mineral mines below Carrock Fell, on a section of the *Cumbria Way*.

You can walk to the remains of tin mines all along the Cornish coast; many engine houses are perched precariously on the sea cliffs as the nearer to sea level they were, the less height water from the mine had to be pumped. A short walk from *Rinsey Head* to Trewavas Head takes you past a good example.

The *Great Orme Mines* (greatormemines.info) are in the Great Orme Country Park near Llandudno. Excavations have uncovered evidence of copper mining right back to the Bronze Age. There is a visitor centre and a tour through the mines.

There are several places where you can experience being in a deep mine. The *Sygun Copper Mine* (syguncoppermine.co.uk), in the Gwynant Valley in Snowdonia National Park, has been restored as a family attraction. The workings can be explored on foot. Also in Snowdonia it's possible to descend into the *Llechwedd Slate Caverns* (llechwedd-slate-caverns.co.uk), a captivating experience that gives some insight into how tough a Welsh slate miner's life must have been. A similar attraction can be found at *Honister Pass* in the Lake District (honister-slate-mine.co.uk). The *Big Pit* National Coal Museum at Blaenavon, South Wales (museumwales.ac.uk/en/bigpit), includes a guided tour 300ft below the surface.

Further reading

The Riches Beneath Our Feet (Geoff Coyle, Oxford University Press) is a knowledgeable account of mining in Britain by someone who was involved in the industry. It covers every type of material extracted from our ground through every age, and ends with thoughts on whether mining is due for a revival

The Geology of Britain: An Introduction (Peter Toghill, Airlife) is a readable and well-illustrated introduction to British geology.

Swaledale: Portrait of a North Yorkshire Mining Community (John Hardy, Frank Peters) is by a long-time inhabitant of Swaledale and frequent visitor to the mine workings. The book is full of anecdotes as well as interesting history. It is, unfortunately, out of print and may be difficult to find other than in libraries.

More walks, ideas and discussion can be found on the *Walkingworld* website at walkingworld.com

16 Canal towpaths

We decided to include the canal in our exploration of British paths because it was the last method of goods transportation that relied to any real extent on travelling on foot. With its dependence, at least in the early decades, on horse-drawn power, the canal sits at the crossover between the age-old methods of commercial transport and the new. It was the final time that horses led by hand played any major part in the movement of goods around the country.

Many of the locks on the Regent's Canal in London are double, though often only one is in regular use today.

We think of the canal as an 18th-century invention but the use of water for inland transport goes back to prehistoric times. Some archaeologists believe that the Preselli bluestones at Stonehenge were carried there by glaciers from the last ice age, but there is no real evidence that the ice reached that far south. It's more feasible that the massive blocks of stone were transported all the way from Preselli in South Wales to the ritual site in Wiltshire entirely by human effort. Dragging them overland seems extremely unlikely. There is, however, a feasible route by water, along the Welsh coast, across the Bristol Channel and then by a series of rivers. It would have been an astonishing feat.

There was a rash of canal building across Britain in the early 19th century as industrialists and entrepreneurs rushed to invest in the exciting new technology. "Canal mania" mirrors in many ways the dotcom boom of the late 20th century. As a method of transporting heavy and bulky goods, canals were far preferable to the poorly maintained road system of the time. The first boat along the Bridgewater canal was supposedly towed by a mule but on most waterways heavier, stronger horses were more popular. A horse pulling a barge could transport 30 tons – 10 times what it could carry in a cart. Between 1760 and 1820 no fewer than a hundred canals were built. In some cases extravagant profits were made, with massive returns on investment. In others the shareholders lost pretty well everything.

In theory it all started with the St Helen's Canal, which was built as an adjunct to the Sankey Brook in 1757, making it navigable down to the river Mersey. A few years later the much better-known Bridgewater Canal was opened, joining the Duke of Bridgewater's coal fields with his customers in Manchester some 10 miles away. With the opening of the canal, the cost of coal in Manchester was reduced by two-thirds. It was a compelling argument for further canal construction.

The canal companies made their returns from charging tolls, from providing services to barges, and sometimes from providing the water in the canal itself to factories on the way. But while there were economic benefits to canal owners and to those trading in the goods carried on them, other interests had to be taken into account. Canals used water draining down from the highpoint to the eventual outflow, albeit more slowly than a river, so the need for water for the canal had to be balanced against the irrigation required by surrounding farmland. There was also the risk of flooding if the canal banks were breached. To control these factors, most new canals required an act of parliament, laying down the rights and responsibilities of all involved.

The ascendancy of the canals was short-lived: they were largely superseded by the railways, although many were actually bought up by the railway companies as they sought to have an integrated transport system. Landowners who had invested in canals sometimes fought hard to prevent railways being built across their land, but the onward push of the railway was irreversible. Canals struggled to compete and had to slash their toll prices; the profits available to boat owners also plummeted.

But the canal has had an enduring effect on our country. Perhaps more than anything, it presaged a new attitude to the landscape and how you could travel through it. Canals couldn't go up and down hills: they had to be punched through the countryside on a level. Surveying canals brought new understandings of geology. William Smith, who over a half a lifetime of research created the first geological map of Britain, first developed his skills as a canal surveyor.

Smith was a man of the new industrial Britain, employed by the wealthy and aristocratic the length and breadth of the country to help drain their fields, survey their canals and tell them where to mine for coal. Like so many pioneers, he was rewarded reasonably handsomely for his practical assistance and treated badly for his seminal contribution to the new academic discipline of geology. Largely ignored by the aristocratic academics of his time, he bankrupted himself in the expectation that the map would make his fortune. Smith spent several weeks in the King's Bench debtors' prison in London. His story, however, ends rather more happily. His contribution to the nascent discipline of geology was finally recognised and a pension was cobbled together to allow him to live out his days in modest comfort.

Grooves cut into handrails and posts on the towpath tell of a time when barges were pulled by horses.

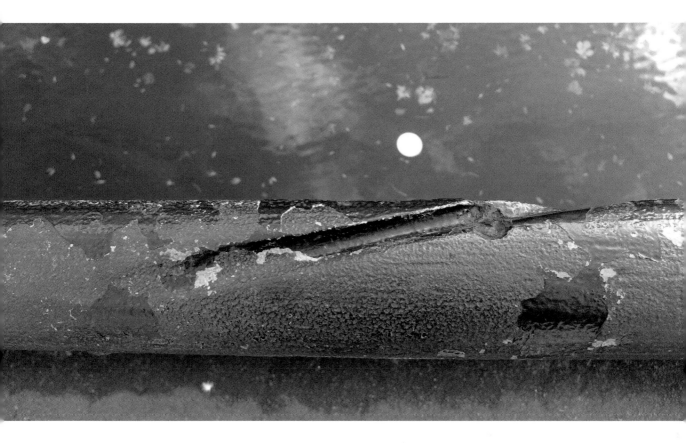

OUR WALK | Regent's Canal

Special halters enable horses to draw heavy barges.

Canals were difficult and expensive things to build. Regent's Canal in London is a graphic example of the difficulties and risks involved in such a major engineering undertaking. The Duke of Bridgewater's canal was funded entirely by him, but most canal enterprises needed to raise share capital, and then an act of parliament was required to push the plans through. The act would place constraints on how the canal was constructed and how commerce on it was managed.

The Regent's Canal project was proposed by the entrepreneur Thomas Homer and the Regent's Canal Act was passed in 1812. One of the directors was the architect and town planner John Nash, who integrated the canal into his masterplan for this whole area of north London and got his friend, the Prince Regent, to lend the new waterway his name. Nash's engineer, James Morgan, was given the task of overseeing construction.

Homer, however, got into personal financial trouble. He was found guilty of embezzling the company's funds in 1915 and sentenced to transportation. The shareholders had to be approached for a fresh injection of cash. There were also bitter arguments with one of the landowners, a Mr Agar, whose gardeners took to having fist fights with the navvies. The first section of the canal, from Paddington to Camden, finally opened in 1816 and four years later the second section was completed through to the Thames at Regent's Canal Dock (now called Limehouse Basin). The whole enterprise cost over £770,000, twice the original estimate.

In 1845 the Regent's Canal company was offered £1m to have the canal basin drained and converted into a railway. The offer was accepted but finance could not be raised for the venture. Another attempt was made in 1883. However, the canal company managed to stage a revival in the late 1920s, buying two connecting canals, the Grand Junction and the Warwick, and combining them to form the Grand Union Canal Company, whose waters stretched from the tidal Thames to Birmingham. A subsidiary bought 186 pairs of narrow boats and aggressive pricing won custom back from the railways. The strategy worked for a decade or more but the final decline was inevitable.

The change to powered craft was also very gradual. The first steam engines weighed over 10 tons and took up a major proportion of the carrying capacity of a barge. Steam-powered craft were sometimes

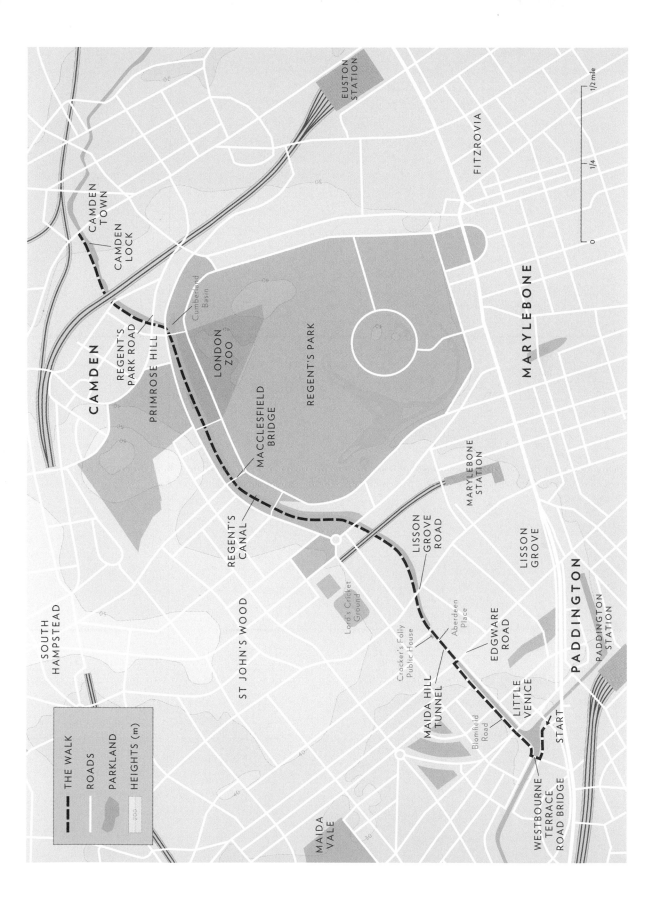

SOUTH
HAMPSTEAD

CAMDEN

CAMDEN
TOWN

CAMDEN
LOCK

REGENT'S PARK ROAD

PRIMROSE HILL

Cumberland
Basin

LONDON
ZOO

MACCLESFIELD
BRIDGE

REGENT'S PARK

REGENT'S
CANAL

ST JOHN'S WOOD

Lord's Cricket
Ground

MARYLEBONE
STATION

MARYLEBONE

FITZROVIA

LISSON
GROVE ROAD

LISSON
GROVE

Crocker's Folly
Public House

MAIDA HILL
TUNNEL

Aberdeen
Place

EDGWARE
ROAD

Blomfield
Road

LITTLE
VENICE

START

PADDINGTON

PADDINGTON
STATION

MAIDA
VALE

WESTBOURNE
TERRACE
ROAD BRIDGE

THE WALK
ROADS
PARKLAND
HEIGHTS (m)

200

0   1/4   1/2 mile

The Kennet Horse Boat Company barge is decorated in the traditional manner.

used by the canal companies to tow boats through tunnels, replacing the slow and laborious work of "legging", in which a team of people would lie on the roof of a barge and propel it through using their feet. Propelled craft really only came into their own after the first world war, when simple single-cylinder diesel engines were installed. On the Regent's Canal the final horses were only replaced in the 1950s, first by narrow tractors chugging along the towpath. The last horse-drawn cargo was towed along the canal in 1956.

EXPERIENCING A HORSE-DRAWN CANAL BOAT

In the interests of research we spend a lazy half day on the Kennet and Avon canal, being pulled along by Freddy the shire horse. The Kennet Horse Boat Company (kennet-horse-boat.co.uk) has a large barge capable of holding well over 50 people, complete with bar. Even with this number on board Freddy is able to tow us with comparative ease, stopping every now and then to munch on vegetation while the barge glides gently through the still water. The quietness is striking, a huge contrast to the chug-chug of the diesel engine one usually associates with canal boats. Progress is also extraordinarily smooth, the only bumps coming as the four young men in charge of the boat manoeuvre it in by hand into locks and under bridges. You can see why Josiah Wedgwood was so keen on canal transport for his fragile pottery.

At sharp corners and other obstacles, pillars and posts on the canal towpath are used to pivot the boat around. Those few still involved in horse-boating are keen to see the remaining posts retained, both for their practical use and also because they are reminders of an important part of canal history. Often they have been taken out and not replaced, perhaps because the repairers have not understood their purpose. Experiencing the canal from a silent craft drifting through the meadows gives us a whole new perspective on this mode of transport. The dog enjoys it too, though he isn't too sure about Freddy. It would be good to see this part of our heritage revived on more of our canals, and then the canal-side "furniture" could resume its proper role.

THE ROUTE | Little Venice to Camden Lock

Grooves cut into metal pillars show where the tow ropes rubbed repeatedly.

David Stewart joins two members of British Waterways on a three-mile stretch of the Regent's Canal, to search for clues to its horse-drawn past.

I am intrigued to learn that there are plenty of relics of horse-drawn canal boating on the Regent's Canal in London. I have arranged to meet up with Gill Owen from British Waterways' marketing department and Florence Salberter, one of its heritage advisers. Gill has promised me that you can find bridge supports and handrails all along the canal where the lines from horse to barge have rubbed deep grooves. It is a walk I must have done a dozen or more times when I lived in London 30 years ago but I don't remember these tell-tale signs at all.

Coming away from British Waterways' plush west London offices, we almost immediately find ourselves at the pretty basin called **Little Venice** (a name supposedly devised by Robert Browning, who lived in a house overlooking the canal from 1862 to 1887). Little Venice is surrounded by graceful Regency mansions with white stucco facades and it's all looking magnificent on this bright autumn day. We sit first in a canal boat café having a cup of coffee and chatting about the history of the canal.

As we set off Florence points out the toll house built in 1812 by Westbourne Terrace Road Bridge, where fees would have been paid by barges heading north on the Grand Junction Canal. It accentuates the fact that these were two separate commercial businesses. Indeed, here at the junction of the two canals a height differential had to be engineered and locks put in place to ensure that the Regent's Canal and Grand Junction Canal companies were not supplying each other with free water. Later an act of parliament in 1816 specifically permitted the Regent's Canal company to act as a supplier of water to the Grand Junction Canal, presumably at a price. The fact that they went to such lengths to regulate their use of water is indicative of its value to them as a limited resource.

We cross the bridge on to the towpath opposite signposted to Camden and Regent's Park. Leaving the pool of Little Venice, we walk alongside the **Blomfield Road** residential moorings, one of the finest waterside locations in London. We are not allowed to use the towpath by these barges, so we turn onto Blomfield Road for a hundred yards or so.

At the end of Blomfield Road the canal disappears into the

The Bloomfield Road moorings are now highly desirable.

THE BOAT PEOPLE

As canal owners were usually prevented from owning their own fleets (to prevent a monopoly developing), another group of entrepreneurs sprang up to provide the boats. Sometimes an owner would have only one boat, on which he would live with his whole family. Others would have a fleet operated by hired boatmen.

The earliest boats were simple open barges, as the distances involved were small enough for the boaters to continue to live on land. But as those distances got greater it became necessary to sleep overnight on the barge. The convention was to have a small cabin at the stern in which whole families lived and slept, often in very cramped quarters.

It was an all-consuming existence, and the boatmen formed a community apart. The forms of decoration that sprang up on their barges are not unlike those on Romany caravans, and it is possible that some of the people were the same (though many boating families firmly resisted the connection). The lack of nautical terms used on inland boats suggests that the people came from the bankside rather than from the sea. Some, perhaps, were navvies involved in canal construction, labourers from the vicinity attracted to a different way of life, or drovers who realised that they had to embrace the new world.

Beautiful white town houses stand over us as we go under Regent's Park Road.

Maida Hill Tunnel, underneath the trendy-looking Cafe Laville. It is immediately obvious that the tunnel has no towpath, a common situation across the canal network. Digging a tunnel capable of containing a full-size horse as well as a narrowboat would have been immeasurably more expensive. Hence the practice of legging; it must have been hard, dirty work.

We cross over Edgware Road into Aberdeen Place and pass **Crocker's Folly** public house on our left. The imposing, if slightly mad-looking, edifice was built in the late 1890s by a Kilburn publican called Frank Crocker. It wasn't named as such by him, of course: he gave it the grander name of the Crown Hotel. He had hoped it would sit right by a new railway terminal but the plans were changed and the trains, with their valuable passengers, eventually came in a mile or more further south at Marylebone. The hotel was a huge failure. The story goes that Crocker, bankrupted, committed suicide by throwing himself out of an upstairs window. The reality is rather more mundane: he died of natural causes in 1904. The property is on sale now for over £4m but there have been no takers and most the time it is boarded up. The day we walk by it is being kitted out for a TV shoot, surrounded by lighting vehicles.

We walk down a flight of steps and back onto the canal towpath as it passes through **Lisson Grove**. There is a strange blue corrugated iron casing by the steps, concealing cabling or pipework. High walls tower over us on our left, making it feel as though the canal is passing through a cutting. As we come down to the towpath, behind us is the exit of the Maida Hill Tunnel, its mouth surrounded by damp mossy brickwork. The darkness in the tunnel is impenetrable; a British Waterways sign tells boat owners to stay within the profile of their boat and switch on their front head lamp.

We come to another short tunnel at Lisson Grove. This one we can walk through, with the towpath running just under the arch on the lefthand side of the canal. The entrance arch has cornerpieces of iron into which thick grooves have been worn by the ropes running from barge to towing horse. At regular intervals along the towpath we see lowered steps in the canal bank. Horses that were accidentally pulled into the canal could be unhitched, brought to these points and extracted.

The canal here is flanked by brand new and renovated buildings, a mixture of office and residential development. We pass a dilapidated brick structure with empty window frames and temporary metal fencing along its top. Coming out from under the next bridge we enter **Regent's Park** and the contrast could not be greater. Nash would have liked the

Camden Lock has become a bustling tourist attraction.

canal to go right through the middle of the park but the fine residents baulked at the idea of having the bad language of the boatmen echoing through their gardens. Nash relented and the canal was directed around the outer edge. He had plans to build over 50 villas in Regent's Park, though only eight were completed.

The canal bends gently to the left to make its detour of the park. The grand villas on our right were built in the late 1880s and early 1890s to Nash's designs. In the garden of one of them a man with a leaf-blower directs the leaves off the immaculate lawn onto the canal side.

We pass under an aqueduct carrying the forgotten River Tyburn over the canal and come to **Macclesfield Bridge**, or Blow up Bridge as it has come to be called. On October 2, 1874 at around five o'clock in the morning Macclesfield Bridge was accidentally destroyed when a barge carrying gunpowder underneath exploded, killing the three boatmen on board. The canal was closed for four days. On reconstructing the bridge, the opportunity was taken to turn the great metal bridge supports around so they could wear on the other side. The grooves are deeper on the older side, suggesting a lessening of wear as horses were displaced by onboard motors.

We make our way through **London Zoo** with its Snowdon aviary, opened in 1965, towering over us on our left. Beyond the zoo the bizarre three-storey Chinese floating restaurant moored in Cumberland Basin appears before us. An arm of the canal used to stretch from here

The great metal pillars of 'Blow up Bridge' were turned round after the accident.

Tow ropes carve even more easily into stone.

towards Euston station. After it was closed the canal bed was largely filled in with bomb rubble from the second world war.

An expensive and time-consuming delay to the original construction of the canal was caused by the installation of an innovative hydro-pneumatic lock at Hampstead Road, designed by restless inventor William Congreve. It never worked properly and in 1819 had to be replaced with a more conventional one. Congreve still went on to receive a knighthood and more justifiable fame for his inventions in the field of military rockets. His perpetual motion machine, however, was a failure.

At the basin the canal takes a sharp turn to the left towards Camden. Beautiful white town houses stand over us as we go under Regent's Park Road. In 10 minutes or so we reach **Camden Lock**, a bustling if now rather touristy market venue. The towpath passes over a footbridge just before the double lock and here the rope grooves cut into the iron handrails and stone walls of the bridge are particularly impressive. We chat for a while to some of the British Waterways canal workers having a break by the lock.

In the past few decades the canals have become busier than they ever were, both for pleasure boating and for canalside walking and cycling. In the 1960s and 70s Westminster and Camden councils opened the towpaths of the Regent's Canal to the general public. Since that time waterside developments have become a major source of income for British Waterways and others lucky enough to own land beside the canals. The draw to water, for boating, walking or living, seems to be deeply embedded in our psyche.

Other towpaths to follow

Britain has hundreds of miles of canals, so you will rarely be far from one. You are generally permitted to walk along the towpath. As far north as the Highlands of Scotland you can walk along the *Caledonian Canal*, linking the east and west coasts of the country by joining up Loch Lochy, Loch Oich, Loch Ness and Loch Dufour. The glorious *Crinan Canal*, on the west coast, links Loch Fyne with the Sound of Jura, forming a channel for vessels through the Kintyre peninsula.

In many of Britain's cities, such as *Birmingham* or *Manchester*, the canal network offers a tranquil haven from urban life. Birmingham, famously, has more length of canal than Venice.

People are always attracted to the more impressive engineering feats of the canal-building age. The Pontcysyllte Viaduct over the River Dee on the *Lllangollen Canal* is breathtaking. If you walk across you have the benefit of a handrail. Travelling across by boat is an airy experience as there is nothing between you and the 128-foot drop to the valley below. The Anderton Boat Lift, in Cheshire, was restored in 2002. Originally built in 1875, it transports boats between the River Weaver and *Trent & Mersey Canal* in two huge water tanks.

The vast majority of British canals are under the care of British Waterways, a government organisation at the time of writing, though likely to become a charity under new proposals. The website, waterscape.com, is a fount of information and ideas on where to walk.

Further reading

There are of course plenty of guides to the canals, mainly directed at the modern leisure boater, many of which have useful sections on canal history. *Canals and Waterways* (History in Camera) (Michael Ware, Shire Publications) is packed with great photographs from the end of the commercial canal era, along with a brief history of the canals.

Canal museums are well worth a visit and sometimes more revealing than books. The *London Canal Museum* is at King's Cross, on the Regent's Canal (canalmuseum.org.uk). Another, in a beautiful setting, is at *Stoke Bruerne* on the Grand Union Canal (stokebruernecanalmuseum.org.uk). *Standedge Tunnel* is the longest and deepest tunnel in the canal network and runs from Marsden in Yorkshire to Diggle in Lancashire. There is a visitor centre and you can take a trip through the tunnel in a glass-topped boat (standedge.co.uk).

The Map that Changed the World: A Tale of Rocks, Ruins and Redemption (Simon Winchester, Penguin) is a compelling account of a man deeply involved in the industrial revolution and a true founder of the discipline of geology. William Smith's involvement in canal surveying was instrumental in his development as a cartographer.

More walks, ideas and discussion can be found on the *Walkingworld* website at walkingworld.com

17 Promenades

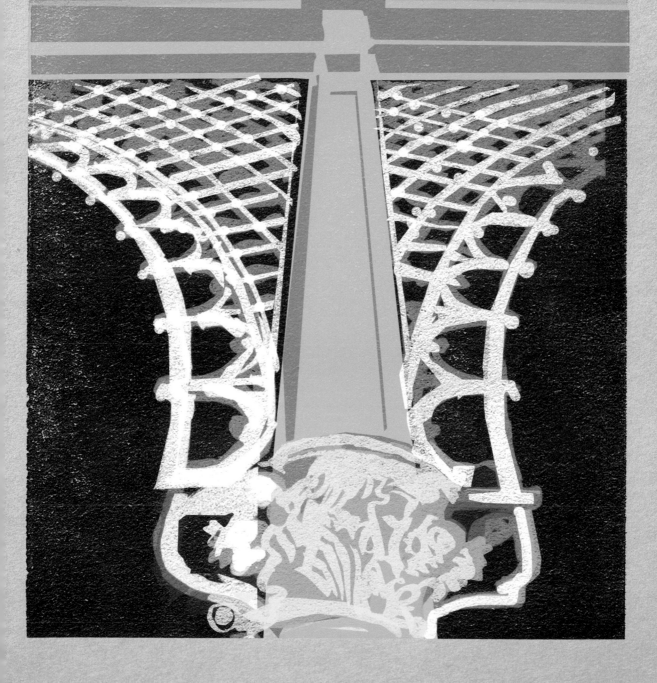

There are accounts from as early as the 1730s of better-off holiday-makers visiting seaside towns, enjoying the bracing weather, having a dip in the sea and perhaps going for a ride on the downs. Maybe these pioneers preferred the freedom of such spots to the social constraints of the inland spas. Those who lived by the sea seem to have always enjoyed the beaches and the water for pleasure as well as for work. But for most middle- and upper-class outsiders the seaside holiday had to be invented, packaged up and delivered on a plate.

During the early years access to the beach and to the sea came to be controlled by physicians. The model was that of the inland spa, varied slightly to promote the special attributes of the coastal resort. The key method by which access to the sea was managed, making it available to those who couldn't swim and allowing it to be charged for, was the bathing machine. Bathing machines varied in design but were generally four-wheeled carriages with canvas or wooden hoods, not unlike those found on Gypsy caravans, and entrances at both ends. You would step in on the beach side fully clothed and undress in private, ready for your dip. Then the whole clumsy machine would be rolled down into the sea, either by hand or with the help of a horse.

It was considered essential that the machine blocked any view of the bather from the shore. Some machines were equipped with a canvas modesty hood on the seaward side, which dropped down to create a private dome. Once in the water, the occupants climbed gingerly down steps into the water. Some bathing machine owners employed attendants, or "dippers" to assist the bathers in and out of the sea. Some of these dippers were renowned for ducking their clients with rather more enthusiasm than was called for, and a few became minor celebrities. Apparently a bit of rough handling during your dipping was considered part of the experience.

However, it was not long before the doctors' grip on the seaside experience began to loosen, although bathing machines were still found at some resorts a good 150 years after their invention and "taking the air" by the sea continued to be prescribed as an antidote to the foul, disease-bearing vapours of the city. People increasingly came for pleasure, to enjoy each other's company, to take in the views – all the things that we go to the seaside for today.

The promenade was a wide open space designed into many seaside resorts, simply because it worked. It acted as a sea defence,

Many piers, like the West Pier in Brighton, have fallen on hard times.

but more importantly allowed visitors of all social classes to saunter along at leisure, showing off their fine clothes and admiring, or criticising, everyone else's.

Like so many seaside structures, the promenade combined business with pleasure: there were opportunities for entrepreneurs to make money in kiosks, cafes and stalls. As resorts vied to attract holiday-makers, the promenades were partnered with seafront parks, complete with lawns, paths, floral displays, bandstands, shelters, paddling pools and ponds. In places the cliff-top walks were made more accessible, to satisfy those with a more adventurous spirit.

The question for seaside resorts ever since the 18th century has been how to make their setting pay. As a present-day business consultant would put it, the object is to "add value" to the natural world and extract some monetary benefit from it. But attempts to control the behaviour of visitors have always been partially subverted by the general public's waywardness. They rejected the doctors' assumption of control and swam in the sea on their own, sometimes naked. They offended the official line in seaside resorts up and down the country by being rowdy and getting drunk, and looking for sexual encounters. They didn't always obey the rules laid down by the archetypal seaside landlady. In fact, the trend by the sea has always been towards pleasure, in this liminal place where norms are overturned and where it's possible, for a short holiday period, to misbehave.

The West Pier in Brighton was derelict for many years and finally destroyed by fire in 2003.

OUR WALK | Brighton

Cast iron is a dominant element in seafront architecture.

Brighton started out as the obscure fishing village of Brighthelmstone. In 1703 and 1705 it was engulfed by great storms and the population dwindled to around 2,000. But the tide turned in the middle of the century, when the local doctor Richard Russell published his influential *Dissertation on the Uses of Seawater in the Diseases of the Glands*, originally in Latin. An English version followed two years later, in 1752. Russell's seawater cures enticed the better-off to take the water at Brighton. His recipes are decidedly unenticing: one contained woodlice, cuttlefish bones, crabs' eyes, bicarbonate of soda, milk and seawater. There is absolutely no evidence that any of his remedies worked, and indeed there were plenty of cynics at the time. But the patients came and, believe it or not, they drank. It is perhaps fortunate that, although the town's sewage went directly out to sea, the population was not yet great enough to make it a serious problem. It would be many years before Brighton was to get even the most basic of sewage systems, enabling the waste to be at least partially treated before it was sent down the outfall.

Dr Russell is sometimes credited with the invention of the seaside health resort but that probably exaggerates his influence. It is just as likely he was stepping onto a bandwagon that had already started rolling. He happened to be practising in an excellent place to develop his business. It was not long before other physicians "discovered" seaside towns all around the coast of Britain that offered equally good access to the perceived restorative properties of the sea air and the water itself.

In Brighthelmstone the movement towards leisure, rather than health, was given a massive boost with the arrival of the Prince Regent in 1783. For several decades George, Prince of Wales – later George IV – brought the fashionable set to his seaside palace, the Royal Pavilion. Between 1815 and 1822 society architect John Nash transformed a drab farmhouse into one of the most dazzling and exotic buildings in the British Isles. Many of the town's elegant squares and crescents were built around this period, reflecting the architectural style of London and inland spas like Bath. The name Brighton came into common use, perhaps because Brighthelmstone was a bit of a mouthful.

The Royal Pavilion was the harbinger of the oriental style that was to dominate seaside architecture for a very long time, though it took a few decades for the fashion to take hold. The style was a mish-mash

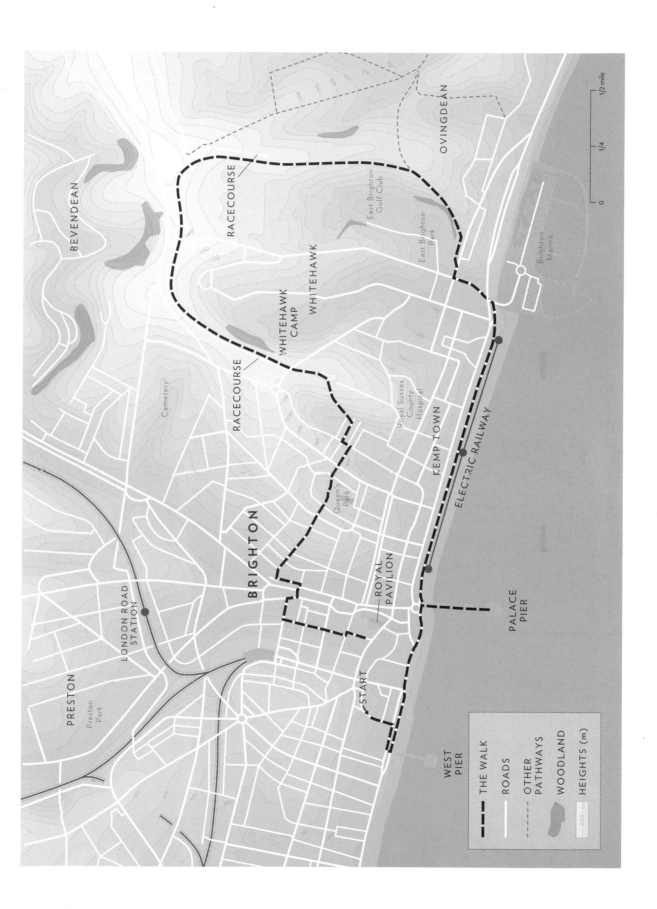

THE WALK
ROADS
OTHER PATHWAYS
WOODLAND
HEIGHTS (m)

PRESTON

Preston Park

LONDON ROAD STATION

BEVENDEAN

Cemetery

BRIGHTON

RACECOURSE

RACECOURSE

WHITEHAWK CAMP

WHITEHAWK

Queen's Park

Royal Sussex County Hospital

East Brighton Golf Club

East Brighton Park

OVINGDEAN

Brighton Marina

START

ROYAL PAVILION

KEMP TOWN

ELECTRIC RAILWAY

WEST PIER

PALACE PIER

0   1/4   1/2 mile

of decorative motifs and features, designed above all to be exuberant and exotic. There were no particular rules: if you fancied a minaret, say, you had one. There was more than an element of British imperialism in the style, each building and structure reflecting the country's global dominance. But on a more innocent level it was a celebration of otherness, of the strange and fantastic places far across the sea.

Queen Victoria and Prince Albert visited the Royal Pavilion in the early 1840s but their trips coincided with another arrival: the train. In 1841 the London-to-Brighton railway line opened. It was massively popular. By 1860 Brighton was welcoming a quarter of a million visitors a year by train alone. The great influx of *hoi polloi* didn't go down particularly well with the royalty, or with the upper classes in general. Resorts across the country tried to sustain elite tourism by erecting gates, opening private gardens and building grand hotels – largely to no avail. By 1850 Queen Victoria had sold the Royal Pavilion to the Corporation of Brighton for £53,000. For her seaside retreats she went to the altogether more isolated Osbourne House, an Italianate villa built on the relatively inaccessible Isle of Wight.

Lack of royal patronage made little impact on the popularity of the town. The sea view became an ever more important ingredient, with the most desirable homes and hotels facing out to the Channel. A prime example is the Grand Hotel, built in 1864 and famously bombed by the IRA during the Conservative Party conference of 1984.

The exuberant architecture of the Royal Pavilion had a huge influence on the look of the British seaside.

The Palace Pier at Brighton retains much of its former glory.

PIERS EVERYWHERE

Cast iron, which could be manufactured as sets of parts and put together like a kit, was the defining technology of seaside architecture. It meant that exciting new attractions could be built relatively cheaply and quickly. Eugenius Birch made the seaside pier his speciality, building a dozen or more, including those at Margate, Eastbourne, Hastings and Weston-super-Mare.

Piers were money-making machines, acting as platforms for an ever-changing array of amusements and kiosks. But they also allowed the visiting public to stand over the sea without having to venture out on a rocking boat. The seaside had its pleasures on balmy sunny days but there was always something elemental about the experience, especially when the weather turned. From the time they were first built people thrilled to the sight of these manmade structures being lashed by the wind and waves in violent storms.

Extreme experiences have long been part of the seaside adventure, with funfairs, rollercosters and towers providing manufactured thrills to match that of the elements. The great achievement of the seaside resort was to provide this excitement with a measure of safety, behind a barrier, a cast iron railing or safely strapped into a roller coaster car.

THE ROUTE | From promenade to downs

David and Chris Stewart, with dog Brough, spend a spring day visiting Brighton beach and the race course on the downs overlooking the town.

We are in Brighton for a bit of seaside strolling. We start our walk in the so-called **Quadrophenia Alley**, not because we are avid fans of the 1979 film but because our son and his girlfriend rent a small flat just next to it. During the 1960s two rival youth cultures, the mods and the rockers, clashed several times in Brighton. The best-known fracas happened over the weekend of May 17–18, 1964, when some 3,000 youths converged on the town. In the film, as this notorious battle rages, Jimmy (played by Phil Daniels) and Steph (Leslie Ash) crash through a door into the alley to escape a gang of rockers. While they hide away Jimmy gets to enjoy a brief moment of ecstasy with the object of his affection. People come from all over the world to find the alley, as evidenced by the (mostly reasonably tasteful) graffiti on the walls.

It is, perhaps, an appropriate place to begin. Sex, and misbehaviour generally, is an ever-present undercurrent in the history of seaside resorts. While the municipal authorities were keen to promote an image of respectability and clean family fun, many holiday-makers were attracted by the freedom from normal constraints that the seaside resorts seemed to confer.

The rather grand architecture of the seaside, too, tells only one side of the story. Promenades, gardens and piers were built to enable visitors to breathe healthy seaside air, take in the views and to mingle socially in an appropriately decorous way. At night, however, the dark spaces under the piers and in shelters and alleys provided other opportunities for intermingling.

Mostly this disgraceful behaviour was ignored, but in a noble attempt to find out exactly what was really going on the Mass Observation Project, set up in the late 1930s, sent its observers to another popular resort, Blackpool. They resorted to pretending they were drunk so they could fall upon couples under the piers and discover exactly what they were doing. In a selfless spirit of exploration they attempted to "achieve copulation" themselves. They succeeded four times and rather sniffily declared that Blackpool was "the most moral town in Britain".

The authorities at Blackpool were surprisingly displeased. They might not have wanted to declare it outright but they knew perfectly well what the underlying attractions of a seaside holiday were. The

Even a popular, relatively affluent, resort like Brighton struggles with the cost of restoration.

marketeers learned quickly how to entice by implication. From the mid-19th century onwards a recurring theme on resort posters is that of fashionably dressed young men and women looking appealing and available.

A few steps through the Lanes brings us out onto the **sea front**. Crossing the busy street, we come onto the promenade. Here we would once have looked down onto elegant Italianate seafront gardens; the present incarnation is rather more utilitarian, with paved pathways and wooden boardwalks linking the bars and cafes housed under the arches. Turning right, we make a short detour to view the remains of the **West Pier**, built in 1866 by Eugenius Birch. Once a magnificent structure, it has been steadily deteriorating since 1975. Fires in 2003 more or less completed the destruction: very little is now left apart from the great metal pillars screwed into the seabed and a collapsing and twisted skeleton out to sea.

Turning back along the beach, we head towards the remaining pier. It's early spring and few people are venturing on to the beach,

Magnus Volk's electric railway runs for just over a mile along the seafront.

let alone into the water. It is a reminder that swimming came late in the development of the town as a popular destination. The first visitors came explicitly for the improvement of their health. Even today Brighton lacks the classic sandy beach that most holiday-makers yearn for, though the pebbles have their own sculptural attraction.

We come to the **Palace Pier**, built in 1899 on the site of a chain pier. Its original name was the Brighton Marine Palace and Pier; it's not surprising it has been shortened. These days dogs are not allowed onto the pier, and indeed they are banned from the beaches for much of the year. Health and safety, rather than morality, has become the controlling theme of the modern seaside resort, with signs telling you where and when you can walk your hound.

So Chris and Brough wait at the entrance while I do a quick tour of the pier. It's early in the year and many of the seating areas are cordoned off for repainting. It's heart-warming to see the woodwork being properly cared for. It's a chilly spring day and there are only a few stragglers like me doing a quick circuit or, in that time-honoured way, gazing wistfully out to sea.

We continue on our way east heading towards the giant marina whose great grey walls dominate the horizon. Just beyond the pier we come upon one of those quaint inventions that characterise the British seaside. In 1883 Magnus Volk built **England's first electric railway** along this part of the Brighton seafront. It remains the oldest operating electric railway in the world.

The railway runs for a mile or so along the edge of the beach. Today it is not open for the public but one of the trains trundles past, a trainee driver and his instructor at the controls. On our left the cliffs have been transformed through the construction of the Madeira Terrace. The terrace demonstrates a long-running tendency in seaside architecture to obscure and tame the natural environment. The iron columns support a wide pathway along what would have been natural cliff, creating a third level of platform along which people could throng. Today it is deserted. On our right is Brighton's famous naturist beach, shielded by a bank of pebbles.

At the terminus of Volk's railway we start to climb up away from the sea, going through an underpass to cross the road. We pass by a huge 1930s-style apartment block and continue upwards towards the downs overlooking Brighton. Skirting the golf course, we find ourselves at one end of **Brighton race course**. It is one of just three courses in Britain that is not a circuit, Epsom Downs and Newmarket being the others. It forms a figure like a horseshoe, with wide left-hand turns along much

The Aquarium Station sits at the western end of the line.

DADDY LONG-LEGS

The Brighton and Rottingdean Seashore Electric Railway was a bizarre addition to Magnus Volk's land-based railway, designed to give the public the exhilarating experience of travelling over the sea. It took two years to lay the track beyond the high tide mark, fixing concrete sleepers into the bedrock. The single car was a pier-like contraption with a 45ft by 22ft platform standing on four 23ft legs. Volk named it the Pioneer, although it was popularly called the Daddy Long-Legs. Regulations meant that a qualified sea captain had to be on board and the car was provided with lifeboats and life-rings.

The railway opened at the end of November 1896; a few days later the Pioneer was knocked on its side in a storm. Volk immediately set to reconstruction and reopened the following July. The attraction was popular, but before long there were problems. The electric motors that drove the car through the water were not powerful enough at high tide, but it was not worth upgrading them. In 1900 groynes built nearby damaged the concrete sleepers and the railway closed for two months for repairs. In a final blow the council decided to build a beach protection barrier, around which the line would have to be diverted. Volk didn't have the funds to do so and closed it instead.

of the course, then a downhill section leading to a level finish in front of the grandstand. The dog, who has been forced onto a lead by the regulations along the beach, gets to run free. From this wide bowl 90 metres above sea level there are views across the town and far out to sea.

The connection with horse-riding harks back to the early aristocratic days of the town, when riding out on your horse was an integral part of the seaside experience. The pleasure of galloping along the downs has probably endured down the centuries, at least for the upper classes. The rest of us have had to make do with donkeys on the beach. In 1783 a group of Brighton's richest inhabitants, including the Duke of Cumberland, the Marquess of Queensbury and Earl of Egremont, initiated the first Brighton races on Whitehawk Down. The two-day event became immediately popular and in its second year attracted the presence of the Prince of Wales.

With the creation of the direct railway link between London and Brighton, the races attracted a more mixed crowd, to the distaste of the upper classes, who felt they were their own. However, unlike the course at Oswestry visited on our Offa's Dyke walk, the owners of this institution stuck with it, and the track and grandstand were repeatedly expanded.

The 1920s saw the emergence of a gang culture within the racing world. This continued on and off until June 1936 when the notorious Hoxton Mob were arrested. Graham Greene's 1938 novel *Brighton Rock* explores the underbelly of the town, with violent London gangs running protection and extortion rackets. It is almost certainly a grossly distorted view of the place, which continued to attract the holiday crowd.

Passing below the main stand, it's just possible to pick out the earthworks of the Neolithic settlement at Whitehawk camp. Built around 3500 BC, it is a causewayed enclosure like Windmill Hill near Avebury. Flint tools, pottery and the remains of butchered animals have been excavated, suggesting that it was used for communal gatherings. It may later have become a burial site, as a few adult burials have been found, along with a young child and a mother interred with her baby.

Coming down from the hill and back into the streets of Brighton, we make our way to **Queen's Park**, set in a sheltered valley. Formerly a Victorian pleasure garden known as Brighton Park, it was later renamed in honour of Queen Adelaide, the adored wife of William IV. The park formally opened to the public on August 10, 1892. There's a lake with ducks to feed, a playground, wildlife garden and scented garden. Exiting on the western side, we make our way through a further series of streets and down a long hill to cross another park and enter into the North Laine area, a bustling collection of shops, cafes and bars. Heading south towards the sea, we complete our eight miles back at the **Royal Pavilion**, where there's a museum into which the dog, of course, is not allowed.

Quadrophenia Alley can be found by walking south-east along Prince Albert Street past the town hall. Turn right into Little East Street. After a 19th-century cottage with walls made from tarred beach pebbles, turn left down an unnamed alleyway marked "To East Street".

Madeira Terrace provides a facade to the natural sea cliff and another level on which to promenade.

Other seaside resorts to promenade through

Promenades can be found all over Britain, but it's the piers that epitomise the British seaside resort. Sadly, more and more are falling in to disrepair, a reflection of the overall decline of many seaside resorts, still suffering from the availability of cheap holidays abroad. In places, however, bold attempts are being made to revive the piers as destinations for a more demanding audience. The Grand Pier at *Weston-super-Mare* has been rebuilt in a modernist style, after a fire destroyed the pavilion in 2008; it advertises itself as a theme park. On the Suffolk coast *Southwold Pier* has the feel of an older, gentler world. The pier company boasts that it has no fruit machines but it does have slot machines in the form of Tim Hunkin's wacky inventions, including a DNA tester and Autofrisk, which pats you down disconcertingly with a pair of rubber gloves.

Following the example of the Tate at *St Ives*, culture and architecture are being mobilised at other seaside resorts to attract a more upmarket crowd. The new Turner Contemporary gallery at *Margate* may start to transform the town. On the north-west coast, *Morecambe's* Midland Hotel, an art-deco classic, has been beautifully restored. A walk along the seafront at Morecambe, with superb views across the wide bay to the Lake District fells, is hugely satisfying. It's just important not to spend too long looking at the forlorn buildings and empty lots lining the seafront.

On the other side of Morecambe bay, *Grange-over-Sands* offers an interesting counterpoint. This genteel town maintains a Victorian ambiance. Arriving by train, you step straight onto the promenade. There's a small-scale seafront park complete with duck pond, and plenty of tea shops and old-fashioned hotels.

Further reading

Designing the Seaside (Fred Gray, Reaktion Books) is a fairly academic study of every aspect of seaside architecture and culture, enlivened by lots of good pictures and a light, humorous style. It covers everything from piers and promenades to swimming pools, beach huts and the seaside postcard.

More walks, ideas and discussion can be found on the *Walkingworld* website at walkingworld.com

18 Municipal parks

The forerunner of the Victorian municipal park was the "pleasure garden". These enclosed spaces, accessible for the price of a ticket, flourished throughout the early and mid-18th century. They became the playgrounds of the gentry and even of royalty. For the middle and lower classes they were the place to gawp at the nobles, who were the celebrities of their day. For the upper classes the possibility of meeting someone masquerading as "one of them", through the simple purchase of some fine clothes and an entrance ticket, no doubt added a certain frisson.

Vauxhall Pleasure Gardens, opened in 1661, offered Londoners a place to promenade on what was then the outskirts of the city, away from the stink and danger of the unlit streets of the bustling metropolis. The gardens became a model for pleasure gardens throughout Europe, their romantic "countryside" layout a contrast to the more formal garden design favoured in France. In fact the generic term "Vauxhall" became used for similar attractions in other British towns and cities. One of the best known, Sydney Gardens Vauxhall in Bath, was frequently visited by Jane Austen. Other "Vauxhall" gardens were to be found in Bristol, Boston, Birmingham, Norwich and Great Yarmouth.

In an effort to keep the public interested, the garden owners put on concerts, fireworks displays, balloon ascents and other entertainments. As time went by, the gardens must have seemed more like early amusement parks. But their popularity waned towards the end of the 18th century. Sydney Gardens in Bath was cut in half by Brunel's new railway and it proved increasingly difficult to entice a paying public. The gardens in Bristol were short-lived, as penny-pinching locals found they could enjoy the fireworks and listen to the music from further up the hill, outside the garden perimeter.

By the beginning of the 19th century the pleasure gardens were either closed down or on their last legs, frequented, it is said, by prostitutes and pickpockets. Today most have been obliterated by urban development. However, some memory of these seminal public gardens must have played a part in the movement to create municipal parks, as semi-rural spaces in which the citizenry of the burgeoning cities could relax and breathe fresh air for free.

The heyday of the municipal park followed the publication of a report by the Select Committee of Public Walks (chaired by R.A. Slancy, MP for Shrewsbury) in 1833. The committee called for the establishment of public parks in towns and cities in order to provide

Oldbury Court in Bristol was a private landscaped garden, now open as a public park.

fresh air and investment opportunities, defuse social tensions, and improve citizens' moral and physical condition.

Behind this was a clear notion that it was beneficial for people of different classes to mix (with the tacit acknowledgement that some were in more need of improvement than others). In typically British fashion the benefit, or otherwise, of the mixing of the upper, middle and lower classes was hotly debated. Some argued that while it might indeed improve the lower orders, equally it might "reinforce feelings of disadvantage". The expectation was ever-present that the lower classes would be unruly. So parks were locked out of hours and park keepers tried to keep order. The fact they were often too old to chase troublesome youths was sometimes bemoaned.

"Appropriate recreational activities" were built into the park design. At Saltaire Park in Yorkshire, the rules stated there were to be "no shooting games, dancing, washing or drying clothes, beating carpets, or the sale or consumption of liquor". Male sports predominated, though football was almost always the last to be catered for. In much of the 19th century women were expected to stroll and look after the children, entertained perhaps by music from the bandstand. Cycling became associated with the movement for female emancipation at the turn of the 20th century; Battersea Park was one fashionable venue for taking to two wheels.

Parks were set up with great ambitions for education, lofty aims that could not always be sustained. The Arboretum in Derby, arguably England's first public park, was conceived as a magnificent botanical garden, with plants and flowers gathered from around the world and lovingly installed by the benefactor. But the flora couldn't withstand the pollution from nearby industrialisation. Within three decades all the exotic planting had gone and most of the carefully labelled specimen trees were replaced with practical London planes and limes, which were much more tolerant of the dirty air.

As for the ordinary working-class park user, we find that their voice is seldom heard. There are, of course, ample records of the generosity of the founders and sponsors, but these need to be taken with a pinch of salt. Often there was a good degree of self-interest in the establishment of the parks, either through the retention of the right to build elegant villas around the perimeter or through the benefits of having a healthier, grateful workforce. Ultimately what we have are the material remains, though much of the original architecture has gone and what does survive is often in a fairly shabby state. The open spaces, however, are still with us and are as valued as ever.

Colourful planting at Snuff Mills in Bristol is a testament to the importance of volunteer labour in Britain's parks.

OUR WALK | The industrial outskirts of Bristol

Parks have always been places to just sit and watch the world go by.

During the 19th century Bristol was a rapidly expanding city, even if its port was losing out to rivals such as Liverpool. In 1801 the population was just 61,000; by 1851 it had swollen to 137,000; and by 1881 it had more than doubled again to 307,000. By 1850 it was considered one of the unhealthiest places to live in Britain.

The north-eastern part of the city, along the banks of the River Frome, was heavily industrialised, though today it is better known for its Tesco superstore and massive Ikea warehouse, and the M32 motorway that runs right through it. A large pottery, run by Joseph and James White, was based at Baptist Mills, a stone's throw from the modern retail park.

There was a working coal pit in nearby Easton, helping to fuel the city's factories and homes. Easton Colliery thrived from the 1830s until the 1870s; after that the pit went into decline, eventually closing down altogether by 1911 (it is shown as abandoned on the 1911 Ordnance Survey map). It was a tough and filthy place to work. As at most mines of the time, young boys were used to enter the thinnest seams and to tug tubs of coal. A government inspector, Elijah Waring, visited the pit in 1841 and found one boy aged seven and half who had already been working underground for a year.

Chocolate-making was a boom industry in the 19th century in Bristol, taking advantage of the imports of cocoa coming into the docks. The business benefited from the fall in duties on imported cocoa from the 1830s onwards – it no longer needed to be smuggled – along with a rise in disposable incomes. The huge Packer factory was built on the hill above the colliery in 1900 by an ex-employee of Fry's. At its height it employed over 1,000 people.

These industries contributed to the wealth but also to the noise and pollution of the city. Ben Tillett (1860–1943), a founding member of the Labour Party, was brought up in a street in Easton, right by the colliery. He described the environment eloquently: "It was a drab and mean street and most of its inhabitants worked in the pit. The outlook was black, gaunt and smoky against the sky line. The buzz and musical clamour of the circular saw, swiftly cutting timber and pit props to length, driven by an engine with a deep-voiced exhaust, added to the industrial orchestra."

In spite of the obvious need, Eastville Park came somewhat late in the roll call of British municipal parks. Since the 1830s a large number

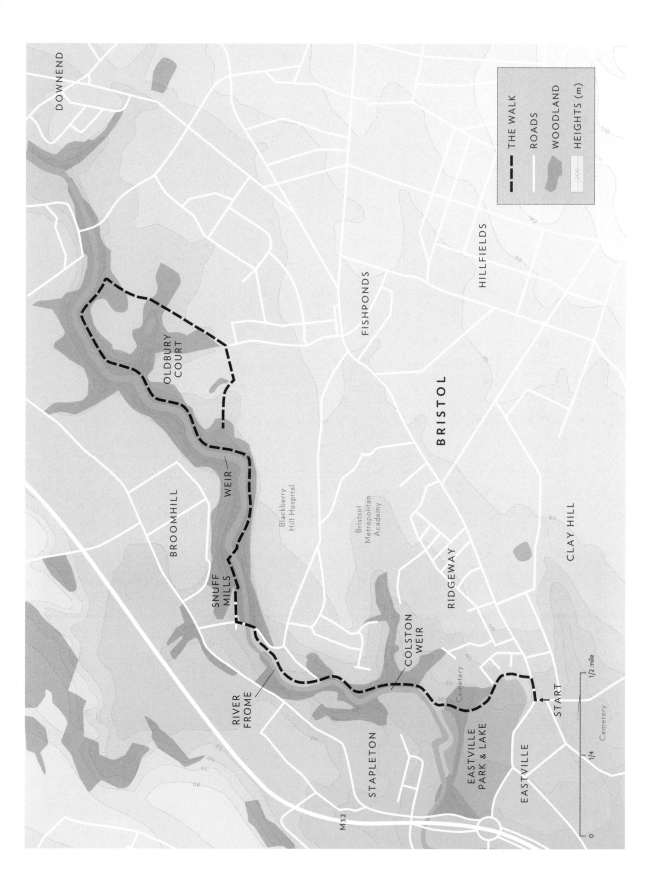

THE WALK

ROADS

WOODLAND

HEIGHTS (m)

DOWNEND

HILLFIELDS

FISHPONDS

OLDBURY COURT

BRISTOL

WEIR

BROOMHILL

Blackberry Hill Hospital

Bristol Metropolitan Academy

SNUFF MILLS

CLAY HILL

RIDGEWAY

COLSTON WEIR

RIVER FROME

Cemetery

STAPLETON

START

M32

EASTVILLE PARK & LAKE

Cemetery

EASTVILLE

0   1/4   1/2 mile

of towns and cities had become the proud owners of such amenities. By the 1880s there were clearly people in Bristol who felt that a place for relaxation and recreation for the working folk of Bristol was long overdue.

The land for Eastville Park, until that point a stretch of farmland on the outskirts of the city, was bought in 1889 by public prescription to the tune of £30,000. Some complained that the location was too remote from the city – though for the colliers of Easton and their families it was right on their doorstep. Some mature trees were kept and avenues of lime trees and London planes were planted. Various paths were laid out, with 100 seats and some small wooden shelters.

Further work was carried out in the early part of the 20th century. The lake was dug out in 1908 and 1909 from an existing water meadow, with labour provided by unemployed applicants under the Distress Committee's Labour Bureau. It is built to a "serpentine" plan, popularised by Capability Brown. By virtue of this design, wherever you stand on the perimeter you will not be able to see the lake in its entirety: there is always some hidden corner folding out of view.

Most of the original built features of the park are long gone. At one time there was a caretaker's lodge, bandstand, refreshment pavilion and a drinking fountain, the octagonal footings for which can still be seen at one of the entrances. The boathouse on the lake burned down in 1913, supposedly set alight by a group of suffragettes. The replacement, built in 1925, has also been removed.

The serpentine lake in Eastville Park is a popular spot for feeding the ducks.

THE GREAT PARK DESIGNERS

Most of the architects of Britain's public parks built on their experience of creating private gardens. Public parks needed to cope with far greater numbers of people, a wider variety of activities and generally much smaller budgets, yet they too wanted to give their visitors a sense of space, exciting vistas and periodic surprises. Designers were expected to make the park a place one would want to visit again and again.

Many designers drew on the ideas of Lancelot "Capability" Brown (1716–83), John Nash (1752–1835), whom we have discussed elsewhere, and Humphrey Repton (1752–1818), who was probably the best known of Brown's followers. Brown's creations epitomised the fashion for idealised but apparently natural landscapes. They were, in reality, the product of a great deal of planning and resculpting of the original environment. Unlike Brown, Repton was rarely involved in the construction of his designs, which meant that many were never realised at all, or were substantially changed from his original conception. He would present his clients with a "red book", of which the most notable features were his "before" and "after" visualisations, allowing the client to appreciate his ideas without having to interpret a plan.

John Claudius Loudon (1783–1843), another well-known landscape gardener, was chosen to design Derby Arboretum, which opened in 1840. Loudon used carefully placed earth mounds to focus attention into the park rather than out to the town that was swiftly growing around it, and to obscure walkers on one path from others nearby. The result was that the park seemed much bigger than it really was, a trick that others were happy to borrow.

Joseph Paxton's (1803–65) influence on park design extended beyond the many he created in England and Scotland. In 1842 he was commissioned to develop a park in Birkenhead. Paxton incorporated a variety of landscapes, building rocky outcrops, digging out lakes and setting out a serpentine route for carriages and horse riders round the boundary of the park. He worked on an even more ambitious design for Crystal Palace Park in the early 1850s, which included the huge glass structure originally erected in Hyde Park for the Great Exhibition, wide terraces and a lake with islands populated by life-size replicas of prehistoric species.

THE ROUTE | Eastville Park and Oldbury Court

Brough the Jack Russell, accompanied by David and Chris Stewart, relives his youth on a scamper through his favourite park and on to the adjoining Oldbury Court, following the banks of the River Frome.

In Bristol we got to know Eastville Park, and the long connecting footpath that leads away from the city along the River Frome, like the back of our hands. Our two years of living in Bristol coincided with the early years of our endlessly energetic Jack Russell, who needed at least two decent walks a day. Brough now knows these parks as his homeland: whenever we are back we are sure to meet at least some of his doggy friends on one of our habitual routes.

To reach the park we have to circuit the cemetery, another oasis of calm from the city, though not one you are allowed to walk your dog through. We pass by the trackbed of a disused railway, now converted into a small nature reserve, and enter **Eastville Park** by Royate Hill. Most of the outer railings of the park are gone, surviving only at a couple of gated entrances. At last Brough can be let off the lead, passing by the bowls club, discreetly hidden behind a dark hedge, and then a bench more often than not occupied by a group of genial alcoholics with cans of liquor in hand. When the park was planned this certainly wouldn't have been allowed. In many cases parks were founded specifically to counter the temptations of the tavern, although the fact that many were closed on Sunday and at night seems to have been counterproductive.

We arrive at the car park and walk past the children's play area. The wide expanse of park opens up before us. At Eastville Park football has arrived in force. There are a few tennis courts but mostly they stand empty. Football pitches fill the once open grassy area, between lines of trees that would have originally been lime and plane trees, now partly replaced with horse chestnuts. When the park opened, the grass was managed by a combination of mowing and grazing; the sheep are long gone.

On our right as we walk down the side of the pitches is a small **outdoor swimming pool**, constructed in 1905. Enclosed on three sides by high brick walls and on the park side by tall iron railings, the pool must have been a pleasant place to bathe and sit in the sun. Now it is drained, a victim of lack of support for outdoor swimming, concern about health and safety and the fact that it is just too small to be worth maintaining. A few years ago the site was overgrown, shabby and permanently locked. Volunteers have tidied it up, repainted the ironwork and planted some

Paved stone steps lead down to the lake at Eastville Park.

reeds and flowers. Despite all the hard work, you hardly ever see anyone in there. With the pit of the pool rather oddly laid out with planting, reached by steps that once would have taken bathers gingerly into fresh cold water, it remains strangely purposeless.

A few metres beyond we bear right to descend some wide stone steps. Brough for some reason likes to wait at the top while we walk down and then bound down at full pelt. It's an odd ritual that maybe has something to do with the likelihood of his meeting a friend by the **lake**, which now appears on our left. The lake has two small islands covered in bushes and trees – shelter for ducks, moorhens, geese and the occasional pair of swans. From time to time we spot a heron standing impassively on a log.

During the spring, conversation at the lake always centres on the numbers of young birds spotted trailing behind their parents across the water. The ducklings always seem to do well. But if the geese and swans have offspring at the same time, the goslings are hunted relentlessly by the male swans and drowned. We all stand and shout, furious and impotent at this cruel display of dominance by one species over another. Why can't they each find space at opposite ends of the lake? Every day one fewer gosling is to be seen, until eventually the adult geese are to be found swimming around totally alone.

Walking on from the lake, we continue by the banks of the **River Frome** towards Colston Weir. At this and various other weirs along the river one becomes aware of the volume of water and the extent to which an apparently lazy river falls in just a few miles. Before the advent of coal the Frome was, along with the Avon, one of the reasons for Bristol's early growth. The river, running between steeply sided wooded banks, was a hive of industry. In the 1700s a substantial brassworks developed near here, doing good trade with the manufacturers of Birmingham. Good trade, that is, until the customers collectively decided they had had enough of "price fixing" by the owners of the Bristol works. In 1781, after a year of industrial espionage and poaching of Bristol staff, they set up their own brassworks, much closer and conveniently serviced by the Birmingham canal network. There must have been some truth in their allegations as the Bristol business could no longer compete and rapidly declined. The site lies right under the M32 junction at the corner of Eastville Park.

At **Colston Weir** it's possible to cross a footbridge and then cross back a few hundred yards further on, using the bridge for the lane that joins Fishponds and Steepleton. If you stick on the right-hand bank of the river, however, you come to a rocky outcrop reaching right down to the water. A small tunnel through the rock leads onto the path on the other side. Whether this tunnel once had a practical purpose, or was cut through (perhaps at a point where there was already a fissure) to give park visitors a bit of a thrill, no one seems to know. All along the Frome riverbank wherever there are rocky outcrops paths have been built through them. It's a hint that the creators of the park had moved beyond the rounded curves of the serpentine landscaping style and embraced the excitement of the Romantics. Perhaps they wanted to create just a little bit of the Alps on the outskirts of Bristol.

We pass through an open meadow with allotments on our right, and then over a busy road to join the street leading down to **Snuff Mills**. The row of terraced houses includes a tiny one converted into a Methodist chapel, complete with arched windows. Now we get to stop for a while at our favourite snack bar. The same bunch of dog-walkers are always hanging around the counter, like regulars at a local pub. We get hot chocolate in proper ceramic mugs and a bacon-and-egg buttie to take round to the covered seating area at the back. Here

The footbridge at Snuff Mills stands close to the site of the original snuff works.

The weirs are tell-tale signs of
the river's industrial past.

we can watch the wagtails, ducks and other waterfowl making use of the broken branches lying in the water. Anywhere along the Frome you will occasionally see a flash of bright blue and orange as a kingfisher darts from one perch to another.

The riverside path continues upstream beside the remains of one of the mills. Although this partially reconstructed building is commonly known as Snuff Mills, this isn't where snuff was ground. That mill was further upstream, owned and run by "Snuffy Jack", whose apron was always dusted with the product. Here the mill was used for various purposes, including the cutting of stone from the quarry that sits right behind it. The building used to be three storeys tall; when it became unsafe it was reduced to one and local enthusiasts protected the remains with a roof. You can see the huge boiler of a steam engine used to supplement the river when the flow was not adequate.

Beyond the mill the path crosses the river once again by an old stone bridge and passes by another substantial weir. Once again one becomes aware of the power of the water as it drops several feet from one level to another. We reach the boundary of **Oldbury Court**. This country house with substantial gardens was in private hands until the 1930s, when it was sold to the council by a member of the Vassell family. Locally it is still known as Vassells Park.

The landscaped gardens of Oldbury Court were designed by Humphry Repton. Here and there it's possible to find elements of the landscaped environment – a planting of trees or a stream turned into a rather genteel rendition of a rocky cascade by the addition of several tons of boulders and the occasional small dam. The house itself was left to rot by the new council owners and eventually had to be pulled down. On the flatter areas of the park a children's play area and several football pitches have taken over.

Everywhere on this five-mile walk grand plans have proved to be short-lived. Eastville Park, Oldbury Court and the intervening stretch along the River Frome would all be considered shabby and dilapidated by their original creators. The pathways are a strange mixture of tarmac, gravel and plain old earth. The signs are worn and sometimes unreadable. Here and there individuals make brave efforts to stamp some civilisation on the general sense of decline: the owners of the cottage by the mill at Snuff Mills are planting out beautiful gardens, and signs plead with dog owners not to let their animals trample over the flowers.

But to most park users it doesn't seem to matter at all. Bristol Council spent a small fortune a few years ago building a concrete platform so that boating on Eastville lake could resume. No one came along to take up the lease. After a while the metal barriers protecting the platform came down and now it's just an odd addition to the lake shore. Nobody has complained that it hasn't happened; they just wonder why the council tried to do it when the money could have been better spent on something else. On the whole people seem to be perfectly happy with the park just as it is. The dogs certainly are.

Oldbury Court was once a private garden designed by Humphrey Repton.

Other parks to visit

Thanks to the Victorians, most larger towns and cities have one or more municipal parks. London is blessed with several, including of course *Hyde Park*. Strictly speaking, this is a royal park, seized from the monks of Westminster Abbey by Henry VIII to satisfy his passion for hunting. William and Mary created a processional way through the park, the "route du Roi", now corrupted to Rotten Row. In the 18th century Queen Caroline fuelled a new fashion in landscaping, damming the Westbourne stream and making the Serpentine into the model for natural-looking lakes.

In Sheffield you can walk from the formal Botanical Gardens through two narrow municipal parks, *Endcliffe* and *Bingham*, following a river valley right up to the Clough Plantation on the edge of the moors. It is a popular walking route.

One of the most spectacular city public spaces must be *Holyrood Park* in Edinburgh. The centrepiece is Arthur's Seat, a 250m hill that provides tremendous views across the city and of the Pentland Hills to the south and the Firth of Forth to the north.

GreenSpace (green-space.org.uk) is a charity that works to improve parks and green spaces by raising awareness, involving communities and creating skilled professionals. The organisation runs Love Parks Week, which was launched in 2006 and has been growing steadily each year.

Further reading

People's Parks: the Design and Development of Victorian Parks in Britain (Hazel Conway, Cambridge University Press) is a superb history of the municipal park in Britain. Unfortunately it is out of print and very expensive when it does appear as a secondhand book. There is a copy in the British Library. A shorter book, *Public Parks* (Shire Garden History) by the same author, is sometimes available secondhand from Amazon.

The English Pleasure Garden: 1660–1860 (Sarah-Jane Downing, Shire Library) tells the fascinating and sometimes racy story of the English pleasure gardens.

More walks, ideas and discussion can be found on the *Walkingworld* website at walkingworld.com

19 Leisure trails

For many people the idea of walking for pleasure would once have seemed utterly bemusing, as it still does to a lot of farmers. Walking was like breathing – it was simply something that happened. But from the start of the 19th century, and largely inspired by the Romantic movement, walking began to be a pastime for the upper middle classes (especially parsons, dons and public schoolmasters, apparently). It was a way of stimulating the mind and body and appreciating the aesthetics of the countryside.

Wordsworth was the chronicler of this new spirit, helping to establish the idea that the ideal way to experience the countryside was to walk in it, covering long distances, accompanied if at all by one or two kindred spirits. The countryside became not merely a workplace but a place of recreation. In his *Guide to the Lakes* he comments: "It is a great advantage to the traveller or resident, that these numerous lanes and paths, if he be a zealous admirer of nature, will lead him on into all the recesses of the country, so that the hidden treasures of its landscape may, by an ever-ready guide, be laid open to his eyes."

In legal terms, the pendulum began to swing back from landowners to walkers with the 1835 act of parliament requiring footpath closures to come before a jury. The first books also appeared to guide the leisure walker. One was Thomas Roscoe's *Wanderings in North Wales* (1836). Walking groups began to be formed, the first of which was the Manchester Association for the Preservation of Ancient Footpaths, set up in 1826. The Commons, Open Spaces and Footpaths Preservation Society was formed in 1865.

At last walkers were coming together, forming local clubs, expressing their views and beginning to put pressure on the government for better legislation. A key moment in the movement towards gaining better access to the countryside was the mass trespass on Kinder Scout in 1932 (see page 285). The simple aim was to improve access to the moors, at a time when 99 per cent of the Peak District was out of bounds to the public and people risked confrontations with gamekeepers and even prison simply by going for a walk.

By 1935 the local and regional walking federations had formed the Ramblers' Association (later renamed the Ramblers) to give a national voice to the views and interests of their members. This coming-together of walkers, combined with the wave of socialist euphoria after the second world war, led to the breakthrough of the

Low Force, near Middleton-on-Teesdale in Durham, is one of the highlights of the Pennine Way.

*It's big stone for a small arrow,
but a wooden sign would not
last long on a boggy moor.*

1949 National Parks and Access to the Countryside Act. This act was described by the minister Lewis Silkin, its proposer, as a "people's charter for the open air, for the hikers and ramblers, for everyone who loves to get out in the open air and enjoy the countryside".

The 1949 act led directly to the creation of the national parks, the formation of the network of long-distance paths and the requirement for every county to draw up a "definitive map" of the public paths within its borders, giving them full legal status and definition for the first time.

The definitive map is now the legal cornerstone of public rights of way in England and Wales, and can be found in every council's offices. It is referred to in any legal matter concerning paths. There is also now an established process for settling path disputes, with the general guideline that, if a path has been habitually used for a period of 20 years or more without objection, it shall be deemed to be public.

The obligations outlined in such acts are seldom enacted as quickly or as well as one would like. It took some counties 20 years to complete the job of creating definitive maps, and it was sometimes done in a rather slapdash way. Some of the maps lacked even the signature of the person who had prepared them, and there are tales of office-bound clerks simply drawing a line from A to B rather than investigating where the path went on the ground. London was never required to draw up a definitive map, although with the shift in favour of pedestrians and cyclists there is a renewed political impetus to put this right.

The trend towards improved access has continued steadily since the 1949 act. In 1968 official signposting of paths became a requirement for councils. This was recognition that paths were now used by people who were unfamiliar with the surrounding countryside, and that walking was becoming an increasing part of the tourist economy, especially in rural areas.

The 2000 Countryside and Rights of Way Act finally granted the freedom to roam over mountain, moor and heath, down and common land in England and Wales. Scotland, on the other hand, has always had an effective "right to roam". Free access is allowed almost anywhere over open countryside, except in the deer-stalking season, when walkers are expected to take reasonable steps to find out where hunting is taking place. As a result, however, there are fewer marked paths and ways and none of them are designated as public rights of way. This means that although one has the right to

Families walk sections of the Pennine Way, whatever the weather.

THE MASS TRESPASS OF KINDER SCOUT

The events of April 24, 1932 have long since entered the realms of rambling mythology. About 400 ramblers set off from Bowden Bridge quarry in the Peak District to campaign for right of access to the moors, which were almost totally blocked off to walkers by landowners who wanted exclusive use of them for rearing and shooting game birds. About halfway up, William Clough, the trespassers' leader, scrambled up towards the Kinder plateau and came face to face with the Duke of Devonshire's gamekeepers, who had been instructed to block their path.

In the ensuing scuffle, one keeper was slightly hurt, and the ramblers pressed on to the plateau. Here they were greeted by a group of Sheffield-based trespassers who had set off that morning crossing Kinder from Edale. After exchanging congratulations, the two groups retraced their steps, the Sheffield trespassers back to Edale and the Manchester contingent to Hayfield.

As they returned to the village, five ramblers were arrested by police accompanied by keepers, and taken to the Hayfield lock-up. The day after the trespass, Rothman and four other ramblers were charged at New Mills Police Court with unlawful assembly and breach of the peace.

All six subsequently pleaded not guilty and were remanded to be tried at Derby Assizes – 60 miles from their homes – in July 1932. Five were convicted and were jailed for between two and six months.

The arrest and imprisonment of the trespassers unleashed a huge wave of public sympathy. A few weeks later in 1932 10,000 ramblers – the largest number in history – assembled for an access rally in the Winnats Pass, near Castleton, and pressure for greater access continued to grow.

roam, it's not always easy to find a way through, especially if you are unfamiliar with an area.

The Marine and Coastal Access Act 2009 went another step towards giving the public full access to its natural heritage. It is intended to create a continuous path (or rather, given the presence of Wales and Scotland, two continuous paths) around the coast of England. Currently, almost half of England's shores have no public right of way. Tom Franklin, chief executive of the Ramblers, has commented: "This act enshrines a very simple principle on the statute books – that everyone, no matter who they are, where they come from or how much money they have, has the right to visit all parts of the coast which is so much a part of our heritage."

One of the arguments that the Ramblers put forward while lobbying for the act was that it would create an estimated extra £284 million income for coastal economies. But as with so much walking legislation, the timing of its implementation is uncertain. It will undoubtedly be affected by the 2010 public spending cuts.

Still, in the last generation the pendulum has swung back after at least 200 years of the landowners holding sway. Paths are now for the most part well signposted, there is growing access to non-cultivated areas and there is the mouth-watering prospect of a pathway right around the English coast.

From Low Force the Pennine Way follows the banks of the Tees towards High Force.

*Two stone rams are forever
heading towards the river.*

OUR WALK | The Pennine Way

Coping with land erosion is an important consideration on National Trails.

The Pennine Way, Britain's first official long-distance path, takes in the changing landscapes of northern England and a very small segment of Scotland. It was the brainchild of the journalist and rambler Tom Stephenson, who was inspired by similar trails in the US, particularly the Appalachian Trail. He proposed the concept in an article for the *Daily Herald* in 1935 and later lobbied parliament for the creation of an official trail. Stephenson had started life as a labourer in the textile industry in grimy, industrial Lancashire when at the age of 13 he began walking on the nearby open moorlands.

As part of intensive lobbying to get the 1948 bill passed, Stephenson arranged for MPs Hugh Dalton, Barbara Castle, Arthur Blenkinsop and George Chetwynd to walk the stretch from Middleton-in-Teesdale to the Roman Wall. Dalton commented afterwards: "After renewing acquaintance with this beautiful part of the country, I am sure that we must in the lifetime of this parliament place on the Statute Book a great measure of liberation, freeing for the health and enjoyment of all our people what for so long has been monopolised by a few."

The Pennine Way was officially opened on April 24, 1965 at a rally by 2,000 walkers on Malham Moor in Yorkshire. The trail runs from Edale in the Derbyshire Peak District, through Yorkshire and Northumberland to finish just inside the Scottish border at Kirk Yetholm. Travelling up the "backbone" of England, the route passes many famous spots, including the limestone cliff at Malham Cove, Tan Hill (England's highest inn) and Hadrian's Wall. It takes in peaks such as Pen y Ghent, Cross Fell and the Cheviot (although this last is a small detour from the official route). The entire trail is 267 miles, of which only 20 is on roads.

For the generation after its opening it became a rite of passage. Celebrated author Alfred Wainwright offered to buy a free half-pint of beer for every walker who finished the route at the Border Hotel in Kirk Yetholm. The pledge is estimated to have cost him some £15,000 between 1968 and his death in 1991. But although the Pennine Way once reigned supreme as *the* long-distance challenge, the emergence of other paths, like the West Highland Way and Wainwright's own Coast to Coast, has diminished its popularity. And more exotic walks, like the Annapurna Circuit or the Inca Trail, have to some extent supplanted it in people's imaginations as they huddle around a table in a suburban bar dreaming of their next outdoor challenge.

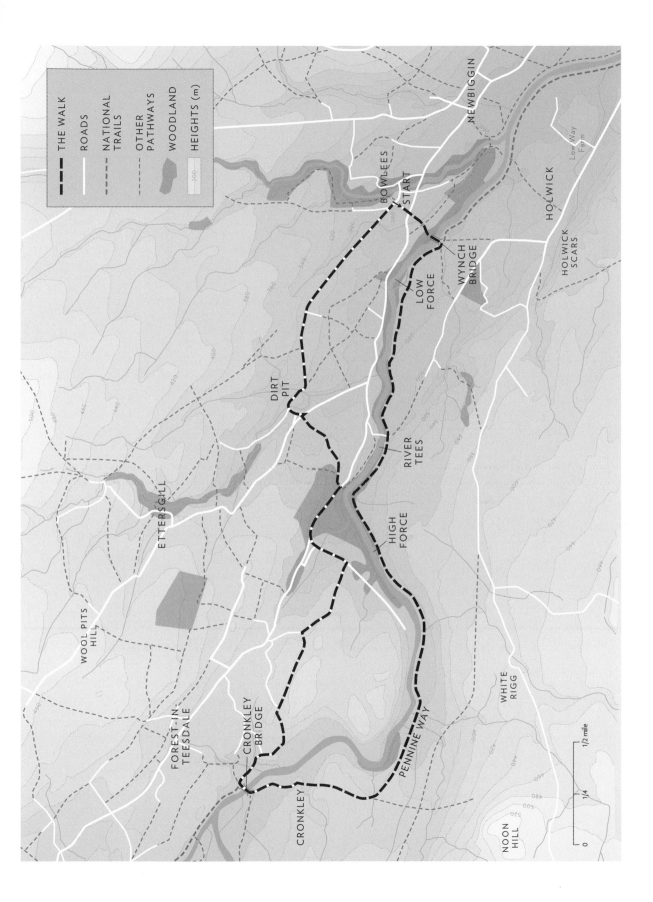

THE WALK
ROADS
NATIONAL TRAILS
OTHER PATHWAYS
WOODLAND
HEIGHTS (m)
200

NEWBIGGIN

HOLWICK

Low Way Farm

HOLWICK SCARS

BOWLEES
START

WYNCH BRIDGE

LOW FORCE

DIRT PIT

RIVER TEES

HIGH FORCE

ETTERSGILL

WHITE RIGG

WOOL PITS HILL

FOREST IN TEESDALE

CRONKLEY BRIDGE

CRONKLEY

PENNINE WAY

NOON HILL

0   1/4   1/2 mile

THE ROUTE | The Pennine Way to High Force

Nicholas Rudd-Jones, his two young sons and an extended Stewart family set out on the same stretch of the Pennine Way that inspired Tom Stephenson and his clutch of enthusiastic MPs.

Despite the promises of the weather forecast, it turns out to be a rather dull and damp morning. But we have spent three hours driving up from Stamford in Lincolnshire, so there's no turning back now. We sit in the back of David and Chris's Volkswagen van, brew up a cup of tea and exchange the books we have been reading. Brough the Jack Russell, meanwhile, is bored and straining to go. He eventually forces us to depart.

From the Bowlees Car Park, the path heads west to cross the River Tees. As we come to the river we immediately get a good view of the Low Force waterfall through a copse of trees. We cross by the very narrow and slightly swaying **Wynch Bridge**, an iron suspension bridge constructed in 1830. It replaced a chain bridge built in 1741, apparently the first of its kind, and somewhat scarier as it had a hand rail on only one side. It was built to provide access for the Holwick lead miners, who used it to get to the mine at Little Eggleshope in the fells to the north. It survived over 60 years before it collapsed, with the loss of one life.

Turning right up the river on the far bank, we come to a stone carving of two rams, with the inscription "A wonderful place to be a walker" – true enough, although as a sentiment it seems a little prosaic. In the river dozens of brightly coloured kayaks are making their way up and down. A few of the craft are carried by hand up into the pool above **Low Force** and are paddled gingerly towards the gushing waterfall. For a moment the paddler is able to hold the flimsy plastic vessel back, but inevitably the force of the water catches them and they shoot over the edge, plunging into the dark pool below. Most of them, astonishingly, end the right way up.

From Low Force we follow the Pennine Way a mile or so up the west bank until we reach **High Force**. With a drop of 21 metres it must be one of the grandest waterfalls in England, and certainly no place to be kayaking. We are here on a day when the river is in spate after heavy rain. It is a magnificent and impressive sight, best viewed from a tiny path heading off to the right as you approach the falls, where you can perch high above the river bed (but take great care of your footing).

The spectacular waterfall, with the peat-coloured mass of water forced between two massive stone buttresses, must have impressed

The Wynch Bridge, an iron suspension bridge constructed in 1830, is a slightly wobbly way across the river.

*The stone walls along the Tees
are made of rounded boulders
collected from the river bed.*

Peat-coloured water plunges 21 metres over High Force.

the MPs and made them appreciate the uplifting qualities of nature at a time when the country was still on rations and looking to raise its spirits. My boys are equally taken with it. For my co-author David, who had walked the Pennine Way 35 years previously as a teenager, it provided something of a memory jolt, as it was one of the few experiences of the whole route that he could vividly recall (well, that and having a drink on Alfred Wainwright at the end). High Force is not a sight that is easily forgotten.

As we continue up-river past High Force the path is increasingly reinforced with large limestone slabs and wooden walkways, a reminder of how erosion has become a problem in popular walking areas throughout the UK. Several of the limestone slabs look as if they have been used previously for some other purpose, odd gouges suggesting that they perhaps served as gateposts. The wooden walkways look as if they may have been railway sleepers in a previous life.

On our left a man is out with his ferret, hunting rabbits. Every now and then the peace of the valley is shattered as he lets off with both barrels. Brough's ears go down and we have to put him on his lead to encourage him on. For a dog brought up on the edge of a shooting moor in an old gamekeeper's cottage, he is surprisingly ill at ease with guns. Chris and David wonder if he was on the wrong end of one in a previous life.

From now on we notice a difference in the type of walkers we pass, as we venture beyond the honey-pot locations of High and Low Force. There is a switch from "leisure day out" walkers – who are after all the majority – dressed in nothing special and often attached to a dog. We start to encounter that slightly more serious type, the genuine long-distance walker, with backpack, waterproofs and compass, map and sometimes a GPS. They are few and far between, though: we probably see a handful during the whole day. It's a reminder that although it was conceived as a long-distance path, the Pennine Way is mostly used for short excursions. Nothing wrong with that, but not quite like the Appalachian Trail after which it was conceived.

As the way veers north we pass alongside a piece of open-access land at Cronkley, a reminder of how much has been achieved since the path originally opened. **The Upper Teesdale National Nature Reserve** is a haven for nesting birds and plants that have colonised the sugar limestone outcrops, a rare habitat that occurs in only two places in the British Isles. On our right, in savage contrast, are the massive corrugated-iron-clad buildings of a large limestone quarry.

A little further on, the path drops down the valley and we come to **Cronkley Farm**. It is one of the joys of Britain that so much of its finest walking lies on the divide between moorland and farmland, interweaving between the two. At Cronkley Bridge we leave the Pennine Way and start to make our way back along the other side of the valley. If we had had more time we would have loved to follow the Pennine Way to High Cup Nick, about eight miles further on and on the other side of the great hump of the Pennines. It is a spectacular natural feature, carved out in the last ice age, with ragged limestone edges open-armed towards the Eden Valley below.

David, who is a volunteer with the Kirby Stephen Mountain Rescue Team, tells us that it is one of the most difficult stretches of the Pennine Way to navigate, with walkers regularly losing their way in poor visibility. He recalls the team being called out to search for a lone walker who had become disoriented by the complex pattern of streams just before reaching High Cup Nick. He was discovered two days after getting lost, having holed up in his tent inside a deserted shooting hut, where he read a book while he waited for the storm to abate. It's a reminder of why these long-distance trails came into being in the first place – to help people explore remote areas in relative ease and safety by providing clearly marked routes. But you still need to keep an eye on the map.

Walking back along the other side of the valley, we observe how dispersed all the settlements are, an armful of whitewashed farms and outbuildings sprinkled across the landscape. This series of non-nucleated settlements means that there is a veritable cobweb of paths taking one from farm to farm as well as from village to village.

The final stage in our eight-mile walk takes us through **Dirt Pitt**, a few quaint cottages thrown into the corner of a hill, with a stream running through. Apparently the name is a corruption of Deer Peth, reference to an ancient hunting forest that was in these parts in the 11th century. The route winds its way through a few dry-stone walled fields to bring us back to our cars.

"And what did you do today?"
"Why, I kayaked down a waterfall."

Other long-distance routes

The Long Distance Walkers Association (ldwa.org.uk) lists more than 700 long-distance routes in the UK. Those that are rightly popular include the *South West Coast Path*, the *South Downs Way*, *Offa's Dyke*, the *Coast to Coast Path*, *Hadrian's Wall* and the *West Highland Way*. It is notable that these routes have a combination of spectacular scenery and a clearly defined feature to follow, or at the very least significant start and end points.

The past few decades have seen a rash of new routes, despite the fact that long-distance walkers are a small minority of the walking public. Many, especially those that pass across lower land, struggle to merit a multi-day walk, though small segments can be pleasurable. A few seem to be grasping at straws or have clearly been created to fulfil a county council's insistence on having its own long-distance path, supported no doubt by EU or regional development money.

Further reading

A Right to Roam (Marion Shoard, Oxford University Press) is an indispensible guide to the issue of access to the countryside, from a campaigner who is passionate about it.

Right to Roam: A Celebration of the Sheffield Campaign for Access to Moorland (Dave Sissons, SCAM) is a detailed history of the movement that is best remembered for the Kinder Scout mass trespass. It includes eight suggested routes to roam.

The Secrets of Countryside Access (Dave Ramm, the Ramblers) is a practical guide to finding, using and enjoying public paths. Topics include the various types of paths, and who is responsible for maintaining them.

Walking in the Countryside (David Sharp, David & Charles) has a brilliant opening chapter on the history of paths in our country.

More walks, ideas and discussion can be found on the *Walkingworld* website at walkingworld.com

20 Pedestrian zones

Raised pavements for pedestrians, separated from the carriageway by kerbs, have existed since before Roman times, but they only became widespread in our towns and cities in the 19th century, as a means of avoiding the muck in the road and also to provide havens from speeding carriages. Their safety role was enshrined in law in the 1835 Highways Act, which made it an offence to "wilfully ride upon any footpath or causeway by the side of any road made or set apart for the use or accommodation of foot-passengers, or wilfully lead or drive any carriage of any description upon any such footpath or causeway."

As motor traffic increased in both speed and volume in the second half of the 20th century, so the physical separation of pedestrians and motor cars became more commonplace. In an effort to stem the rising tide of casualties, traffic lights, guard rails, staggered crossings and a proliferation of road signs sprang up along the pavements. All these measures were put in place with pedestrian safety in mind, but at a price – they made the car the undisputed king of the road and they made the pedestrian feel hemmed in and a second-class citizen.

The apogee of this belief in the separation of pedestrians and cars was in the 1960s, and its bible, published in 1964, was the book *Traffic in Towns*, by the town planner Colin Buchanan. He was convinced that motorists and pedestrians should be separated completely through the use of flyovers, clearways and gyratory systems. This doctrine informed the thinking of town planners for the next two decades and led to pedestrian-unfriendly city centres, encircled by hostile one-way systems and ugly rails at every street corner.

But that process encountered serious resistance in the 1980s, with the emergence of the concept of "shared space" – the belief that breaking down the barriers between motorist and pedestrian could make the former more alert and aware of his surroundings. Doing so would reduce pedestrian injuries.

The most notable exponent of shared space was Hans Monderman, a Dutch road traffic engineer and innovator. He pioneered the concept of the "naked street" by removing all the things that were supposed to make it safer for the pedestrian – traffic lights, railings, kerbs and road markings. He thereby created a completely open and even surface on which motorists and pedestrians "negotiated" with each other by eye contact. His maxim was: "If you treat drivers like idiots, they act as idiots. Never treat anyone in the public realm as an idiot – always assume they have

New pedestrian footbridges were built to flank Hungerford Bridge in London. They were opened in 2002 and are properly called the Golden Jubilee Bridges.

*The Millennium Bridge
connecting The Tate Modern
with the City must be one
of the best loved pedestrian
bridges in the world.*

intelligence." He was a driving instructor in his spare time, so he must have known a thing or two about scary traffic situations.

To prove his point, Monderman was known for boldly walking out on to his naked streets and junctions, turning his back on the moving traffic and walking to the other side to show that drivers would not run him over. Research in Holland also showed that naked streets cut speeds far more than speed humps because they increased drivers' sense of uncertainty.

Britain has only recently become an enthusiastic adopter of the shared space concept. The Commission for Architecture and the Built Environment, founded in 1999, began to champion Monderman's work and it is now the accepted wisdom of all the main political parties' traffic policies. Today streets all over Britain

are being stripped of traffic lights, kerbs and other street furniture deemed to be lulling motorists into a false sense of security. Recent schemes include Kensington High Street and Exhibition Road in London, and New Road in Brighton. There are now more than a hundred shared space streets under development in Britain.

The Department for Transport's Design for Streets manual was recently rewritten to encourage local authorities to redesign on shared space principles, and 12 councils have pledged wholesale redesign of their streets. The result is a more pleasant environment for us to walk in – or rather for most of us, as the shared space environment is considered much more challenging for people with visual impairments.

OUR WALK | The City of London's Pedway scheme

The underbelly of the Millennium Bridge, a reminder that form has to be underpinned by function.

The epitome of the separation between pedestrians and motorists was (or very nearly was) the City of London's Pedway scheme, initiated in the mid-1960s. It envisaged a 30-mile elevated walkway network around the City, from Liverpool Street to the Thames, and from Fleet Street to the Tower.

The devastation of the second world war, in which a third of the City was razed, gave planners the impetus to devise this network. The architect Charles Holden and the planner William Holford came up with a blueprint for rebuilding London's financial centre in 1947 that included walkways "as fit for the traffic it carries as any of the main streets". Plans were also drawn up for the Barbican and Paternoster Square developments, to include towers, podiums and walkways.

By 1965 a City of London Corporation document, named Drawing 3400B, made specific mention of the Pedway for the first time. As the whole Pedway plan was part of a vision for levelling much of the capital, the future had to be created by stealth. But straight away there were problems, including the fire brigade struggling to find equipment suitable for the raised walkways. The corporation's maintenance, cleaning and lighting bills soared.

But the biggest, and ultimately insurmountable, problem was the growth of the conservation lobby. Ironically, its seat of power was in the Barbican development, and its activists the very users of the one successfully completed network of "highwalks". They didn't object to the Pedway system itself, but to the service roads and loading bays springing up at street level in anticipation of its completion.

So in the great tradition of British planning, the Pedway vision never materialised. However, several stretches of the network were built, notably through the Barbican. A number of footbridges across major roads were also constructed. Additionally, as developers in the 1970s were required to provide walkways as a condition for planning consent, there are bits and pieces in several other places. Stroll around parts of the City of London today and you stumble across strange walkways, stairwells and bridges, all seemingly heading nowhere. You have found the Pedway.

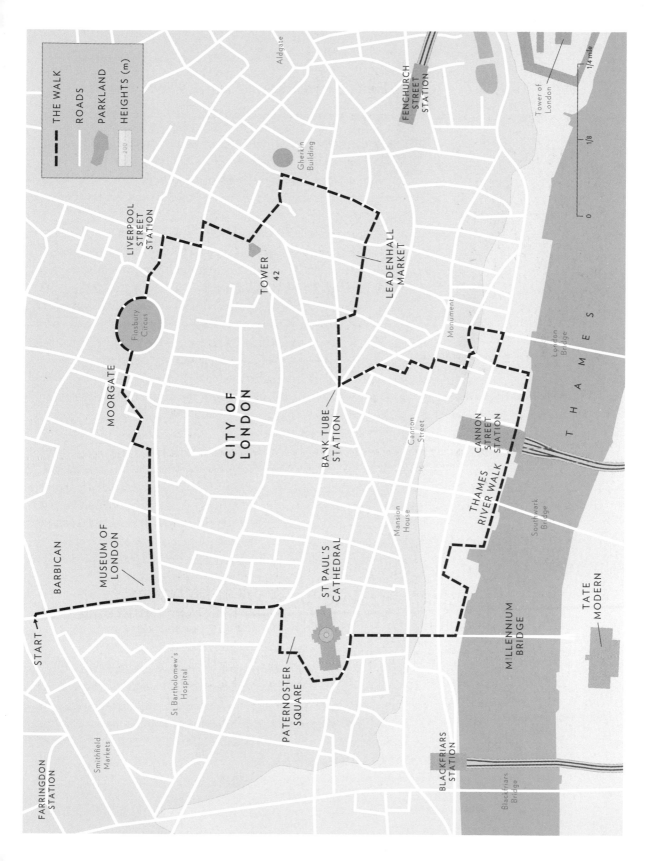

THE WALK
ROADS
PARKLAND
HEIGHTS (m)
200

START

FARRINGDON
STATION

BARBICAN

Smithfield
Markets

MUSEUM OF
LONDON

St Bartholomew's
Hospital

MOORGATE

Finsbury
Circus

LIVERPOOL
STREET
STATION

Aldgate

Gherkin
Building

TOWER
42

FENCHURCH
STREET
STATION

Tower of
London

CITY OF
LONDON

LEADENHALL
MARKET

PATERNOSTER
SQUARE

ST PAUL'S
CATHEDRAL

BANK TUBE
STATION

Mansion
House

Cannon
Street

Monument

THAMES RIVER WALK

CANNON
STREET
STATION

London
Bridge

T H A M E S

BLACKFRIARS
STATION

Blackfriars
Bridge

MILLENNIUM
BRIDGE

Southwark
Bridge

TATE
MODERN

1/4 mile

1/8

0

OUR WALK | Remnants of the Pedway

An office block near London Wall looks down on a Pedway bridge.

Nicholas Rudd-Jones and David Stewart went to London one day to discuss a book they were planning to write on the history of paths; you're reading it! While they were there, they thought they would see if they could find those bits of the Pedway that did make it to the light of day.

Tracing the remaining parts of the Pedway is surprisingly easy. Starting at the Barbican tube station, the only listed part of the network takes you past the flats on Seddon Highwalk to the **Museum of London**. This part of the walk is well maintained and, although the main building material is concrete, there is quality in much of the material. The slate covering at several points on the walkway sides is impressive.

Most people walk purposefully along these rather impersonal walkways. We must make an unusual sight to the inhabitants of the Barbican apartments above, stopping every few yards to take photos and admire the views across to yet more towers and apartments. Our fascination with the construction of a concrete walkway must seem a little odd – troubling even.

Passing through **Albangate**, we reach a 1969 adjunct to the Pedway plan: kiosks, built to encourage pedestrians off the streets and on to the walkways. A green marble building, now unoccupied, was originally a Midland Bank; nearby is an empty row of tailors' shops and an empty pub with the tell-tale name the Podium. Maybe Podium pubs would have popped up all over the UK in much the same way as the Packhorse Inn did in a past era, if the pedway concept had taken root. The day we visit there are problems with the drains, leaving a vast puddle across the path. The whole scene is a stark reminder of the challenges of maintenance and the difficulty of persuading people up from the street level to shop. The Pedway separated people not just from traffic, but also from existing commerce. It didn't work.

The trail runs cold at **Moorgate**, though abutments for a never-built bridge can be seen above the station. From time to time people look nervously over the edge of the walkway, puzzled that there is no way down. We manage to pick the path up again at the footbridge in Wormwood Street, heading towards **Tower 42**, previously known as the NatWest Tower. This bit of the walk is a passageway between offices, and workers give us puzzled looks as we pass by; it makes us realise that very few people use this route today. Coming out right at the base of Tower 42 is a thrilling experience, like suddenly happening

The Millennium Bridge's south bank destination is The Tate Modern, its power station chimney silhouetted against the sky.

THE THAMES PATH

The Thames Path, opened in 1996, is the only long-distance path to follow a river for most of its length. It is 184 miles long, beginning at the source of the Thames near Kemble in Gloucestershire and finishing at the Thames Barrier at Teddington. A significant part of its length is along the towpath, a reminder that the Thames was once a vital trade route, bringing produce from the farming regions in the west and taking back goods from the London docks.

By the 18th century London was the world's busiest port and Reading, for example, received 95 per cent of its goods by barge towed along the River Thames. The towpath between Lechlade and Putney, along which much of the Thames Path now travels, was established towards the end of the 18th century by the Thames Commissioners. It was a difficult task since many landowners refused permission for the towing path to enter their land, or there were natural obstacles. As a result in many places the towpath switched from one bank of the river to the other and ferries were used to transfer the towing horses across the river.

The Pedway encircles the base of Tower 42, previously known as the NatWest Tower.

A Pedway bridge is still in use across Thames Street.

The Pedway at the Barbican is the one stretch that most Londoners will be familiar with.

upon a huge beast about to pounce.

The next bit of the walk takes us through the heart of the City, past recent iconic landmarks such as the Gherkin and the Lloyd's Building, but also past the old London: St Helen's Church, dating from the 13th century, and **Leadenhall Market**, which from the 14th century became established as a thriving market for cheesemongers and poulterers.

It is striking how walking-oriented the City is today – the streets and squares are full of pedestrians, both workers and visitors, and motor traffic is relatively light thanks to the congestion charge. The eerie separatedeness that we felt walking along the Pedway is replaced by a throng of people – much more of an upbeat, market feel. The naked street concept, the blurring of pedestrian and traffic, seems to have taken hold in this part of the City and it's working.

After Leadenhall we explore a network of passages leading to **Bank tube station**, a reminder of the medieval origins of the City and a fabulous chance to get away from the hubbub of the main streets. From Bank, the landscape changes again and we find ourselves going slightly

downhill. We start to get the sense of a grand river getting closer, when suddenly we spy it along one of the north-south vistas. An old stretch of the Pedway gets us across Upper Thames Street and then we join the **Thames River Walk**.

The River Walk takes us all the way to the **Millennium Bridge**, with a brief detour as it goes back onto Upper Thames Street. This turns out to be a boon for Pedway detectives, as we pass a now defunct Pedway stairway, boarded up and quite forlorn, and two working Pedway footbridges. Returning to the River Walk, we get our first good view of the Millennium Bridge, opened in June 2000, long after the Pedway dream had died.

Londoners nicknamed the bridge the Wobbly Bridge after participants in a charity event to open it felt an unexpected swaying motion. The movements were caused by a phenomenon known as synchronous lateral excitation: the natural swaying motion of people walking caused small sideways oscillations in the bridge, which in turn caused people on the bridge to sway in step. This increased the amplitude of the bridge oscillations and so the effect was continually reinforced. It was a wonderful demonstration of the communal power of walkers, but not so welcome for those who had built the structure. The bridge was closed for almost two years while modifications were made to eliminate the wobble entirely (a shame, some felt). It reopened in 2002.

The Millennium Bridge is a pedway that most definitely works. People simply love walking across it, enjoying the juxtaposition of land and water. In it beauty and function are perfectly combined. It is one of the most glorious bridges in the world, and it's just for walkers! As we cross towards the great brick bulk of **Tate Modern**, we have to navigate round dozens of tourists taking souvenir pictures.

But in case you feel you haven't seen enough famous landmarks for the day, turning back along the Millennium Bridge **St Paul's Cathedral** is elegantly framed between the buildings ahead. We step off the bridge and head back past the cathedral into **Paternoster Square**. We bear right, past a glorious Shepherd and Sheep sculpture by Dame Elisabeth Frink. Paternoster Square was long the site of a livestock market, which this sculpture is designed to celebrate. Perhaps this represented the end of the journey for some of the Welsh drovers met in our earlier chapter.

We complete the three-mile walk by returning to the **Museum of London** and are delighted to meet up once again with our long-lost friend, the Pedway, which takes us safely back to the Barbican station.

The Millennium Bridge instantly feels like a natural part of the topography of London.

Should we have got this close?
Property rights still reign
supreme in the City of London.

Other pedestrian routes to explore

London is undergoing a sea change in favour of the pedestrian over the motorist, and the end of segregation between the two. And right across the country, cities are once again becoming more enjoyable places to walk in, from the redevelopment of dockyard areas in the likes of Liverpool, Portsmouth, Sunderland and Bristol to the elimination of traffic in historic town centres, such as Cambridge.

If you are new to a town or city, a good place to start is often the tourist information centre, which is likely to have a map of a "heritage trail" of the centre. Die-hard pedestrianisation addicts should head for "new towns" such as Bracknell or Milton Keynes. In many ways these places are a vindication of the move to separate people from traffic: walking or cycling along the walkways and through the underpasses is surprisingly enjoyable. But this is chiefly because they were designed from scratch.

The Millennium Bridge in London is not the only pedestrian river crossing to lift the spirits. Its counterpart in Gateshead, linking the city of Newcastle with the arts quarter on the south bank of the Tyne, has the added attraction of being a lifting bridge. Having been sponsored by Gateshead alone, the bridge and its lifting mechanism are pointedly sited entirely on the southern bank; the bridge barely touches the Newcastle quayside. The stunningly beautiful new footbridge over the River Aire at Castleford is a further example of a pedestrian bridge acting as a catalyst for urban regeneration.

Further reading

London (Michael Hebbert, Wiley) is a very readable book chronicling the capital's haphazard development and its refusal to bend to any master plan. It includes a small section on the Pedway.

Traffic in Towns (Colin Buchanan, Penguin Books) turned out to be a very influential book. Buchanan, a town planner, was convinced that motorists and pedestrians should be separated and his case was very persuasive at a time when there were more road deaths than today.

Hans Monderman (Frederic P. Miller, Agnes F. Vandome and John McBrewster) will give you much more detail on the thinking and practice of this influential traffic engineer.

Living Streets (livingstreets.org.uk) is the oldest campaigning organisation for pedestrians in the world, formed in 1929. It aims to create safe, attractive and enjoyable streets, prioritising people over traffic.

After the group called for pedestrian-safe crossing places, the government introduced the first pedestrian crossing experiments in 1934. Leslie Hore-Belisha was the transport minister at the time, hence the name Belisha beacons. These crossings provided easily constructed "bridges" over the flow of traffic – an urban version perhaps of a packhorse bridge over a roaring stream.

More walks, ideas and discussion can be found on the Walkingworld website at walkingworld.com

INDEX

Boldface page numbers denote
photographs; italic page numbers
denote maps.

A

Acton Castle *185*, 192
Aethelbald, King 56, 67
Aird da Loch *201*, 208
Albangate *303*, 304
Aldreth Causeway 76, **77**, **78**
Alfred, King 22, 57
Anderton Boat Lift 247
Antonine Wall 42, 70
Appalachian Trail 288, 293
Aquarium Station 261
Atkinson, Richard 78
Atthil, Henry 166
Aubrey, John 35
Avebury 16, 28, 32, 35, 36, **38**,
    38, 70

B

Bank tube station *303*, 306
Barbury Castle 16
Barker, Adam 226
Barrell, John 170
Baxter, Warren 132, 134
Beag loch *201*, 210
Bealach a' Bhuirich loch 210
Becket, Thomas 100, 102, 105
Belloc, Hilaire 50, **51**, 52
Beornred, King 67
Beowulf 64
Bessy's Cove **184**, 184, *185*, **189**, 190,
    191, 191, 192, **193**
Bewick, Thomas 138
Bignor Hill 46, *47*, 48, 52, 54
Birch, Eugenius 259
Bishop's Castle 26
Blackstone, Sir William **116**, 116
Blades *217*, 222
Blomfield Road 240, **241**
"Blow up Bridge" 244, **244**, **245**
Borrow, George 60
Boughton Aluph *101*, **104**, 104, **105**,
105, **107**
Bowden Bridge 144, 285
Bridgewater Canal 232

Brighton Marine Palace and Pier
    260
Brighton race course *255*, 258, 260
Brighton Rock (Greene) 262
Brighton and Rottingdean Seashore
    Electric Railway *255*,
    261
Brigsweir Bridge *115*
British Waterways 240, 246, 247
Brough (dog) 34, 36, 64, **65**, **90**,
    92, **92**, 102, **133**, 174, 204, 205,
    210, 258, 260, 274, 290, 293
Brown, Lancelot "Capability"
    272, 273
Browning, Robert 240
Buchanan, Colin 298
Bwlch y Rhiwgyr *155*, 158

C

Cadair Idris 154, 160
Camden Lock *237*, 240, **243**, 246
Canterbury Cathedral 100, 166
Canterbury Tales, The 96, 97, 100,
    108
Car Dyke 76
Carn Ricet 86
Caroline, Queen 280
Carter brothers **182**, 184, 186, 188,
    190, 191, 192, 196
Channel Tunnel 102
Charlemagne, King 67
Charles I 116
Chat Moss Bog 73
Chater, Daniel 187, 195
Chaucer, Geoffrey 96, 97, 100, 108
Chichester Cathedral 50
Chilham Castle 106
Chilham Station *101*, 102
City of London 122, **300**, 302,
    306, **309**
Clare, John **168**, 168, 170, **171**, 172,
    174, 176, 178
Cliff Cottage **191**, 192
Clough, William 285
Coast to Coast Walk 288, 296
Coghill, Nevill 108
College Cottage *169*, 174
Colston Weir *271*, 276, **277**
Commission for Architecture and
    the Built Environment 300
Common Stream, The (Parker) 166

Commoners' Association 120
Congreve, William 246
Council of British Archaeology 40
Countryside and Rights of Way
    Act (2000) 284
Countryside Commission 18
Craig Goch Reservoir 88, **89**, **90**
Crinan Canal 247
Crocker, Frank 242
Crocker's Folly *237*, 242
Cronkley *289*, 293
Crowden Tower **139**, *141*, 142
Cudden Point *185*, 188, 192, 194
Culloden, Battle of 200, 202
Cumberland Basin 244
Cunliffe, Barrie 23
Cwm Marteg 90
Cynethryth, Queen 67

D

Daily Herald 288
Davies, John 221
Defoe, Daniel 74
dendrochronology 80
Derby Arboretum 268, 273
Devil's Dyke/Ditch 56, **69**, 69, 70
Devil's Tor 136
Diamond, John 187
Dirt Pitt *289*, 294
Disarming Acts (1716) 157
Doggerland 12, 72
Domesday Book 110, 164
Dorset Cursus 29
Dragon Hill *17*, 24, **25**

E

Eastville Park 270, *271*, 272, **272**,
    274, **275**, 276, 278
Edale Cross *141*, 142, 144
Edale Head Farm 144
Edgware Road *237*, 242
Edward I 120
Eis a' Chual Aluinn **199**, *201*, 204, 210
Elizabeth II 48, 64
Elliot, John 208, 210
Ely Cathedral 74
Enclosure Acts (1750) 16
English Heritage 79, 94
Epping Forest 122
Ermine Street 43

F

Feetham Pasture 136, 222, 224
Fishbourne Roman Palace 52
Fitz Walter, Milo 119
fitz Waryn, Walter 97
Fitzwilliam, Toby 52
Flag Fen 73, 79, 80
Fleam Dyke 56, 57, 70
Fleming, Andrew 94
Forest of Dean 112, **114**, 114, 116,
    118, 119, **120**, 120
Forestry Commission 116, 120
Fosse Way 42, 178
Franklin, Tom 286
Frome river 270, *271*, 274, 276, 278

G

Galley, William 187, 195
Game Act (1831) 199
Gatescarth Pass *129*, 132
General History of Quadrupeds
    (Bewick) 138
George IV 254
Gilbert, Alison 154
Glencoul loch **199**, *201*, **204**, 204,
    206–7, 208, 210
Glendhu bothy **203**, 205, **206–7**
Glendhu loch 201, *204*, 204,
    206–7, 208
Glorious Twelfth 199
Golden Jubilee Bridges **299**
Gordon, Elizabeth 209
Gors-y-Gedol **159**, 160
Gouther Crag 134
Gower Peninsula 107, 195
Grand Junction Canal 236, 240
Grand Pier (Weston) 264
Grand Union Canal 236, 240, 248
Great North Road (A1) 176
Great Orme Mines 229
Great Ouse 76, 78
Greene, Graham 262
Grindsbrook Clough *141*, 142
Grinton church 136
Guide to the Lakes, The
    (Wordsworth) 282
Gumber Farm *47*, 50, **51**
Gunnerside 222
Gus (walker) 205
Gutenberg, Johann 317

H

Hadrian's Wall 42, 70, 288, 296
Halnaker Windmill **43**
Hans Monderman (Miller/
    Vandome/McBrewster) 311
Hard Level (Force Level) 225–6
Hardwell Lane *17*, 18, 20
Harker, "Captain" Jammy 220
Harter Fell 128, 132
Haweswater **127**, 128, *129*, 132,
    134–5
Hawkhurst Gang 187
Hawkins, John 48
Helpston **165**, 168, 170, 172, 174,
    175, 176
Henry I 119
Henry II 100, 112
Henry VIII 82, 84, 280
Hereward the Wake 76
High Cup Nick 293, 294
High Force **286**, *289*, 290, **292–3**,
    292, 293
Hilly Wood *169*, 176
Hog's Back 48
Holden, Charles 302
Holford, William 302
Hollins Cross 146
Holme, John 128
Homer, Thomas 236
Honister Pass 229
Hore-Belisha, Leslie 311
Hoxton Mob 262
Hrothgar, King 69
Hudnalls 116, 119, 120
Hungerford Bridge **299**

I

Icknield Way 18, 26, 57
Icknield Way Association (IWA)
    26
*Idea of Landscape and the Sense of
    Place 1730–1840, The* (Barrell)
    170

J

Jackson, William 187
Jacob's Ladder **140**, 140, *141*, 142, **143**,
144, **145**, **146**
Jagger's Clough 146
James, Edward Renouard 100
John Clare Trust 174, 176

K

Keiller, Alexander 35
Kempe, John 97–8
Kempe, Margery (of Lynn) 97–8
Kenneggy Sands *185*, 188, 194
Kennet and Avon Canal 238
Kerry Hills Ridgeway 26
Kinder Low **146**
Kinder Scout **139**, 142, 282, 285
King Street (Helpston) 176
King's Cove **182**, *185*, 190
King's Wood **97**, 104, **103**, **105**
Kylesku *201*, 204, 205, 210–11

L

Lakeland Fells 135
"Lament of Swordy Well, The"
    (Clare) 174
Law Force **283**
Lawes of the Forrest (Manwood)
    110
Leadenhall Market *303*, 306
Lee Farm 144
Level House *217*, 226
Limehouse Basin 236
Lisson Grove *237*, 242
Little Venice *237*, 240
Llechwedd Slate Caverns 229
Llangollen Canal 247
London (Hebbert) 311
London Canal Museum 248
London Road (Canterbury) 104
London Zoo *237*, 244
Long Mynd 26
Longsleddale 132
Loudon, John Claudius 273
Low Force **283**, **286**, *289*, 290, 293
Lych Way 136
Lydford church 136

M

Macclesfield Bridge *237*, 244,
    244, **245**
Mackay, Ishbel 208
Mackid, Robert 210
Maengwyngweddw *87*, 91
Maeshowe tomb 39
Magna Carta 112
Maida Hill Tunnel *237*, 242
Maldie Burn 205

Mam Tor 26, 140, 144, 146
Manners, Thomas 93
Manwood, John 110
Mardale church 128
Margary, Ivan 54
Marine and Coastal Access Act
    (2009) 286
Marshall, Jacob 144
Mawddach estuary 154, **157**, 158,
    158, 160
Maxham's Green Lane 174
Mere, Kate 18
Midsummer Night's Dream, A
    (Shakespeare) 124
Millennium Bridge **300–1**, **302**,
    303, **305**, 308, 310
Monderman, Hans 298
Monks' Trod **83**, 86, 88, 90, **91**, 94
Moor House *217*, 226, **227**
Moorgate *303*, 304
'Moorhens Nest, The' (Clare) 168
Morgan, James 236
Mosedale *129*, 132
Mountain Bothies Association
    132, 205
Museum of London *303*, 304, 308

N
na Gainmhich loch *201*, 210, **211**
Nannerth *87*, 90–2
Nant y Sarn 86, *87*, **91**, 91
Nash, John 236, 242, 254, 273
National Parks 39, 46, 50, 93, 122,
    128, 212, 229, 284
National Trails 16, **58**, 70, 108, **288**
National Trust (NT) 16, 34, 37, 38,
    48, 50, 144, 192
NatWest Tower *303*, 304, **307**
Nero, Emperor 107
New Forest Act (1877) 122
Newcomen, Thomas 223
Noel Stool 142
North Downs Trail 108
North Downs Way 100

O
Offa, King 58, **61**, 64, 67
Offa's Dyke 56, **58**, *59*, 58–68, **61**,
    62–3, **65**, **68**, 70, 88, **113**, *115*,
    118, 262, 296

Old Corpse Road 128–31, *129*,
    130–1, 134
Old Gang Mine **215**, **219**, **220**, 221,
    222, **223**, 224–6, **225**, **228**
Old Straight Track, The (Watkins)
    78
Old West river *75*, 76
Oldbury Court **267**, *271*, 274, 278,
    279
Outhlaw Crag 134
Owen, Gill 240
Oxey Wood *169*, 174

P
Pagoda Rocks 142
Palace Pier (Brighton) **255**, **257**,
    260
Parker Pearson, Michael 36
Parker, Rowland 166
Parliamentary Enclosure Acts
    (1750–1850) 166–7
Paxton, Joseph 273
Peddars Way 43, 54, 195
Pedway scheme 302, 304, **304**,
    306, **307**, 308, 311
Penda, King 69
Pennine Way 142, 212, **283**, **285**,
    286, 288–93, *289*
Pen-y-Dyffryn Hotel 64
Perran Sands *185*, **186**, 194
Pilgrims' Way 26, **97**, **99**, **100**, 100,
    101, 102, 108
Piskies Cove **181**, **184**, 184, *185*, 192
Pont Fadog **154**, *155*, 158
Pont Marteg *87*, 90
Pont Scethin 156, 160
Poor Law Amendment Act (1834)
    218
Porth-en-Alls 190
Portleah Cove 184
Pryor, Francis 79

Q
Quadrophenia Alley 258, **263**
Queen's Park (Brighton) 262
Quick, Oliver 118, 156

R
Racecourse Common *59*, 64, **66**, **68**
Raffan, Peter 142
Ramblers' Association/Ramblers

282, 286, 296
Reach church 69
Re-Afforestation Act (1667) 114
Red Lady of Paviland 107
Reddystore Scoutgate 142, 149
Rees, Diana 76
Regent's Canal **233**, 236, *237*, 238,
    240, 246, 248
Regent's Canal Act (1812) 236
Regent's Park *237*, 240, 242, **243**,
    244
Regent's Park Road *237*, 246
Reign of Terror (France) 190
Repton, Humphrey 273, **279**
Rice Wood *169*, 176
Ridgeway **12**, 16–25, **16**, *17*, **23**, 26,
    32, *33*, 36
Robert of Clairvaux 82, 83
Roger of Hoveden 102
Roscoe, Thomas 282
Royal Pavilion (Brighton) 254,
    255, 256, **256**, 263
Russell, Richard 254

S
St Briavels Castle *115*, 116, 118, 119,
    121, 120
St Cuthbert's Way 108
St Eustace's Well 102
St Helen's Canal 232
St Helen's church 306
St Martha's Hill 108
St Michael's Mount **186**, 194
St Paul's Cathedral 214, *303*, 308
St Peter's Chapel 195
St Swithun shrine 100
St Thomas Becket chapel 100
St Thomas's shrines 105–6
Salberter, Florence 240
Sanctuary 32, *33*, 36, 37
Savery, Thomas 223
Severn river 114, 116
Shap church 128
Sherwood Forest 122
Ship of the Fens 74
Silbury Hill 32, *33*, 34, 36, 37
Skara Brae 39
Slade Bottom *115*, 118
Slade Brook 118
Slaney, RA 266
Slindon Estate 48

Smith, Thomas 221
Smith, William 234, 248
Smugglers' Way 195
Snowdon 154, 229, 244
Snuff Mills **269**, *271*, 276, **277**, 278
Snuffy Jack 278
South Downs Way 50
Southwold Pier 264
Spanish Armada 48, 114
'Splitmate Meg' 226
Spurrells Cross 149
Standedge Tunnel 248
Stane Street **43**, 46, *47*, 48, 50, 52
Starr Carr 12, 72
Stephenson, George 73
Stephenson, Tom 288, 290
Stewart, Chris 34, 64, 88, 102, 188,
    204, 222, 258, 260, 274, 290,
    293
Stewart, David (of Garth) 202
Stewart, Greg 132, 134
Stewart, Ian 204
Stonehenge 7, 13, 20, 26, 29, 35,
    36, 38
Stones of Stenness 39
Strata Florida 86
Strata Marcella 86
Strethall church 78
Stretham Engine Trust 80
Stukeley, William 35
suffragettes 272
Surrender Bridge 224
Swaddywell Pit 174
Swale river *217*, 222
Sweet, Ray 80
Sweet Track 72, 80
Swindale Head **125**, 128, *129*,
    130–1, 132–4, **133**
Sydney Gardens 266
Sygun Copper Mine 229

T
Tan Hill 216, 225
Tate Modern **300**, *303*, **305**, 308
Tate (St Ives) 264
Tees river **283**, **286**, *289*, 290, **291**
'telephone-box leys' 78
1066 56, 86, 110, 164
Thames Barrier 305
Thames Path 305
Thames River Walk *303*, 308

Three Peaks of Yorkshire 149
Tillett, Ben 270
timber trackways 80
Toby's Stone 48, 50, 52
't'Old Man" 218
Toulson, Shirley 156
Tower 42 (City) *303*, 304, **307**
Traffic in Towns (Buchanan) 298,
    311
Travertine Dams **117**, 118
Trent & Mersey Canal 247
Trollope, Sir John 176
Tupper, Mr (farmer) 52
Turner Contemporary 264

U
Uffington Castle 7, *17*, 18, 20, 22, **23**
Uffington Hill 22, 24, **25**
Upper Teesdale National Nature
Reserve 293

V
Vassells Park 278
Vauxhall Pleasure Gardens 266
Vermuyden (engineer) 74
Victoria, Queen 122, 256
'Village Minstrel, The' (Clare)
    170
Volk, Magnus **260**, 260, 261

W
Waden Hill 32, 37, 38
Wainwright, Alfred 288
Walkers Hill 70
*Walking, Literature and English
    Culture* (Wallace) 167
Wallace, Anne 167
Wanderings in North Wales
    (Roscoe) 282
Wansdyke 34, 56, *57*, 70
Waring, Elijah 270
Warwick Canal 236
Wasdale Head 133
Wat's Dyke 58
Watkins, Alfred 78, 80
Watling Street 43
Wayland's Smithy **16**, *17*, 18, 20,
    21, 22, **23**
Wedgwood, Josiah 238
Wesley, John 222
Wesley-Methodist 184

West Kennet 20, **32**, 32, *33*, 34, **35**,
    37, 37
West Pier (Brighton) 251, *255*, 259
Westbourne Terrace Road Bridge
    237, 240
Wharton, Lord 226
White Horse Trail 70
White Horse (Uffington) 7, 14, *17*,
    22, 24, **25**
White Horse Way 36
'White widow's stone' 91
Whitehawk Camp *255*, 262
Whitland Abbey 86
Wicken Fen 80
Wild Wales (Borrow) 60
William the Conqueror 76, 110,
    164, 166
William IV 262
William and Mary 280
Willingham Drain **74**
Windmill Hill 32, 262
Winnats Pass 285
Wobbly Bridge 308
Woden's Dyke 56
Wool Packs 142
Woolstone Hill *17*, 22
Wordsworth, William 282
Wycliffe, John **98**, 98
Wye river *87*, 88, 90, 116
Wye Station *101*, 118
Wye Valley 92, 118
Wynch Bridge *289*, 290, **291**

Y
Yr Wyddfa 154, 229, 244

A NOTE ABOUT TERMINOLOGY

We have used a number of common terms to describe the inhabitants of the British Isles and periods of time. They are simply useful shorthands in a complex story.

Britain, Great Britain and the separate countries of Wales, England and Scotland are ways of defining geographical areas using modern political boundaries. It should be remembered, however, that the national entities, and the subsequent union, only came into being part-way through our story. The "United Kingdom of Great Britain", for instance, was formed with the union of England and Scotland in 1707. Hence many of the peoples we refer to as British, English, Welsh or Scottish would not have seen themselves as such. In fact, in the early part of our tale most folk's horizons would have been much closer: they would have considered themselves part of a local tribe and no more.

National identities are often ascribed to people after the event, sometimes with political intent. Celtic is a term we have avoided because it is fraught with difficulties over whether it refers to a genetic group or to a distinctive culture that was taken up by many groups across northern Europe. Likewise, the Scandinavian invaders of the late eighth to mid-11th centuries most likely used the word viking to mean an overseas expedition. It only came to be used for the people and culture in the 18th century, and then in a highly romanticised way.

Even terms such as Anglo-Saxon are problematic when applied to an entire population. The period following the Romans, from around 410 AD, saw an influx of Angles, Saxons and Jutes from continental Europe. But it is by no means certain that they completely displaced the existing Romano-British population: they may simply have become the dominant elite, and as such been the people who got to write their name into history.

We have kept to the commonly used prehistoric "ages", although they have a tendency to suggest a sharp transition of culture or even of people. In reality the ages blended into one another, as the uptake of a new technology, such as bronze or iron, or a new way of thinking was almost always gradual. The people, too, were very likely one and the same. The notion that new ideas and technologies must have been brought in by invading immigrants who drove out the existing population is gradually losing ground.

The Mesolithic (or Middle Stone Age) is generally taken to last from around 9000 BC to 4000 BC. It covers the period in which ice sheets retreated across present-day England, Wales and Scotland and the land became habitable once again. The Neolithic (New Stone Age) runs from approximately 4000 BC to 2200 BC. The Bronze Age is typically set at around 2200 BC to 750 BC, followed by the Iron Age (750 BC to 43 AD, the date of the Roman invasion).

Of course, these ages refer to the approximate dates of arrival of farming and metals in our own small corner of Europe; in other places the technologies took root very much earlier. The separation of the Roman period in Britain is also somewhat artificial as it was in effect a continuation of the Iron Age under new rulers. Some historians regard the entire period up to 500 AD as the Iron Age, well after the Roman withdrawal from Britain.

The Medieval (or Middle) Ages are often said to start from around 500 AD and we follow this convention by considering that the "Anglo-Saxon" period was an Early Medieval one. It is also often known as the Dark Ages, although this relates more to the lack of surviving literature and the absence of currency than to a significant lack of material wealth or culture. In many ways Early Medieval is a better description, as during this period methods of social organisation were developed, both in agriculture and in the creation of towns, that contributed greatly to the relative affluence of the ensuing 500 years.

The end of the Medieval Age is rather wooly. Some put it at the invention of the movable-type printing press by Johann Gutenberg in the mid-15th century, while English historians have tended to use the Battle of Bosworth Field (1485) when Henry became the first Tudor monarch. The dates seem rather arbitrary; what matters is that around this time ways of thinking and behaving that we would regard as modern began slowly to evolve.

The industrial, agricultural and transport "revolutions" all suggest a sudden change in social and economic organisation. It is true that there were periods of particularly rapid transformation but, as our story shows, the uptake of new technologies unfolded over several centuries. The same applies to the enclosure movement. The term implies that all the common land was parcelled up and made private over a few decades at most. In fact enclosure had been taking place gradually over many decades, if not centuries: sometimes an enclosure act merely legalised an existing situation. In common with many historians, we use the terms "movement" and "revolution" to highlight the pace of change over a shorter period and to emphasise that, in Britain and beyond, the effects of the change were far-reaching indeed.

ACKNOWLEDGEMENTS

We would like to thank the following for their support and help:

All those who inspired us with a love of the outdoors, of history and of language, particularly our parents, John and Anne Stewart and Derek and Joan Rudd-Jones. Everyone involved in the creation and maintenance of the Walkingworld website, including shareholders Barrie Gibson and Oliver Quick (who also gave valuable feedback on the first draft), walk administrators Chris Stewart, Jo Clark and Frances Clark, web developers Ant Tickner and Paul Heywood, accountant Ray Ormsby, the walk contributors (too numerous to mention by name) and the tens of thousands of members without whom the website would not exist at all. All those we walk with regularly, including those who joined us on the walks for the book, our families and of course our dogs, Sally and Brough (one of whom features throughout the book while the other was a little young at the time). The whole team involved in the publication of the book, especially our publisher from Guardian Books Lisa Darnell and our editor Phil Daoust, both of whom were very patient with us as first-time authors. And, perhaps most importantly, the many people who work tirelessly to maintain our public footpath network and keep these important walking routes open.